"*The approach that Fry and Nisiewicz have taken is fresh, appropriately reflective, and uniquely grounded. Contrary to 'soft' treatments of this popular theme, their book links spirituality to effective leadership and more concretely defines spiritual leadership.*"

—KENT RHODES, Pepperdine University, Family Business Consulting Group, and Founder, OnCourse Network, Inc.

"*I've met many leaders who feel inspired and called to run organizations that are more sustainable and more nurturing to the human spirit, but they didn't know where to start. With this book, not only can they get started—they have guidance for the whole journey. We've been waiting a long time for a book like this.*"

—JUDI NEAL, Tyson Center for Faith and Spirituality in the Workplace, University of Arkansas and Author, *Edgewalkers: People and Organizations That Take Risks, Build Bridges, and Break New Ground*

"*This is a book long overdue. The authors complement their compelling case for an organization's multiple bottom line by providing a model and practical tools for effectively implementing spiritual leadership. Fry and Nisiewicz are on to something important here and the wise leader stands to benefit from their advice. Find a place to keep the book within arms' reach. You'll refer to it often.*"

—PETER C. HILL, Co-editor, *The Psychology of Religion and Workplace Spirituality* and Co-author, *The Psychology of Religion*

"*Spiritual leadership appears as our next threshold for resolving the paradox of profitability and humanity's most profound needs. This book offers a holistic approach, pragmatic business cases, success stories, accessible concepts, and how-to methods that encourage leaders to break through antiquated business models and apply creative solutions.*"

—RICHARD MAJOR, Former Worldwide Director of Human Resources, Hewlett-Packard and former Vice President, Human Resources, Global Business Partners, and Worldwide Operations, Solectron Corporation

"*It is easy enough to see that personal spiritual values inform the way that one leads in business. Co-authored by one of the foremost champions of research and training in spiritual leadership, this book goes a step further, arguing that spiritually-informed leadership improves performance in terms of profits, people, and the planet.*"

—JONATHAN GOSLING, Centre for Leadership Studies, University of Exeter

"*For many people in the worlds of business and politics, juxtaposing the words 'spiritual' and 'leadership' is off-putting, and quite possibly both pretentious and risible. This book exposes the pitfalls of such a position, giving practical examples of successful leaders and effective leadership practices across a range of organizations in which spiritual leadings have played an explicit role. It is a 'must read' for anyone interested in either leadership or the spiritual dimension of organizational development.*"

—ANN LIMB, Chair, Helena Kennedy Foundation

"*A powerful, well written, and engaging book from keen thought leaders!* Maximizing the Triple Bottom Line through Spiritual Leadership *is full of real-world examples which underscore the fact that sustainable business models balance profit with wider concerns that, at a fundamental level, have a spiritual foundation.*"

—JONATHAN SMITH, Anglia Ruskin University

"*By looking at the importance of love, altruism, and reflective personal practice to leadership, Fry and Nisiewicz enable us to take these fundamental notions into consideration in the way that businesses want to: to impact the bottom line.*"

—KATHRYN GOLDMAN SCHUYLER, Alliant International University and President, Coherent Change

Maximizing the Triple Bottom Line Through Spiritual Leadership

Maximizing the Triple Bottom Line Through Spiritual Leadership

Louis W. Fry and
Melissa Sadler Nisiewicz

STANFORD BUSINESS BOOKS
An Imprint of Stanford University Press
Stanford, California

Stanford University Press
Stanford, California

For more information on spiritual leadership or about the use of the models, methods, and tools contained in this book, please contact:

The International Institute for Spiritual Leadership
7804 Pebble Creek Rd.
Georgetown, Texas 78628
iisl@iispiritualleadership.com

Special discounts for bulk quantities of Stanford Business Books are available to corporations, professional associations, and other organizations. For details and discount information, contact the special sales department of Stanford University Press. Tel: (650) 736-1782, Fax: (650) 736-1784

Printed in the United States of America on acid-free, archival-quality paper

Library of Congress Cataloging-in-Publication Data

Fry, Louis W., author.
    Maximizing the triple bottom line through spiritual leadership / Louis W. Fry and Melissa Sadler Nisiewicz.
        pages cm
    Includes bibliographical references and index.
    ISBN 978-0-8047-7636-3 (cloth : alk. paper) — ISBN 978-0-8047-8508-2 (pbk. : alk. paper)
    1. Leadership—Moral and ethical aspects. 2. Leadership—Religious aspects.
    3. Industrial management—Moral and ethical aspects. 4. Industrial management—Religious aspects. 5. Spirituality. I. Nisiewicz, Melissa Sadler, author. II. Title.
    HD57.7.F788 2013
    658.4'092—dc23
                                                                    2012016183

Typeset by Westchester Publishing Services in 10.5/15 Minion Pro

Contents

Chapter Seven
IMPLEMENTING ORGANIZATIONAL SPIRITUAL
LEADERSHIP   193

Chapter Eight
SPIRITUAL LEADERSHIP:
THE DRIVER OF THE TRIPLE BOTTOM LINE   238

Chapter Nine
CO-CREATING A CONSCIOUS, SUSTAINABLE WORLD
THROUGH SPIRITUAL LEADERSHIP   283

Tables and Figures

Acknowledgments

We are truly grateful for all the people who have encouraged and helped us to develop our book. These same people have often gone out of their way to share the thoughts and ideas of spiritual leadership with leaders everywhere. First and foremost, we want to acknowledge Professors Jerry Hunt and John Slocum for their pivotal role and support in the early development of the spiritual leadership model. We also express deep gratitude to Stanford University Press and our editor, Margo Fleming, for shepherding us and this project along. Her kindness and graciousness were always present, along with a steely resolve to draw from us and accept nothing less than our best. This book would also have not been possible without our generous clients sharing their stories: Robert Ouimet, Earl Maxwell, Lynne Sedgmore, and the countless others who have worked with us but were not named in this book.

We are also grateful to Melanie Cohen, Dave Geigle, Dorianne Cotter-Lockard, Hermant Khanna, Gaston Sauvé, B., Jan B. King, and Dave Sherman for taking the time to give their most helpful comments.

Maximizing the Triple Bottom Line Through Spiritual Leadership

Chapter One

Maximizing the Triple Bottom Line: The Need for a New Business Model

In 1965 Robert Ouimet bought J. René Ouimet Holding Inc. (OHI) and became president of a leading Canadian frozen-food processing company. Today OHI is Canada's largest manufacturer of low-cost frozen dinners and entrées. From the beginning, Robert envisioned leading a company based on spiritual principles. This vision is the core management philosophy of OHI, and Robert Ouimet has demonstrated that his company can generate profits while simultaneously improving the lives of employees and the communities in which they operate—what has come to be called the Triple Bottom Line, with an integrated focus on people, planet, and profit (Mele and Corrales 2005).

However, before he could bring such unity to his company, Robert discovered that he needed to first find unity in himself. Since his childhood, he had carried with him a nagging, obsessive, and recurring sense of guilt about being a "privileged" person because of his father's business success. Based on that sense of guilt and on his early working experiences, Robert became certain that there is an inner longing in every person's heart, regardless of their spiritual or religious orientation, for the Infinite or the Absolute, and he felt compelled to make a difference in the way he did business (Ouimet 2009).

Robert's personal dilemma—how to succeed in business and honor his and his employees' spiritual longings—drove Robert to meet with Mother Teresa of Calcutta, who had served some of the poorest and most afflicted people on earth. Robert had always admired Mother Teresa because he thought she was doing "so many beautiful things on earth." He felt called to seek her spiritual guidance and wrote her a letter; he told her what he was doing in trying to manage his company on spiritual principles and asked for a brief audience, which took place on April 16, 1983, in Calcutta.

He only asked her one question: "Should I give away everything I have, Mother?"

She immediately replied: "You cannot give it, it has never been yours. It has been loaned to you by God. If you want, you can try to manage it . . . with Him . . . which is very different than 'for Him.' And if you want to manage 'with Him,' you have to follow His hierarchy of Love. . . . So, for you, His hierarchy of Love is: First Him; second, your wife; third, your four children; fourth, the four hundred employees and their families; and in that order. Not first the employees, and last the wife" (Ouimet 2009). In that moment, Mother Teresa radically changed the priorities of Robert Ouimet's life. His real calling was not to give away his riches and responsibilities as a business leader but instead to love and serve his God, his family, his employees, and others through his various business interests. Mother Teresa told Robert to not try to manage with God without praying a lot; she suggested the motto *Orare ad gerendum in Deo* ("Pray to manage in God") for his company.

Through this window to inner unity and through his subsequent personal spiritual journey, Robert created the possibility of reconciling human development and economic success ("Our Project: Reconciliation of Human Well-Being with Productivity and Profits" n.d.). This unification was made possible by the model of organizational spiritual leadership that Robert experimented with and put into practice.

Like Robert, many leaders today want to implement business models that accentuate and promote the Triple Bottom Line that focuses on people, planet, and profit. Organizations are increasingly being held responsible for the impact their activities have on their employees, suppliers, customers, and communities. They must account not only to shareholders and investors but also to politicians, the media, employees, community groups, government agencies, environmentalists, and human rights organizations. This trend has fundamentally changed the operating environment for organizational leaders.

This shift, along with the Fortune 500 scandals of the last decade and the current world financial crisis, has only served to increase the pressure on corporate leaders to reevaluate current business models in an attempt to find answers that might solve these problems. Companies such as SAS Institute, Google, Shell Oil Company, NEC Corporation, and Procter & Gamble have committed their organizations to implementing new business models that accentuate ethical leadership, employee well-being, sustainability, and social responsibility without sacrificing profitability, revenue growth, and other areas of financial and performance excellence.

In a recent survey of 900 global corporations conducted by PricewaterhouseCoopers, 80 percent of CEOs said they believe "sustainability" is or soon will be vital to the profitability of their company, and 71 percent said they would consider sacrificing short-term profits to move their company toward sustainability (Savitz and Weber 2006). One of the greatest challenges facing leaders of both large and small organizations today is to develop business models that can achieve this holistic balance.

One answer to this call to maximize the Triple Bottom Line lies in the implementation of spiritual leadership. Drawing on workplace spirituality, spiritual leadership, and conscious capitalism, the International Institute of Spiritual Leadership has developed and refined two models—the Spiritual Leadership Model and the Spiritual Leadership Balanced Scorecard Business Model. The two models have been developed based on years of research on diverse organizations, including government agencies, municipalities, military units, schools, manufacturers, and retailers. These research efforts form the foundation of this book.

You may have asked when you read the title of this book: What is spiritual leadership? Is it about religion? If not, how is it different? Why do I need to know about this approach to leadership? The answer is simple: regardless of your spiritual or religious tradition or whether you are an atheist or an agnostic, and if you are a CEO, an entrepreneur, a small business owner, or just someone who believes that the old ways of leading don't work and you want to be part of creating a sustainable world that works for everyone, an understanding of Spiritual Leadership is necessary to be effective in the twenty-first century. *Maximizing the Triple Bottom Line Through Spiritual Leadership* offers case examples that will give you this understanding, plus tools we have developed through years of scientific research to help you achieve your vision both for yourself personally and at work.

This chapter will provide a general overview of the Models for Personal and Organizational Spiritual Leadership plus the Spiritual Leadership Balanced Scorecard Business Model. In addition, we discuss the importance of workplace spirituality, the distinction between spirituality and religion, and the relationship between corporate culture and leadership as important contexts for performance excellence and maximizing the Triple Bottom Line.

Spiritual Leadership: The Driver of the Triple Bottom Line

What is spiritual leadership anyway? Spiritual leadership involves intrinsically motivating and inspiring workers through hope/faith in a vision of service to key stakeholders and a corporate culture based on altruistic love. While there are innumerable theological and scholarly definitions of love, we focus here on a definition based on the Golden Rule. We define altruistic love in spiritual leadership as "a sense of wholeness harmony and well-being produced through care, concern, and appreciation of both self and others."

The purpose of spiritual leadership is to tap into the fundamental needs of both leader and follower for spiritual well-being through calling and membership; to create vision and value congruence across several levels—the individual, the empowered team, and the organization as a whole; and, ultimately, to foster higher levels of employee well-being, organizational commitment, financial performance, and social responsibility—in short, the Triple Bottom Line.

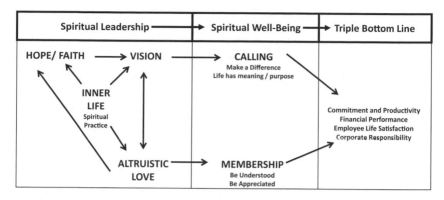

FIGURE 1.1 Model of Organizational Spiritual Leadership
Source: International Institute for Spiritual Leadership

Essential to spiritual leadership are the key processes of:

Creating a vision in which leaders and followers experience a sense of calling so that their lives have meaning and make a difference.

Establishing a social/organizational culture based on the values of altruistic love whereby leaders and followers have a sense of membership, feel understood and appreciated, and have genuine care, concern, and appreciation for *both* self and others.

As shown in Figure 1.1, the source of spiritual leadership is an inner-life practice—possibilities range from spending time in nature to prayer, religious practice, meditation, reading, yoga, or writing in a journal. An inner-life practice positively influences spiritual leadership through the development of hope and faith in a transcendent vision of service to key stakeholders that keeps followers looking forward to the future. Hope/ faith in a clear, compelling vision produces a sense of calling—the part of spiritual well-being that gives one a sense of making a difference and, therefore, a sense that one's life has meaning.

Spiritual leadership also requires that the organization's culture be based on the values of altruistic love. Leaders must model these values through their attitudes and behavior, which creates a sense of membership—the part of spiritual well-being that gives one a sense of being understood and appreciated. The dimensions of spiritual leadership and the process of satisfying spiritual needs then positively influence the key individual and organizational outcomes that comprise the Triple Bottom Line.

THE CONTEXT FOR WORKPLACE SPIRITUALITY

Spiritual Leadership can be viewed as an emerging paradigm within the broader context of workplace spirituality and an even broader framework of sustainable models of twenty-first-century business (Fry, "Toward a Theory of Spiritual Leadership" 2003). A person's spirit is the intangible, life-affirming force in all human beings. As part of their spiritual journey, people are struggling with what this force means and how it can be applied to their work. A major change is also taking place in the personal and professional lives of leaders as many of them attempt to integrate their spirituality and their work (Benefiel 2005).

Many people agree that this integration leads to very positive changes in workplace relationships and in their effectiveness as leaders (Neal 2001). There is also evidence that workplace spirituality programs counteract the trend toward seeing "employees as expendable resources", leading not only to beneficial personal outcomes, such as increased employee health and psychological well-being, but also to improved employee organizational commitment, productivity, and reduced absenteeism and turnover (Fry and Cohen 2009). There is mounting proof that a spiritual workplace is not only more productive but also more flexible and creative, and that it is a source of sustainable competitive advantage. Initial research on spiritual leadership to date in schools, municipal governments, police, for-profit organizations, and active-duty military units found that the spiritual leadership model predicted between 45 percent and 60 percent of variance in productivity, 60 percent to 80 percent variance in organizational commitment, 20 percent in life satisfaction, 32 percent in social responsibility, and 13 percent in sales growth.

The power of spirituality is increasingly impacting our personal lives and is spreading into the workplace to foster a moral transformation of organizations. This trend has been identified as "a spiritual awakening in the American workplace." Patricia Aburdene states in *Megatrends 2010* (Aburdene 2005) that the focus on spirituality in business is becoming so pervasive that it stands as "today's greatest megatrend." She contends that more people are making choices in the marketplace as "values-driven consumers."

Spirituality in the Workplace on the Rise

For many of us, work serves as an integral part of our self-concept and greatly affects the quality of our lives both at work and at home. As the two-decade trend to spend more time at work increases, we actively seek opportunities for meaning, purpose, and a sense of connection and belonging from our work. Employees have come to expect their employers to provide these opportunities. Unfortunately, the tumultuous social and business changes brought on by the Internet age and globalization have led employees to believe they are viewed as expendable resources rather than as valued human beings. This has led to increasing distrust in organizations and leaders.

One reason the interest in workplace spirituality is increasing is the desire by some organizations to nurture employees' dedication to their work and connection to the workplace. Another is that global awareness has brought on a growing social/spiritual consciousness. People are increasingly motivated by their spiritual needs to serve others. According to George Platt, CEO of ViewCast Corporation, "People don't come to work to be Number 1 or 2 or to get a twenty-five percent return on net operating income. They want a sense of purpose and come to work to get meaning from their lives" (Aburdene 2005).

Organizational scholars have begun to study this rising interest in workplace spirituality, arguing that the spirit-work connection is based on definable and measurable aspects of the work environment.

In their *Handbook of Workplace Spirituality and Organizational Performance*, Giacalone and Jurkiewicz define workplace spirituality as "a framework of organizational values evidenced in the culture that promotes employees' experience of transcendence through the work process, facilitating their sense of being connected to others in a way that provides feelings of completeness and joy" (Giacalone and Jurkiewicz 2003).

Subsequently, a special issue of *The Leadership Quarterly* on spiritual leadership found that what is required for the emergence of workplace spirituality is an *inner life* that nourishes and is nourished by *calling or transcendence of self* within the context of a *community* based on the values of altruistic love. Employees who view their work as a "calling" and the workplace as a source of community approach their work very differently from employees who see work primarily as a means to satisfy their pecuniary needs.

Workplace spirituality incorporates those values that lead to a sense of transcendence and interconnectedness such that workers experience personal fulfillment on the job. This sense of transcendence and the need for a sense of belonging, community, or social connection through membership are essential for both workplace spirituality and spiritual leadership.

Spirituality and Religion

In his book *Ethics for the New Millennium*, the Dalai Lama speaks to the relationship between spirituality and religion:

> Religion I take to be concerned with faith in the claims of one faith tradition or another, an aspect of which is the acceptance of some form of heaven or nirvana. Connected with this are religious teachings or dogma, ritual prayer, and so on. Spirituality I take to be concerned with those qualities of the human spirit—such as love and compassion, patience tolerance, forgiveness, contentment, a sense of responsibility, a sense of harmony—which brings happiness to both self and others. (Tenzin Gyatso 1999)

Spirituality as manifested through these qualities provides the foundation for the world's spiritual and religious traditions. Nondenominational spiritual practices and world religions are fundamentally based on love and service of others. This explains what some people and organizations (for example, Alcoholics Anonymous) mean when they claim to be spiritual and not religious. Consequently, spiritual leadership can be implemented and practiced with or without religious theory, beliefs, and practices. In our work on leadership in general and this book in particular, we use the term spirituality to allow for its application to any organization interested in implementing workplace spirituality and/or religion. However, this is in no way meant to imply that nondenominational or nontheistic spiritual practices are superior to the religious traditions and their beliefs and practices.

CORPORATE SOCIAL RESPONSIBILITY, CONSCIOUS CAPITALISM, AND THE TRIPLE BOTTOM LINE

Sustainable businesses recognize that we operate in an interdependent, global environment in which all living beings depend on one another and on their natural environment. Andrew Savitz and Karl Weber, in their best seller *The Triple Bottom Line: How Best-Run Companies Are Achieving Economic, Social, and Environmental Success—and How You Can Too,* define a sustainable organization as one that is financially prosperous while being socially responsible and improving the lives of its employees and the key stakeholders with whom it interacts (Savitz and Weber 2006). Organizations need a business model that enriches the lives of its employees, customers, suppliers, and the community while still maintaining adequate levels of financial performance. Doing so requires finding ways to work with all of a company's stakeholders for mutual benefit that will create more profit for the company while benefiting its employees and society.

In response, leaders of such admired organizations as Whole Foods, Procter & Gamble, Starbucks, and Southwest Airlines have adopted a stakeholder approach to managing strategic issues facing their firms. These leaders acknowledge that stakeholders have a legitimate moral stake in the organization's performance. Key stakeholders often have the power to negatively affect an organization's performance if their expectations are not met. The fundamental problem for top management is how to maximize performance while meeting the needs and safeguarding the rights of its stakeholders. To achieve such an outcome, employees must jointly define a set of core vision and values that meet or exceed the expectations of stakeholders while also establishing those expectations as the basis for organizational behavior.

Other organizations provide examples of business models that drive innovative and sustainable business processes. New Balance reduces or eliminates negative impact on the environment by designing and building products with end-of-product-life in mind. Nike Inc. recognizes the impact of declining natural resources and the need to move to a low-carbon economy. Nike's vision is to reach a closed-loop business model, achieving zero waste throughout the supply chain with products and materials that can be continually reused with no pre- or postconsumer waste. The Walt Disney Company is a pioneer among American companies in thinking about and caring for the planet. Disney has launched a variety of programs and resource conservation initiatives that educate customers on the importance of a healthy environment. Recently Disney introduced new goals in the areas of waste, carbon emissions, energy, water, ecosystems, and inspiration to substantially reduce its impact on the environment and further enact environmentally responsible behavior among employees, guests, consumers, and business partners.

Unfortunately, traditional financial measures, including return on investment, return on equity, and return on assets, do not fully reflect a company's performance in the environmental and social arenas. Many companies, including Unilever PLC, Dow Chemical Co., Amoco Corp., and Ford Motor Company are examining how they are approaching their Triple Bottom Line. According to Tom Gladwin, professor of sustainable enterprise at the University of Michigan, they have created education programs and new executive positions focusing on sustainable development as a means to implement the Triple Bottom Line (Gladwin 2012).

Out of all of this has emerged a new breed of "conscious" capitalism consisting of organizations that are aware of the untallied cost of capitalism. This is an increasingly popular, decentralized, broad-based crusade to heal the excesses of capitalism with transcendent human values. It is a new way of business that acts out of a deeper purpose than merely profit maximization. Its leadership is based on creating sustainable learning organizations that deliver to stakeholders a system of values by which the interests of customers, employees, suppliers, investors, the community, and the environment are harmonized and aligned to the greatest extent possible.

CEOs like Jeff Swartz of Timberland and John Mackey of Whole Foods have embraced conscious capitalism and the Triple Bottom Line through integrity, transparency, and enlightened governance; they have established higher social and environmental standards that address the interests of other key stakeholders while still meeting the demands of investors. They embody the idea that profit and prosperity go hand in hand with social justice and environmental stewardship. Their organizations and employees recognize and benefit from the connectedness and interdependence of all stakeholders.

MEASURING PERFORMANCE EXCELLENCE

Organizations that focus on sustainability and strategic performance measurement have been at the forefront of the movement to maximize the Triple Bottom Line. Proponents of sustainability and strategic performance measurement stress the need for a new business model that emphasizes nonfinancial predictors of financial performance such as leadership, operating/internal measures, quality, customer satisfaction, employee well-being, and social responsibility.

Measuring organizational performance in this new way requires the adoption of a stakeholder approach. Organizations need to embrace the various internal and external parties that have a legitimate strategic and moral stake in the organization's performance. Each group of stakeholders has its own values, interests, and expectations, as well as particular relationships with other individuals, groups, and organizations. The main purpose of the stakeholder approach is to define the common good of the organization, while meeting the needs and safeguarding the rights of the various stakeholders. By achieving congruence between customer, worker, and other stakeholder values and expectations, leaders will enhance rather than detract from corporate profitability.

A Brief Look at the Triple Bottom Line

At the turn of the twentieth century, classical management theory gurus Henri Fayol and Mary Parker Follett argued against using a centralized, hierarchical model for organizations. Fayol maintained that authority should not be concentrated at the top of the organizational hierarchy; instead, employees needed to develop skills to improve organizational efficiency, and managers should encourage an esprit de corps around a common cause. Follett asserted that power and leadership in organizations should stem not from a manager's position of authority, but from knowledge and expertise. This idea of the importance of employee participation and motivation has continued throughout the twentieth century into the present day.

In the 1980s, total quality management became a prescription for management to decentralize decision-making authority and empower individuals and teams with the authority needed to make processes more efficient and effective. Total quality management also ushered in the establishment of the Malcolm Baldrige National Quality Award, which recognizes areas of performance excellence for organizations in the United States. The award focuses on business results in six categories: customer focus, products and services, financial and market, human resources, organizational effectiveness, and governance and social responsibility.

In the 1990s, measuring performance excellence took center stage when Kaplan and Norton introduced the Balanced Scorecard (Kaplan and Norton 1996) as a way to capture metrics at the executive level, based on the categories of product and service quality, customer satisfaction, employee learning and growth, and financial performance. Nonfinancial measures provid the balance needed to supplement financial measures and align employees with the organization's strategy. By examining monthly trend data and performance versus targets, managers can identify performance gaps that, if closed, provide their firms with significant competitive advantage.

The development of quality and performance metrics has played a pivotal role in identifying the impact employees have on the Triple Bottom Line. Central to an organization's success is recognizing the knowledge, skills, creativity, and motivation of all employees. Valuing employees by committing to employee development, learning, and well-being leads to continuous improvements in key processes and produces higher-quality products and services. According to Baldrige, (Baldrige National Quality Program 2005) organizational and personal learning will lead to a more flexible, responsive, and efficient organization, which will result in a sustainable, distinctive competency and market advantage. Kaplan and Norton assert that the learning and growth perspective is *the* driver for achieving performance outcomes in the other categories.

The Spiritual Leadership Balanced Scorecard Business Model

The Spiritual Leadership Balanced Scorecard Business Model (see Figure 1.2) draws from the latest developments of the Baldrige and Balanced Scorecard approaches to performance excellence. It emphasizes stakeholder satisfaction and spiritual leadership as key to maximizing the Triple Bottom Line. It utilizes a vision and values-driven stakeholder approach to achieve congruence across the individual, team, and organizational levels that fosters high levels of employee well-being, stakeholder satisfaction, and financial performance.

As shown in Figure 1.2, the strategic management process begins with the development of a vision, a purpose, and a mission, followed by an internal and external stakeholder analysis that forms the foundation for meeting or exceeding the expectations of key stakeholders. This analysis forms the basis for developing organizational strategic objectives and action plans. In turn, as the dotted line shows, the spiritual leadership process is linked to the organization's strategic management process so that it drives the Learning and Growth category, which produces continuous improvement in operations and the development of high-quality products and services. That improvement increases levels of customer and stakeholder satisfaction, leading to better financial performance and sustainable organizations that maximize the Triple Bottom Line. Ultimately, the Spiritual Leadership Balanced Scorecard Business Model facilitates the integration of individuals and teams with the organization's vision

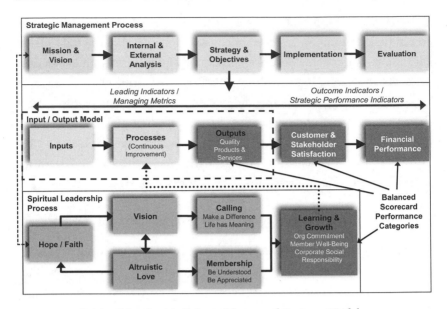

FIGURE 1.2 Spiritual Leadership Balanced Scorecard Business Model
Source: International Institute for Spiritual Leadership

and values. As one result of this integration, empowered teams emerge, allowing workers to utilize their talents and abilities to effectively deal with key strategic stakeholder issues.

SPIRITUAL LEADERSHIP IN PRACTICE: CORDON BLEU-TOMASSO

Robert Ouimet's meeting with Mother Teresa in 1983 marked a transition phase on his spiritual journey. He could have easily given up on the spiritual path and enjoyed his more materialistic pursuits. Or he could have gone back to a more traditional way of doing business. Robert did neither of these things. Instead, he chose to focus on his inner life, to deepen his spirituality and continue moving his business on the path of spiritual transformation.

In seeking advice from Mother Teresa, Robert discovered that his business *was* his ministry. By putting his spiritual values first, Robert regained renewed energy and vision. In doing so, he put his business back on course and further reaffirmed his dedication to spiritual leadership. Through trial and error he gradually discovered how to further articulate and deepen the company's dedication to workplace spirituality through spiritual leadership.

The next decade proved to be a time of many ups and downs as he gradually moved to implement workplace spirituality in J. René Ouimet Holding Inc. On Mother Teresa's advice, Robert initiated several management activities to foster the inner-life development of his employees. He fitted out a room for inner silence and reflection, decorating it to evoke an atmosphere of peace and serenity. He believed that a fundamental condition for self-realization or awareness of any human being was to have a sense of transcendence. For him transcendence was as a Christian seeking God. However, he appreciated that, since his employees embraced other spiritual traditions—including Jewish, Muslim, Buddhist, new age, agnostic, and atheist—each person must be able to seek inner strength, wisdom, and courage in his or her own way.

It took about ten years from when the silence room was installed for everyone in the organization to feel secure and to not be afraid of others trying to convert or proselytize them. They slowly realized that people who went to the room for silence and reflection did not necessarily get promotions or avoid demotions. The rules were: you don't talk in the room; you relax; you do not prepare for a meeting with papers; you do not stop a production line when you are in the silence room. Some managers acknowledged that they particularly found it useful when they were facing difficult or important decisions. In the room for silence and reflection they could take momentary refuge from the hectic pace of company life. They found it an ideal place to meditate, safe from interruption; it was a place where peace and calm were tangible.

Next, Robert implemented a biannual organizational climate survey. He also introduced the practice of one-on-one personal conversations; each manager was required to conduct such a personal conversation with each employee at least once a year. This conversation had nothing to do with the annual performance evaluation. Rather, it was about the two parties coming to know, understand, and appreciate each other and their concerns with the purpose of fostering a solid sense of trust. This activity proved to be one of the most difficult to implement because, at first, employees were wary of telling their bosses what they really thought. It took several years to convince employees that the conversation had nothing to do with their evaluations. However, in time this practice fostered a sense of trust between managers and workers.

In the mid-1980s, Robert suggested to his managers the possibility of performing a "gesture" once or twice a year. Such a gesture might be a manager and his direct reports visiting the needy to offer some kind of service, such as serving food to the homeless at a shelter and then having a coffee afterward to share their experience. Some managers take their direct reports to serve meals to street people in parts of town that are so poor and dangerous that taxis refuse to drive people there unless they're offered a big tip. Others serve meals in hospitals, nursing homes, and prisons. For most of those who participate, the gesture is a transformative experience that causes them to see themselves and the less fortunate in a new way.

All of these activities take place on company time. Introducing these activities to managers and employees and getting them to accept them was a slow process, but Robert was unwavering in his purpose, even though he knew the results might not become apparent for several years. Participating in these activities also meant embracing the primary values of the dignity of every human being and the ideal of justice, including equity and authenticity in telling the truth in words and deeds. The coming years saw Robert and his company moving ever more deeply into articulating and living out these values. With each step forward, despite occasional fierce debate and uncertain outcomes, Robert, his board, and his key executives chose to stay true to their values; in doing so, they deepened both their personal values and those of the organization.

The CBT Acquisition

One of the J. René Ouimet Holding Inc. (OHI) companies that the International Institute of Spiritual Leadership has worked with is Cordon Bleu-Tomasso (CBT). Today CBT's products can be found in the frozen-food section of supermarkets in Canada from coast to coast. To maintain its leading market position in such a highly competitive industry, CBT strives for continuous growth in quality and innovation as well as productivity, sales, and profits, while maintaining a commitment to corporate social responsibility—the Triple Bottom Line. With three exceptions, sales growth and profits have been superior to those of the industry in general. Absenteeism is low and, although the company is unionized, there have been no strikes, lockouts, or voluntary work slowdowns

OHI purchased CBT in 1985. At the time Paolo and Marco Tomasso, two sons of the founder, Giovanaia, were in need of expansion capital. They approached Robert Ouimet at that time, and he agreed to acquire 100 percent of CBT's capital stock. The company continued to be managed by the Tomasso brothers, and they continued their characteristic management style. At that time CBT had twenty employees and annual sales of Can$2 million. The culture was characterized by the workers as a "family relationship." The Tomasso brothers were close to their workers and treated them with great consideration and affection. The workers also held the brothers in high regard for their caring management style and their concern for the workers' personal problems.

In the 1990s CBT began to grow rapidly. Several large Canadian retailers showed interest in CBT's products, and the company started exporting to the United States and Mexico. By the end of the 1990s the production facilities were undersized and obsolete. To meet the increasing demand, a modern frozen-foods manufacturing plant was built on the outskirts of Montreal in 2000. When the company moved to the new facility, Robert decorated the corridors of the office building with photographs and mottos that evoked such values as serenity, peace, understanding, service, etc. After the move, CBT went to three shifts. Even though the surroundings were pleasant and modern, the nature of the work was as hard as ever— a constantly moving production line, damp conditions, and refrigeration that held the temperature constant at 6°C (42°F) to meet processing requirements.

From the beginning, the Tomasso brothers showed little enthusiasm or desire to have CBT implement workplace spirituality and spiritual leadership as had been done in Robert's other companies. For the most part Robert let them have their way, although he did gradually introduce some spiritually oriented activities into CBT, where they were well received by managers and workers. The first, in 1993, was the organizational climate survey, followed by the moment of silence at board meetings, the room for inner silence and reflection, charitable activities like the "gesture," and the annual one-on-one conversation (but only between senior managers and between managers and their immediate subordinates).

As in Robert's other companies, there was mistrust and suspicion at the outset. Many wondered, "Why's he doing that?" "What's his hidden agenda?" "Aren't we being had?" "Is he really impartial?" "Isn't he trying to get us wound up in his Catholic faith?" For a long time, Robert found he was the only one meditating during the moments of silence and prayer at the beginning and ending of board and management committee meetings. He often asked himself if he wasn't really trying to impose this practice or if his insistence wasn't actually subtly disguised pride or if he shouldn't just stop the practice or conduct it less frequently.

Another example of the difficulties in introducing a management practice was the introduction of invited testimonials. This activity was inspired by the experience of prayer breakfasts and Alcoholics Anonymous meetings. It took more than five years to convince CBT workers that they were really free to attend or not attend and that they were not being manipulated or "sucked in" to some religious activity against their wishes.

The results of these activities are reflected through CBT's vision, mission, and values and serve as examples of the vision of service to key stakeholders through a culture based on altruistic love inherent in spiritual leadership

CBT's Vision

- Joyful and passionate people serving enthusiastic customers.
- To lend full meaning to our work and to our lives.

- By nurturing each others' happiness and well-being.
- By shining God's love upon those with whom we work each day, upon our families, our customers, and everyone we encounter in the life of our enterprise.
- By respecting the diversity and the dignity of each person we work alongside.
- By living, in full freedom, universally authentic human, spiritual, and religious values.
- By sustaining a safe, healthy work environment where ideas flourish, teamwork and initiative are encouraged, and success is rewarded.

To be a world-class leader and the "go to" supplier in the development and manufacture of top-quality consumer meal solutions,

- By maintaining the highest standards for quality and food safety.
- By meeting our customers' changing expectations for product innovation.
- By controlling costs and offering consistently high-quality products at reasonable prices. ("Our Project" 2008)

CBT's Mission

To be a leading and profitable North American supplier of niche quality innovative entrées and meal components with differentiated branded and private label offerings, superior service capabilities, tailored to specific customer channel needs. We are centered on and driven by our people in cooperation with God, to innovatively generate continuous growth in human well-being as well as sales and earnings, with a relentless sense of values, human respect, and dignity ("Our Project" 2008).

CBT's Values

- Solidarity, brotherhood
- No "us versus them." No "big bosses." Together, we are the company. We share a common dream, a common mission.

- We accept, therefore, the spiritual obligation to love and care for everyone, more today than yesterday. Authenticity, humility, every day, in everything we do.
- Listening to others, growth of human dignity. No one is a number or a cog in a wheel. Everyone deserves to be treated with respect.
- We are, each of us, inhabited and loved by God. We are ends in ourselves and not means to some other end.
- Hope and faith in the love, wisdom, and caring of God, as freely lived by each of us in our own personal rhythm and way. ("Our Project" 2008)

These statements relate CBT's commitment to spiritual leadership, through hope/faith in its vision and the values of altruistic love for both the company and its people, with the intention to find meaning in work (calling) and a sense of brotherhood/solidarity (membership). The company's activities reflect human, spiritual, and economic priorities that serve to establish the various aspects of spiritual leadership while working to maximize the Triple Bottom Line.

CBT's Integrated System of Management Activities

By now, Robert was wholly convinced he must generate profits while at the same time improving the spiritual lives of his employees. That initial concern was to become the core for the management philosophy underlying the economic and human activities he calls the Integrated System of Management Activities (ISMA). The ISMA would lead to maximizing employee well-being and development, service to the community, and the company's productivity and profitability. Not all the employees in the company take part in the ISMA, but the activities are made available to all, and the company encourages employees to take advantage of them.

CBT's Economic ISMA

The Economic ISMA is derived from three main principles: serving consumers, efficiency, and profits. These principles are further developed into a set of six guiding ideas ("Our Project," 2008).

- A level of profitability and productivity is maintained at least equal to that of their competitors. CBT finds it essential, if it is to continue to exist as a financially solid organization, to generate and invest capital in support of ongoing developments and to secure the collective future of CBT stakeholders.

- CBT's vision is to be recognized, across North America, as a world-class leader and the "go to" supplier in the development and manufacture of frozen dinners and entrées.

- CBT is determined to provide customers products of the highest quality, delivered on time, at prices consistent with the expectations of the people who consume them. At all times their products must conform to the directives of the appropriate government bodies.

- CBT distinguishes itself through competence, authenticity, and the desire to work within a team of each of its people; by the quality of their products and services; through technological innovation and efficient production; through a continuing commitment to research and development.

- CBT favors highly organized, strongly disciplined but flexible management characterized by the decentralization of responsibilities and authority. This permits people to act quickly and cohesively, and it promotes the initiative and participation of everyone in the company.

- CBT accepts its responsibility to protect the environment and to contribute to the economic and social development of the country.

CBT's Human ISMA

The Human ISMA contains the concepts of human dignity and human well-being at work, which are supported by five key principles ("Our Project" 2008).

- Offer fair and equitable wages and benefits that compare favorably to those of other companies of similar size and type.

- Provide safe and secure working conditions for each person and foster the growth and development of the individual and collective values that exist within the company.

- Promote a just and equitable working environment while respecting the dignity of each person. No discrimination or harassment will be tolerated. People will work together in a beautiful and healthy climate of individual and collective freedom and thought.

- Make every effort to give full, lasting meaning to our daily work. Work exists for men and women; men and women do not exist for work. The lasting meaning of our work will allow us, at the end of each day, to return home to our families with more love, compassion, serenity, courage, and wisdom.

- Accept our responsibility to contribute to the human, material, and spiritual development of our country.

In order for the organization to achieve the full potential of the Human ISMA, the company wants employees to discover and develop their inner life and values: solidarity and brotherhood, peace and serenity, humility and reconciliation between people, justice and equity, along with authenticity and honesty between everyone throughout the enterprise.

Management Practices to Reinforce CBT's ISMAs

In addition to a room for inner silence, testimonials, a moment of silence before meetings, and one-on-one personal conversations, CBT established other management practices to further reinforce CBT's culture and the Human ISMA. Taken together, these activities include:

Nonstereotyped, Warm, and Authentic Communication. The company works to establish authentic ways of being and communicating at all levels and among all members of the company, starting with the top managers.

A Biannual Organizational Climate Survey. All workers are surveyed every two years as an anonymous way to raise issues of concern and for Robert to obtain feedback about the effectiveness of his attempt to implement workplace spirituality.

A Moment of Silence During Meetings. This activity centers around brief moments of inner silence, sharing, reflection, or meditation and prayer in which the participants feel at ease.

Meetings Between Three Employees and a High-Ranking Manager. On a rotating basis, three people working in the company meet with a high-ranking manager for about ninety minutes. The meetings take place about once a week, and participants choose the subjects to discuss. No notes are taken during the meetings; the focus is on learning to listen to others.

The Prize of the Heart. Every year, a prize is awarded to one person who has over the years exhibited behavior that radiates solidarity, joy for life, helping others, compassion, and human dignity.

The Annual One-On-One Personal Conversation. During an annual meeting, two people, one having authority over the other, reflect together on the previous year. They exchange thoughts about concrete events that have both negatively and positively marked their interpersonal relations. This activity completes the professional evaluation of the subordinate's performance, but the professional performance evaluation and the one-on-one personal conversation are never held at the same time.

A Room for Inner Silence. This room is available to people in the company and allows those who feel the need to take time out, in an atmosphere of inner silence, relaxation, and reflection. This time away from the job should not affect the work of the person's department.

Testimonial Meetings. By opening themselves and their reflections to others, invited guests share their personal life choices with those people in the company who desire to listen. They speak of the human, moral, and often spiritual experiences that have guided them in their lives.

A Dinner for Four and Pre-Hiring Interviews. After all the pre-hiring interviews have been completed and the number-one candidate has been chosen, but before the final decision to hire the candidate, the manager in question invites the candidate, with his or her spouse (or significant other), to dinner with the manager and his or her spouse. This activity links the spouse and the family to the final hiring process.

A Spiritual Support Group. Employees are invited to attend, on a voluntary basis, a celebration during which the members of the group, led by a competent guide, can discuss their faith or any other opening to transcendence. This discussion is often followed by a fraternal dinner and a shared reflection on a spiritual text.

A Gesture. Some employees are called on to contribute and share with others. The specific gesture can take various forms: serving meals to street people, working in a prison or hospital, or collecting clothes, toys, or food to be distributed to those in need. Immediately after this experience, the participants spend thirty minutes afterward sharing their experience. Participating in a gesture is done on company time and with no reference to the company's trademarked products.

Community Meals. Twice a year, before Christmas and the summer vacation, a simple community meal, generally a buffet, is planned for all the personnel. At the summer event, management serves the meal and eats after everyone else.

Meetings with Laid-Off or Dismissed Employees. Each manager who has dismissed someone meets with that person at least twice in the first twelve months following his or her departure. The first meeting takes place generally around a light meal or a coffee and is most of the time very hard and tense, which is very understandable. Some months later, in the second meeting, a different atmosphere is generally felt: one of reconciliation and of a human, authentic, humble, and brotherly relation. In addition, the people who have been dismissed are invited to the two community meals. Such meetings provide moral support to the former employees, who are naturally suffering because they lost their jobs.

A Shared Bonus. This activity is an attempt to share the wealth created by the work of all the people in the organization. The size of the bonus depends on how successfully budgetary and departmental objectives have been reached. This bonus is not part of the salary system: it is an addition.

Sponsoring. Someone in their department introduces newly hired employees to colleagues and familiarizes them with the organization's procedures, customs, and culture. The sponsors also introduce the new employees to the activities of the Human ISMA. Sponsoring usually takes place during the first six months after being hired. ("Our Project" 2008).

The Keystone

These activities are incorporated, with love as the keystone, to reconcile the two ISMAs and CBT's values (see Figure 1.3). Robert Ouimet believes that when employers emphasize religion in the workplace, negative consequences may result. For example, religious practices, if taken to the extreme, can lead to attempts to proselytize other employees with different beliefs, which can conflict with the social, legal, and ethical foundations of business and law, as well as with public and nonprofit administration. Thus religion can lead to the arrogant attitude that a particular company, faith, or society is better, morally superior, or more worthy than another. An emphasis on the distinction between religion and spirituality in regard to workplace spirituality is therefore essential. CBT attempts to avoid these pitfalls through periodic surveys and by allowing openness to spirituality, religion, and transcendence in full freedom through adherence to its core values.

CBT makes this clear by publicly proclaiming:

> All actors in the company's life freely interpret the value of transcendence in their own way. This value occupies the keystone in the illustration of the Economic and Human ISMAs. Transcendence can mean the Creator; the higher power; God Love; God the Father, Son, and Holy Spirit; Allah; Jehovah; Buddha; or any other openings to Transcendence. To this value of Transcendence can be added, for those who so desire and according to their personal choices, different forms of reflection, meditation, and, for some, silent and personal prayer during work. This is quite possible without stopping work ("Our Project" 2008).

OUR PROJECT AND THE GOLDEN BOOK

The implementation of nearly all the management activities intended to facilitate the implementation of the Human ISMA and to guide CBT initially were met with resistance that sometimes took years to overcome.

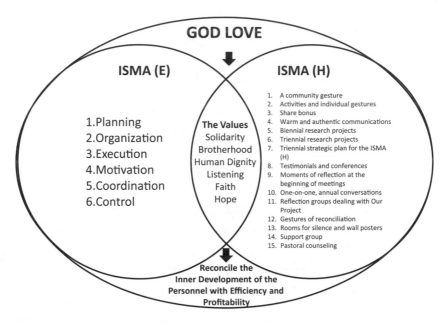

FIGURE 1.3 Reconciliation of CBT's Economic and Human ISMAs
Source: Ouimet, R., *Spirituality in Management Reconciles Human Well-Being—Productivity—Profits*, 4th ed., Montreal: Holding O.C.B. Inc., 2005; "Our Project: Reconciliation of Human Well-Being with Productivity and Profits," *Notre Project*, n.d. http://www.notreproject.org/homepage-our-project.html (accessed November 19, 2008).

Despite the apparent success of various management activities in implementing the Human ISMA, challenges remained.

Even before the new plant was built, expansion and the arrival of new managers had brought about a noticeable change in the workplace climate at Tomasso. The family atmosphere had begun to evaporate, and growth had brought about the implementation of a more conventional bureaucracy and organization chart that clearly defined hierarchical reporting relationships within the company. The Tomasso brothers were still greatly respected, especially by the older employees. However, because the company had grown so rapidly, it was impossible for them to know everyone. The company had also become unionized, and relations between union and management were generally tense. An organizational climate survey also revealed that workers felt they received little recognition for their efforts. They also complained that their managers were too harsh and unbending.

This, on top of the various problems encountered in transferring to the new factory and the use of new state-of-the art machinery, had a significant negative impact on customer sales and service. Before the move the company had been profitable and growing; now suddenly sales were dropping and many customers canceled their contracts because of these problems.

By the end of 2001 there was a 20 percent reduction in working hours, and it was clear that the current management could not resolve these problems. Subsequently the Tomasso brothers left the company to start another business. The brothers' departure was deeply felt, especially by the veteran employees. Some described this as a bigger shock than the transfer to the new factory. Consequently, Robert hired Benoit Gauthier, a consultant the company had used regularly, to serve as interim president until a permanent president could be found.

After fifteen years of growth, the company had stagnated under the traditional bureaucratic model its new managers had brought with them. CBT's organizational climate survey revealed that, although the workers had responded favorably to the Human ISMA initiatives instigated by Robert, the failure of top management to enthusiastically embrace them reduced their effectiveness. For example, 86 percent of the respondents wanted to keep the room for silence and reflection. More than 40 percent reported that they used it. This reinforced Robert's conviction that it could take years to create a climate of real freedom and that there was still much work to do in this regard.

In 1998, after ten years of hard work, Robert received his PhD from the University of Fribourg; the degree was based on his experience with spiritual management activities as they reflected his management philosophy. Subsequently he summed up the contents of his thesis in a small book, known as the Golden Book because of its cover (Ouimet 2005). The basic ideas in the book became the foundation for what Robert started to call Notre Project (Our Project). In 2001, with the help of an independent management consultant, Robert presented the basic outline of Our Project to CBT employees, stressing that maximizing the Triple Bottom Line was the ultimate objective. Management also emphasized that participation in most of the activities was optional, that there would be no coercion, and that multiculturalism in CBT would be respected at all times.

Robert and the board then embarked on a vigorous search for a new president who would give fresh impetus to Our Project and overcome the current problems faced by CBT. Robert, in particular, wanted a president who had operational experience running a company and who shared the values of Our Project. They all agreed that the successful candidate must meet three major criteria. He or she must be:

Professionally and technically competent, and must have earned an MBA.

Absolutely authentic.

A humble person with drive, dynamism, and a desire for success, both economically and for the people employed by the company.

In mid-2002, after a laborious process, a new president was hired. He was given the full support of Robert and the board of directors to do what he felt was necessary to turn CBT upward, in a new direction after three profitless years. Armed with a good understanding of Robert's management philosophy, before initiating any changes he first took the time to get to know personally the senior managers in the company, as well as to further assess the nature of the problems CBT faced. At the same time he concentrated on improving relations with customers and managed to regain most of the lost contracts.

One of the new president's first major activities was to hold a series of weekly meetings, organized based on seniority, with employees in groups of three. These meetings lasted ninety minutes and were designed to be relaxed, personal encounters in which the employees were invited to have refreshments and coffee. It became clear from his conversations with the company's managers and employees, along with the results from the workplace climate survey, that the behavior of the managers was the root cause of CBT's problems. CBT's values had been clearly defined and key activities had been initiated for their implementation, yet these values were not demonstrated in the managers' daily activities.

The problems were centered in a group of about a dozen people representing both short- and long-term employees hired by the Tomasso brothers, the previous president, and even Robert Ouimet himself. Some had been good at managing a business making Can$10 million a year but were incapable of managing the much larger enterprise CBT had become. The group included most of the members of the management committee: the operations director, the human resources director, the maintenance and production director, and the packaging and logistics director. By mid-2004, all of these people were replaced. The new president brought in a dynamic group of people hired primarily based on whether they embraced CBT's core values and spiritual management practices.

In the end CBT's vision and values won out. The laborious process of introducing Our Project and the painstaking search for a new president had clarified to Robert and CBT what was most important to them. Staying in business was not a viable option if it meant the company would lose its spiritual values. Their vision and values were the greatest good.

In 2007 Robert created the To God Go Foundation when he transferred the family food processing business to his son, Jean-René (Ouimet 2009). The Foundation is rooted in the Catholic faith and lived out in a perspective of ecumenical and human openness. It has as its mission to make known the business experiment of Our Project to leaders and managers of various workplaces and companies all over the world. It also aims at reaching professors and researchers in the management field. The diffusion of knowledge gained from the experiment is done through lectures, visits to factories, and assistance in editing case studies based on the experimentation of Our Project and applied to business education, conferences, and publications.

Since then, CBT has initiated another significant new multimillion-dollar plant expansion. And although it has encountered the same challenges as other organizations due to the global economic recession that began in 2008, it has remained committed to workplace spirituality, spiritual leadership, and the Triple Bottom Line. CBT also initiated a restructuring to further integrate Our Project into the very DNA of the business. For example, the position of Chief Spiritual Officer (CSO), was created to oversee the functioning and promotion of the management activities and to reinforce God Love as the keystone that links the Economic and Human ISMAs. This position reports directly to the CEO and is on the same level with the Chief Operating Officer (COO) and the Chief Financial Officer (CFO).

CBT and the Spiritual Leadership Model

CBT's vision of love and service to stakeholders helps its employees overcome the inevitable obstacles and difficulties everyone has to face. It helps them fulfill their desire to achieve inner unity and meaning in their lives and to have a sense of calling, and it opens the door for them to personal growth and long-term happiness.

CBT's values exemplify the values of altruistic love in spiritual leadership. These values promote dignity by drawing on people's capacity for knowing, feeling, and cooperating with others to experience a sense of membership in working together to realize their life goals. Because of their sense of calling and membership, they become highly committed to continuously improving key processes, products, and services—to the delight of their customers—and ultimately to achieving superior financial success.

The Economic and Human ISMAs contain both the performance excellence and spiritual components required for the Spiritual Leadership Balanced Scorecard Business Model. The ISMAs contribute to the inner development of all people, both individually and in their relations with others. The balance between the Human ISMAs and the Economic ISMAs produces an organization that focuses on sustainable business strategies that maximize employee well-being, sustainability, and financial performance—the Triple Bottom Line.

ROAD MAP FOR THIS BOOK

Look Ahead

In this chapter we have explained the importance of spiritual leadership, provided an overview of the spiritual leadership models, and offered an example of a pioneering organization that has developed specific leadership and management practices and activities to implement them. The rest of the book will focus on further describing the elements of these models and explaining how personal and organizational leadership can be put into practice. The book can be viewed as three sections: The first four chapters explore the "Spiritual Leadership Model," the next three chapters focus on "Implementing Spiritual Leadership," and the final chapter issues "The Call for Spiritual Leadership."

"Exploring the Spiritual Leadership Model," presents a detailed explanation of the model components and how they interact as a whole.

> Chapter 2, "The Spiritual Leadership Model", explains how hope/faith, vision, and cultural values based on altruistic love combine to create organizational spiritual leadership as an intrinsic motivating force that satisfies our fundamental needs for spiritual well-being.

> Chapter 3, "Inner Life: The Source of Spiritual Leadership," explores the role of inner life as the source of spiritual leadership.

> Chapter 4, "Spiritual Leadership and the Values of Altruistic Love," elaborates on the power of the values of altruistic love that, along with hope/faith and vision, define the qualities of spiritual leadership.

> Chapter 5, "Spiritual Leadership and Spiritual Well-Being," defines the nature of spiritual well-being as rooted in calling and membership, and explores the relationship between spiritual well-being and spiritual leadership.

"Implementing Spiritual Leadership," demonstrates the spiritual leadership models' methods, tool, and techniques for continual improvement and growth to maximize the Triple Bottom Line.

> Chapter 6, "Developing the Qualities of Personal Spiritual Leadership," offers a modification of the twelve steps used in recovery programs as one approach for undertaking the spiritual journey that is essential to personal spiritual leadership development.

> Chapter 7, "Implementing Organizational Spiritual Leadership," provides a roadmap for implementing organizational spiritual leadership and details how to use the spiritual leadership survey and other tools and strategies for organizational transformation and development.

> Chapter 8, "Spiritual Leadership as a Driver of the Triple Bottom Line," describes the Spiritual Leadership Balanced Scorecard Business

Model and how to use it as the driver of the key performance categories necessary to maximize the Triple Bottom Line.

The final chapter, "The Call for Spiritual Leadership," discusses the need for maximizing the Triple Bottom Line through spiritual leadership.

Chapter 9, "Co-Creating a Conscious, Sustainable World through Spiritual Leadership," covers various movements whose purpose is the creation of a conscious, sustainable world; the commitment of the International Institute for Spiritual Leadership to this journey; and the call for you to join us in the quest of co-creating organizations dedicated to a world that works for everyone by maximizing the Triple Bottom Line through the Spiritual Leadership Balanced Scorecard Business Model.

Conclusion: Practical Tools

For those interested in maximizing the Triple Bottom Line, the major tools introduced in this chapter include the following:

The Spiritual Leadership Model serves as a guide for optimizing important individual and organizational outcomes—such as life satisfaction and spiritual and psychological well-being—as well as personal and organizational commitment and performance.

The Spiritual Leadership Balanced Scorecard Business Model provides a roadmap for using the Spiritual Leadership Model to optimize four key performance categories to maximize employee well-being, sustainability, and financial performance—the Triple Bottom Line.

Management practices reinforce workplace spirituality, spiritual leadership, and the Spiritual Leadership Balanced Scorecard Business Model.

Chapter Two

THE SPIRITUAL LEADERSHIP MODEL

Interstate Batteries is an active laboratory for the implementation of organizational spiritual leadership. In his book, *Beyond the Norm*, company chairman Norman Miller writes, "The bottom line of Interstate is to love people and try to meet their needs, all in the context of top performance and reasonable profitability" (Miller and Miller n.d.; N. Miller 1996). But, early on, Norm's leadership style was not so spiritual. During his high school days, Norm's mother would say, "College! Hell, I just hope I can keep him out of jail and get him out of high school!" (N. Miller 1996). Back then, Norm, known by the nickname Bubba, was many things: petty thief, bootlegger, budding alcoholic, rebellious, ignorant, and rude—not a kid you would pick to eventually become one of America's best and brightest entrepreneurs. Today Norm has helped make Interstate Batteries the leader in battery marketing and distribution, providing consumers with "Every Battery for Every Need."

Norm Miller's success comes from understanding the role that change plays for individuals and the organizations we lead. To succeed in today's world of global competition, organizations must be willing and able to change. Flexibility of this magnitude requires the total commitment of all employees. It cannot be found in the traditional centralized, standardized, and formalized bureaucratic organizational paradigm. Instead, it requires an organizational transformation to a learning organizational paradigm that is love-led, customer-obsessed, intrinsically motivated, empowered, innovative, team-based, flat (in structure), flexible (in capabilities), diverse, global, and networked in alliances with suppliers, customers, and even competitors.

The learning organization strives to develop, lead, motivate, organize, and retain people who are committed to the organization's vision, goals, culture, and values. The employees of learning organizations are characterized as being open, generous, and capable of thinking in group teams; they are risk-takers with the ability to motivate others (Ancona et al. 2004). Furthermore, they must be able to abandon old alliances and establish new ones, view honest mistakes as necessary to learning, and exhibit a "do what it takes" attitude versus the more traditional "not my job" outlook that is endemic to bureaucratic organizations. In the learning organization, employees are empowered to act as coaches who constantly listen, experiment, improve, innovate, and create new leaders (Ancona et al. 2004; Bass 1990; McGill and Slocum 1992). Developing, leading, motivating, organizing, and retaining people who are committed to the organization's vision, goals, culture, and values is the major challenge.

In this chapter we will show that spiritual leadership is necessary for the transformation of an organization to become a learning organization and for its continued success. First, we review spiritual leadership as a source of intrinsic motivation and discuss the distinction between leading and leadership. Then we describe the personal and organizational spiritual leadership models, the latter of which was briefly introduced in Chapter 1. Finally, we explore in more detail Interstate Batteries as an example of a learning organization and its leader as a model who makes both personal and organizational spiritual leadership fundamental to his and his company's approach for maximizing the Triple Bottom Line.

MOTIVATION AND LEADERSHIP FORM THE FOUNDATION FOR SPIRITUAL LEADERSHIP

So how are leadership and motivation connected? At its heart, leadership is about motivating people to change. Spiritual leadership draws on the general definition of leadership developed by Kouzes and Pozner in *The Leadership Challenge*: "Leadership is the art of mobilizing others to want to struggle for shared aspirations" (Kouzes and Pozner 2003). From this perspective, leadership is motivating followers by creating a vision of a long-term, challenging, desirable, compelling, and different future. When the organization's vision is combined with its mission it establishes a company's culture. Comprised of an ethical system and core values, culture provides a moral imperative for right and wrong. A powerful vision and a strong ethical culture give the learning organization a roadmap for change.

Intrinsic Motivation and Spiritual Leadership

Why is motivation so important to leadership? Motivation includes the forces (either external or internal) that arouse enthusiasm and persistence to pursue a certain course of action. Motivation is primarily concerned with what energizes human behavior, what directs or channels such behavior, and how this behavior is maintained or sustained. Motivation in the workplace happens when leaders create an environment that brings out the best in people if they receive individual, group, and system-wide rewards contingent on their performance. Motivated workers exert effort above minimum levels, are spontaneous, and exhibit exploratory/cooperative behaviors.

Examples of external or extrinsic motivations include promotions, pay increases, bonus checks, pressure to perform, supervisory behavior, insurance benefits, and vacation time. Under extrinsic motivation individuals feel compelled to engage in a task in order to satisfy a lower-order need (for example, money) to survive. Our modern concepts of bureaucracy and extrinsic motivation are rooted in the experience of early efforts to create large military, religious, and feudal organizations. The primary basis for motivation in these traditional centralized, standardized, and formalized bureaucratic organizations has been fear (Daft 2008). The main benefit of bureaucracy and leading by fear is to create a control and motivation system that ensures minimum levels of effort, organizational commitment, and performance. However, fear-led bureaucracies also can prevent people from feeling good about their work and lead to avoidance behavior, feelings of powerlessness and low confidence, and low levels of commitment, enthusiasm, and imagination (Deci and Ryan 2000). Most important is the effect of reduced trust and communication so that important problems and issues are hidden or suppressed (Nyhan 2000).

To remain flexible to change, leaders are challenged with creating a work environment that is intrinsically motivating (see Figure 2.1). Intrinsic motivation—the primary source of motivation in learning organizations—is defined as interest and enjoyment of an activity for its own sake and is associated with active engagement in tasks that people find interesting and that, in turn, promote growth and satisfy higher-order needs. Intrinsic motivation has been associated with better learning, performance, and well-being (Deci and Ryan 2000). All of us have some activities we do for our own sake, whether having fun with family or participating in a favorite hobby such as golf or knitting. Learning organizations rely on this type of motivation to promote an environment of empowered freethinkers.

Intrinsic motivation at work requires some degree of autonomy or self-management, competence, and relatedness. Autonomy tends to increase intrinsic motivation through the control individuals feel to freely exert extra effort in following their own interest while accomplishing a task. Employees feel competence and relatedness when working with empowered teams, when they are directing their activities toward a meaningful purpose while doing something they regard as significant and meaningful. Individuals in empowered teams have a sense of ownership of the work and are highly engaged in the group's tasks, which require their best thinking and creativity. They take pride in their work and are excited about having a sense of progress and seeing the results of their efforts (Conger and Kanungo 1988; Spreitzer 1996; Thomas 2002).

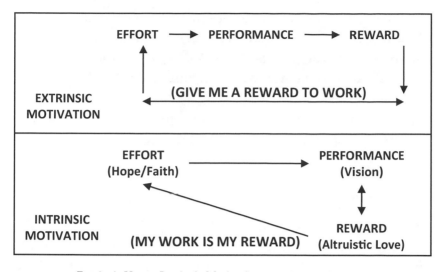

FIGURE 2.1 Extrinsic Versus Intrinsic Motivation
Source: International Institute for Spiritual Leadership

Rewards in intrinsic motivation are internal and under control of the individual. These rewards result from the internal experience one has in performing a task and the feeling of satisfaction through its performance and achievement. Such rewards could be solving a problem that benefits others, fulfilling a personal mission or purpose, being part of a "winning" team, or the completion of a complex task. For individuals experiencing intrinsic motivation the performance of the task becomes the reward. In this sense performance and rewards are fused and indistinguishable—in other words, they become one and the same.

Intrinsic motivation at work can also occur through goal identification, which occurs when employees have internalized into their own value systems the vision and values of the organization and the team goals or sub-goals the organization is pursuing (Galbraith 1977). The goals have value to the individual because they are acquired through a long process of socialization in the organization or because the individuals have participated in developing the organization's vision, values, and goals and therefore are highly committed to them.

Referencing Figure 2.1, spiritual leadership is, fundamentally, an intrinsic motivation process based in an effort–performance–reward process. In spiritual leadership, the interaction between a vision of service to key stakeholders (performance) and a culture of altruistic love (reward) based on care and concern for both self and others, creates the belief, conviction, trust, and action necessary for hope/faith. Hope/faith in turn becomes the source of self-motivation (effort) necessary to achieve the vision.

Leading Yourself Versus Leadership in Organizations

It is important in spiritual leadership to distinguish between leading and leadership. Leading and leader development focus on the individual to develop individual-based knowledge, skills, and abilities associated with a formal leadership role. Such a role often centers on intrapersonal skills and abilities such as self-awareness, self-regulation, and self-motivation. Leading typically concentrates on the influence leaders have among their followers.

On the other hand, leadership focuses on the social influence process that engages everyone and enables teams of people to work together in meaningful ways. This involves building the capacity for better individual and collective adaptability and performance across a wide range of situations. Leadership places emphasis on the leader's development of followers and using the interpersonal skills of a leader to foster mutual trust, respect, and, ultimately, organizational commitment and performance. In this way each person who exercises positive influence to enhance performance is developing as a leader and is capable of exercising spiritual leadership.

There is a growing understanding that leadership is a multilevel influence process involving followers, leaders, peers, and emergent collective (for example, team) dynamics. Thus, spiritual leadership applies both at the individual-level and group or work-unit-level. At the individual level it is about leading and leader development whereas at the group level it reflects spiritual leadership that is shared or experienced by all team members.

So why is intrinsic motivation and the distinction between leading and leadership important? Intrinsic motivation, leading, and leadership form the foundation for spiritual leadership. Intrinsic motivation inspires and empowers both leaders and followers. As we will demonstrate in the following sections, the development of spiritual leaders and organizational spiritual leadership helps increase individual and group intrinsic motivation, thereby enhancing leader and employee well-being, sustainability, and organizational performance.

A BIRD'S-EYE VIEW OF THE SPIRITUAL LEADERSHIP MODEL

Spiritual Leadership requires:

> Hope/faith in vision that motivates both the leader and followers; both experience a sense of calling: their lives have purpose, meaning, and make a difference.

> A personal ethical system and organizational culture based on the values of altruistic love so leaders and followers have a sense of membership and belonging, feel understood and appreciated, and act based on genuine care, concern, and appreciation for both self and others.

> An inner-life practice (for example, spending time in nature, prayer, meditation, reading inspirational literature, yoga, observing religious traditions, writing in a journal) that positively influences development of both hope/faith in a vision of service to key stakeholders and the values of altruistic love.

Personal Versus Organizational Spiritual Leadership

From this bird's-eye view, one can see that the Spiritual Leadership Model can be applied at the individual, group, and organizational levels. There is an old saying that you can't lead others if you can't lead yourself. Therefore, unless individual leaders guide themselves spiritually, organizational spiritual leadership of groups and organizations is impossible. The key distinction between the two models is that one focuses on individual intrinsic motivation and leading through personal spiritual leadership, while the other focuses on leadership and intrinsic motivation of teams and organizations and through organizational spiritual leadership.

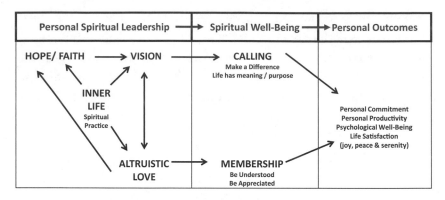

FIGURE 2.2 Personal Spiritual Leadership
Source: International Institute for Spiritual Leadership

Personal Spiritual Leadership

CEOs cannot lead companies to become spiritual organizations without strong personal spiritual leadership. Personal spiritual leadership, as illustrated in Figure 2.2, requires hope/faith in a vision of service to others through altruistic love. The source of personal spiritual leadership springs from an inner-life practice based on spiritual principles. When we are committed to a vision of service to key stakeholders we have a sense of calling, in that we are making a difference in other peoples' lives and our life has meaning. In authentically living the values of altruistic love, we have a sense of membership in that we are understood and appreciated. The combined experiences of calling and membership form the foundation for spiritual well-being, which is the source of the individual outcomes of personal spiritual leadership—personal commitment and productivity, positive human health, psychological well-being, and life satisfaction. Chapter 6 further explores the spiritual journey and developing the qualities of personal spiritual leadership.

Organizational Spiritual Leadership

Organizational spiritual leadership is essential in learning organizations. The organizational spiritual leadership model views group relations between leader and follower, follower and leader, and peer and peer as being dynamic and reciprocal over time. It is well known that, through role modeling, behaviors, and other means, leaders can alter the self-concepts, attitudes, goals, and beliefs of followers. Through group member interactions an emergent process occurs in which individual perceptions over time form group and, ultimately, organizational perceptions of spiritual leadership. As this process unfolds, leaders and followers in the organization begin to form compatible mental models of hope/faith in a vision of service to key stakeholders through altruistic love. In turn, this unfolding process increases the team's sense of calling and membership, and individuals ultimately influence one another toward increasingly greater levels of performance. As group members high in spiritual leadership interact, they continually bolster the level of spiritual leadership of one another and the group.

For example, as workers approach one another with care, concern, and mutual appreciation over time, they increase the intensity of membership each person experiences in the group, as well as reinforce future altruism in other group members. Altruistic love then becomes a shared part of the culture and "the way we treat people around here." Indeed such leaders exemplify personal spiritual leadership and serve as prototypes representing a form of idealized behavior that members of the organization come to identify with over time and come to be influenced by in terms of their self-concept.

The Components of the Spiritual Leadership Model

While it's helpful to have a bird's-eye view of the Spiritual Leadership Model, it is the individual components and their interconnection that brings the model to life. The Spiritual Leadership Model is comprised of four basic components: inner life, spiritual leadership, spiritual well-being, and personal and organizational outcomes that comprise the Triple Bottom Line.

We have researched and tested these components for more than twelve years in an effort to understand the true nature of how and why the model works to maximize the Triple Bottom Line.

Inner Life

The source of the Spiritual Leadership Model is inner life. An inner life can be thought of as a type of personal spiritual practice that can range from spending time in nature to prayer, meditation, reading inspirational literature, yoga, observing religious traditions, or writing in a journal. Inner life is important for enabling personal spiritual leadership and facilitating work that is meaningful and takes place in the context of a community.

Inner life is not only the source for personal spiritual leadership. It is also the basis for spiritual leadership of groups and organizations. Organizational cultures that support their workers' inner lives have employees who are more likely to develop their own personal and organizational spiritual leadership. A work context that supports these practices is the source of both personal and organizational spiritual leadership and workplace spirituality.

Many companies are beginning to recognize the importance of supporting employees' inner lives. Cordon Bleu-Tomasso Corporation has established a room for inner silence. Australia and New Zealand Banking Group Ltd (ANZ) has developed training programs focusing on "high performance" mind techniques and "quiet rooms" for individual spiritual practice. Missouri's Ascension Health is committed to a workplace that deepens personal spirituality through the adoption of an ethical discernment process that fosters self-reflection.

These organizations and many others recognize that employees have spiritual needs (that is, inner lives) just as they have physical, mental, and emotional needs, and none of these needs are left at the door when they arrive at work. At the root of the connection between spirituality and leadership is the recognition that everyone has an inner voice that is the ultimate source of wisdom for the most difficult business and personal decisions (Levy 2000). Observing, witnessing, and cultivating this inner voice is the purpose of an inner-life or spiritual practice.

The existence of an inner life relates both to one's individual identity and to social identity. An individual's identity is part of their self-concept or their inner view, while the expression of that inner life is in part an

TABLE 2.1
Qualities of Spiritual Leadership

Vision	Altruistic Love	Hope/Faith
• Broad Appeal to Key Stakeholders • Defines the Destination and Journey • Reflects High Ideals • Encourages Hope/Faith • Establishes Standard of Excellence	• Trust/Loyalty • Forgiveness/Acceptance/ Gratitude • Integrity • Honesty • Courage • Humility • Kindness • Compassion • Patience/Meekness/ Endurance • Fun	• Endurance • Perseverance • Do What It Takes • Stretch Goals • Expectation of Reward/ Victory • Excellence

SOURCE: International Institute for Spiritual Leadership

expression of social identity. A job is more intrinsically motivating when there is a high level of correspondence between the job, its context, and a person's self-concept. We will explore the specific characteristics and ways to develop an inner life in the next chapter.

Spiritual Leadership

Spiritual leadership, with inner life as its source, emerges from the interaction of hope/faith, vision, and altruistic love. The qualities of spiritual leadership are shown in Table 2.1.

Vision

Vision refers to a picture of the future with some implicit or explicit commentary on why people should strive to create that future. Cordon Bleu-Tomasso Corporation's vision of "Joyful and Passionate People Serving Enthusiastic Customers" is an example. Another is the vision "We Make Happy Campers" of the Outdoor Recreation Center, located at Fort Hood, in Texas, which rents outdoor camping equipment to soldiers and their families. In order to motivate change, visions serve three important functions: clarifying the general direction of change, simplifying hundreds or thousands of more detailed decisions, and helping to quickly and efficiently coordinate the actions of oneself and team members. A vision defines the journey and the reason the leaders and followers are taking it. It energizes workers, gives meaning to work, garners commitment, and establishes a standard of excellence. An effective vision has broad appeal, defines the destination and the journey, reflects high ideals, and encourages hope and faith (Daft and Lengel 1998).

Hope/Faith

Hope is a desire with an expectation of fulfillment. Faith adds certainty to hope. Taken together, hope/faith is a firm belief in something for which there is no evidence; it is based on values, attitudes, and behaviors that demonstrate absolute certainty and trust that what is desired and expected will come to pass. Individuals with hope/faith have a vision of where they are going and how to get there. They are willing to face opposition and endure hardships and suffering in order to achieve their goals. Hope/faith is also the source for the conviction that the vision, either personal or organizational, will be fulfilled. Hope/faith is demonstrated through effort, action, or work. In action, hope/faith is like a race that has two essential components—the victory (vision) and the joy in preparing for the race itself. Both components are necessary and essential elements if hope/faith is to generate the necessary effort to pursue the vision.

Altruistic Love

For spiritual leadership, altruistic love is defined as "a sense of wholeness, harmony, and well-being produced through care, concern, and appreciation for both self and others" (Fry 2003). There are great emotional and psychological benefits from separating love or care and concern for others from need, which is the essence of giving and serving others unconditionally. The fields of medicine and positive psychology have begun to study and confirm that love has the power to overcome the negative influence of such destructive emotions as resentment, worry, fear, and anger. Underlying this definition are the values of integrity, patience, kindness, forgiveness, humility, selflessness, trust, loyalty, and truthfulness. Altruistic love defines the set of key values, assumptions, understandings, and ways of thinking considered to be morally right. Spiritual leaders embody and abide in these values through their everyday attitudes and behavior.

Chapter 4 further develops and explores hope/faith, vision, and the values of altruistic love.

Spiritual Well-Being

The emergence of spiritual leadership then taps into the fundamental needs of both leader and followers for spiritual well-being by positively enhancing their sense of calling and membership. Calling or being called (vocationally) gives a sense of making a difference in the lives of others. Membership gives a sense of belonging or community. These two elements of spiritual well-being are universal and interconnected human needs.

Calling

Calling refers to how one makes a difference through service to others and, in doing so, finds meaning and purpose in life. Many people seek not only competence and mastery for realizing their full potential through their work, but also a sense that work has some social meaning or value (Pfeffer 2007). The term *calling* has long been used as one of the defining characteristics of a professional. Professionals in general have expertise in a specialized body of knowledge. They have ethics centered on selfless service to clients/customers, an obligation to maintain quality standards within the profession, a commitment to their vocational field, a dedication to their work, and a strong commitment to their careers. They believe their chosen profession is valuable, even essential to society, and they are proud to be a member of it. The need for calling is satisfied through both personal and organizational spiritual leadership

Membership

Membership includes a sense of belonging and community; it involves the cultural and social structures we are immersed in and through which we seek what William James, the founder of modern psychology, called man's most fundamental need —to be understood and appreciated. Having a sense of membership is a matter of interrelationships and connection through social interaction. Individuals value their affiliations, being interconnected, and feeling part of a larger community (Pfeffer 2007). As we devote ourselves to social groups, membership enmeshes us in a network of social connections that go as far as the group has influence and power, and backward and forward in relation to its history.

Companies have begun to recognize that calling and membership are essential for employee well-being. Medtronic's Medallion Ceremony honors employees with a medal depicting the company's spiritual logo, a patient rising from the operating table fully healed. This helps foster a sense of community while reinforcing the company's calling to prolong life through its medical products and services. Memorial Herrman Healthcare System celebrates their membership in community through a moving "Blessing of the Hands" ceremony for all caregivers. Spoken by a chaplain, the CEO, or unit manager, the blessing includes these simple words, "May the God that created you bless the care you give others." The optional ceremony, which the company has offered more than 5,000 times, helps nurses, therapists, housekeepers, physicians, and others renew their calling. Cordon Bleu-Tomasso Corporation's Prize of the Heart is awarded yearly, in a company-wide ceremony, to one person in the workplace who has demonstrated a joy for life in helping others through compassion and human dignity.

Spiritual well-being, however, is not obtained by striving for it directly. Employees cannot experience a sense of spiritual well-being through calling and membership by trying to manufacture it. It is not produced when a company focuses on its monetary goals, but instead occurs when leaders first establish a healthy workplace culture grounded in altruistic values and a transcendent vision. Chapter 5 provides additional discussion on spiritual well-being through calling and membership.

Personal and Organizational Outcomes

The positive personal and organizational outcomes that comprise the Triple Bottom Line are generated as a result of satisfying employees' fundamental need for spiritual well-being. Socially responsible companies such as the Body Shop, Timberline, Procter & Gamble (P&G), Weleda, Starbucks, and Ben and Jerry's are widely acknowledged for having vision and values that go beyond short-term profit while growing a sustainable enterprise that also places great emphasis on employee well-being. These organizations demonstrate the qualities of spiritual leadership that positively influence spiritual well-being and the Triple Bottom Line.

People

Mainstream medical research during the past twenty years tends to support a positive relationship between spirituality and health and has begun to recognize the power of spirituality in maintaining health. Individuals in work groups that experience high levels of spiritual well-being have higher levels of positive human health, psychological well-being, and life satisfaction (Fry, "Introduction to the Special Issue," 2005; Ryff and Singer 2001). More specifically, they have a higher regard for themselves and their personal histories, good-quality relationships with others, a sense that life is purposeful and meaningful, the capacity to effectively manage their surrounding world, the ability to follow inner convictions, and a sense of continuing growth and self-realization.

Planet

Attending to the sustainability of our planet requires an ongoing commitment to corporate social responsibility that rests on the underlying assumptions inherent in stakeholder theory (Freeman 1984). Organizations based on a vision of service to stakeholders through altruistic love are dedicated to being socially responsible. Corporate social responsibility feeds into and flows from the attainment of goals consistent with the need for the organization and its workers to function in society as a whole (Fry, "Toward a Theory of Ethical and Spiritual Well-Being," 2005; Paloutzian, Emmons, and Keortge 2003). When members of an organization have a sense of belonging (membership) and a commitment to a common purpose (calling), the organization as a whole is more successful in meeting or exceeding all stakeholder expectations, including those focused on sustainability.

Profit

Figure 1.2 from the previous chapter shows that the Spiritual Leadership Balanced Scorecard Business Model links spiritual well-being to financial performance. Relative to organizational performance and profits, the intrinsic motivation process in spiritual leadership that is based on vision, altruistic love, and hope/faith results in an increase in one's sense of spiritual well-being and ultimately increases:

> Organizational commitment: People with a sense of calling and membership will become attached and loyal to and will want to stay in organizations that have cultures based on the values of altruistic love.

> Productivity and continuous improvement: People who have hope/faith in the organization's vision and who experience calling and membership will "do what it takes" in pursuit of the vision to continuously improve and be more productive.

The field of performance excellence has signaled the need to go beyond reporting financial metrics, such as profit and sales growth, to include nonfinancial predictors of financial performance, such as customer satisfaction, organizational outputs such as quality and delivery, process or internal operating measures, and employee commitment and growth. Employee commitment is the central and leading indicator of these other performance categories. In other words, a high degree of spiritual well-being as a driver of organizational commitment and productivity ultimately drives the level of quality products and service. This then leads to high levels of customer satisfaction and, ultimately, growth in sales and profits.

There is a rich diversity of organizations that place great emphasis on Triple Bottom Line outcomes. The Body Shop is a successful international company that sells high-quality natural skin and hair products. The company explicitly embraces spiritual principles and holds to high ideals of social justice, straight talk, socially responsible activism, volunteerism, and environmental sustainability, which inspires its stakeholders—employees, vendors, customers, and the communities it touches—locally and globally. Timberland, the $1.5 billion manufacturer and retailer of rugged, outdoor-tested, environmentally conscious gear for men, women, and kids, is an organization of creative, hard-working people who share a deep belief that people united in service can change the world. Their core values of humanity, humility, integrity, and excellence are the foundation for everything they do every day as they endeavor to make their communities better places to live. Procter & Gamble is one of America's oldest and most pioneering, admired, imitated, and profitable companies. Dedicated to corporate social responsibility and sustainability, P&G uses technology to help people in developing companies cheaply disinfect water in their homes. The consumer giant also supports minority-owned banks and invests in venture capital funds for minority business. Core values at the heart of P&G's culture—integrity, respect, trust, personal mastery, passion for winning, external focus—communicate a dual concern and caring for both the consumer and the people of P&G.

A STUDY OF SPIRITUAL LEADERSHIP: INTERSTATE BATTERIES

One company that we have worked with directly that embraces both personal and organizational spiritual leadership is Interstate Batteries, which provides more than 7,000 types of batteries for households and businesses. The Dallas-based company has revenues of more than $1.5 billion and holds the largest share of the replacement car-battery market. More than 300 franchise distributors service Interstate Batteries' 200,000 retail dealers, who provide automotive, commercial, marine/RV, motorcycle, lawn and garden, and specialty batteries almost everywhere in the United States, as well as in Canada and select international locations.

The company has received the Toyota Excellence Award for demonstrating "sustained effort, uncompromising attention to detail, and a commitment to performance excellence." Interstate demonstrates its commitment to improving the environment through an active battery-recycling program and by being a sponsor of National Recycling Month in April and Earth Day on April 22. They take pride in being the number-one battery recycler in the United States, with more than 850 million pounds of batteries recycled last year alone. The company also sponsors the highly successful Interstate Batteries Winston Cup team and an NHRA Funny Car Team.

Norm Miller, Interstate's chairman, is a devout believer in God's power to change lives. He chronicles his journey in his book, *Beyond the Norm*, which details his beginnings as a traveling salesman, his conversion experience, how he turned his will and his life over to God after his third DWI, and how he envisioned Interstate Batteries as an organization based on workplace spirituality (N. Miller 1996).

At Interstate, Miller and Interstate's workers do not hide their faith (predominately Christian), but he insists that neither do they want to "cram religion down anyone's throat." There is a corporate chaplaincy program that is available for ministry to employees. Whenever employees or visitors gather to eat, there is a prayer. The company sponsors prayer breakfasts and other spiritual studies before and after work and maintains an e-mail prayer chain. Employees may elect to have up to $5.00 per paycheck deducted for a catastrophic relief fund administered by the corporate chaplaincy. These funds help Interstate employees who need temporary financial assistance for catastrophic emergencies that aren't covered by Interstate's generous employee benefits. A company library lends employees reading material and videotapes. A monthly pizza get-together hosts spiritual speakers and offers employees free pizza.

Norm Miller's Personal Spiritual Leadership

Norm began to show signs of following in his father's footsteps, as a gifted salesman, as early as age ten. "I used to get my dad to bring home soft drinks from his service station. Then I would put them on ice, load them in my wagon, and sell them at construction sites. There was a great profit, because I never paid Dad back for the drinks!" says Norm (N. Miller n.d.).

By the time he entered college, Norm was hawking harder stuff, smuggling alcohol into the dry county of Denton, Texas, and selling it; as time went on, he began sampling more of the product than he should. When he first entered college, Norm intended to stay for only about a year. But during that first year he realized that if he wanted to compete with his peers, he should at least make sure he was on the same playing field. This required him to do everything he needed to graduate. So he stuck it out until he obtained a degree in business. It was during this period that he met his future wife, Ann.

After graduation, Norm's father suggested he get involved in a fledgling company called Interstate Batteries whose owner, John Searcy, was looking for people to open up distributorships. Soon Norm was driving all over the place, peddling batteries out of the back of his Studebaker. In just over two years, Norm became so successful that he was offered a job at Interstate's headquarters. Together with his younger brother Tommy, whom Searcy also hired, Norm started helping other distributors improve their business. Due to Norm's natural affinity for sales and his penchant for hard work, Searcy soon made him second in command, complete with an option to buy out Searcy's share of the company once he retired.

But Norm's life had another side that was not so positive. Although he had managed to work his way up the corporate ladder, he did not give up his party lifestyle. "We never came home," Norm says of his days out on the road with Tommy. "We stayed out and partied. We were pretty self-centered, both of us. . . . And if it was convenient, we'd worry about our wives" (N. Miller n.d.). It wasn't long before Norm's wife began to entertain thoughts of leaving him. Norm's life reached its lowest point when he was stopped by the police early one morning in 1974 after he had been out drinking. He managed to talk his way out of being arrested for drunken driving—it would have been his third arrest—but as he lay in bed that morning, it dawned on him: he was an alcoholic, just like his father. "That just shattered me," says Norm. "I blurted out in a half-yell, 'God help me, I can't handle it!'"

Norm started attending meetings of Alcoholics Anonymous, began studying the Bible, and ultimately became a Christian. He noticed changes in himself almost immediately. Most important, he was able to quit drinking. He no longer struggled with a fear of failure, and he developed a sense of love and caring for others that was in stark contrast to his earlier, self-centered lifestyle. As Norm was undergoing his transformation in personal spiritual leadership, Interstate was changing, too. In 1978 Searcy retired and sold his share of the company to Norm, who suddenly found himself president and chairman of a multimillion-dollar company. At first he wasn't sure if he could do the job, but Searcy's encouragement, combined with his faith in God and the fact that Tommy was also with him, convinced Norm to forge ahead.

Organizational Spiritual Leadership at Interstate Batteries

Norm's soul isn't the only thing that has prospered over the years. His business has thrived as well. When Norm joined Interstate in 1965, it was a five-man operation with approximately 35 distributorships. Now it boasts more than $1.5 billion in sales with more than 1,000 employees and 315 distributorships, making Interstate Batteries the largest distributor of batteries in the world. Today, as chairman, Norm is not involved in the day-to-day operation, allowing him time to speak to a variety of audiences interested in how he found the truth of Christianity and how he learned to effectively apply Biblical principles to implement spirituality in the workplace and create a more successful business.

One of Norm's first initiatives as president was to make organizational spiritual leadership a primary component of the business. Part of what makes Interstate a unique company is its unabashed mission to conduct business in a way that honors God. That was Norm Miller's vision when he became president in 1978, and it is clear from Interstate's current mission statement that Interstate Batteries has found a way to incorporate workplace spirituality and both personal and organizational spiritual leadership to maximize the Triple Bottom Line:

> To glorify God as we supply our customers worldwide with top-quality, value-priced batteries, related electrical power-source products, and distribution services. Further, our mission is to provide our partners and Interstate Batteries System of America, Inc. (IBSA) with opportunities which are profitable, rewarding and growth-oriented. (Miller and Miller n.d.)

While it is not necessary to be a Christian to be employed at Interstate, workplace spirituality is a part of the daily work life for Interstate team members. Norm Miller makes sure he and his staff apply the spiritual principles that underlie Christianity to everything they do, although they also make sure that the practices of all spiritual and religious traditions are respected and supported. Today Interstate and its employees support all sorts of charitable projects all around the world. These include their battery recycling program; the Family Care Fund, which assists Interstate team members and their immediate families faced with urgent short-term financial needs; a camp scholarship program to make it possible for indigent children to attend summer youth camps; the Angel Tree Christmas Project, which buys gifts for children of prison inmates under the umbrella of the Prison Fellowship outreach program; and women's, men's, Dallas Warehouse BBQ (off-site) and pizza luncheons that provide opportunities for spiritual encouragement and growth.

So what does this former bootlegger, petty thief, and recovered alcoholic think about his success? "To me, success is having an abundant life. That does not necessarily mean lots of money. To me, an abundant life is one that is rich, full, meaningful, significant, and adventuresome" (Miller and Miller n.d.).

Measuring Interstate Batteries' Implementation of the Spiritual Leadership Model

To study and confirm their dedication to organizational spiritual leadership, Interstate requested our assistance in conducting a study to capture and examine any differences in organizational spiritual leadership between corporate headquarters and their growing number of company-owned distributorships. At the time, only 43 of the more than 300 distributorships were owned and operated by Interstate. However, the company wanted to pursue a strategy of owning distributorships. Top management felt confident there was a high level of organizational spiritual leadership among employees at their corporate headquarters, which is housed in an office complex in north Dallas. They were less sure of the level of organizational spiritual leadership across the distributorships, which ranged in size from five to twenty-seven employees and were scattered throughout the United States.

The resulting study of Interstate Batteries supported the spiritual leadership model (we will discuss how to measure spiritual leadership in more detail in Chapter 7). The results of the study were first presented in "Maximizing the Triple Bottom Line Through Spiritual Leadership" at the international conference of the Academy of Management and then published in *Organizational Dynamics* (Fry and Slocum 2008). A sample was taken of approximately 350 workers employed in 43 company-owned wholesale distributorships who serviced automotive, commercial, marine/RV, motorcycle, and lawn and garden retail dealers, along with almost 400 workers at the home office. The three dimensions of spiritual leadership (hope/faith, altruistic love, vision), two spiritual well-being dimensions (calling/meaning and membership), and organizational commitment and productivity were measured. In addition, two measures of performance were provided from each distributor—percentage increase/decrease in sales and profit.

The averages of the spiritual leadership variables were all significantly higher for employees at the corporate headquarters than for those in the distributorships. Headquarters employees also reported higher levels of spiritual well-being than distributorship employees. The findings provided empirical support for top management's view that there was a need to establish a baseline to assess the effectiveness of future organizational development strategies to more closely align corporate and distributor vision and culture.

Further analysis revealed that meaning/calling and membership explained 13 percent of distributor sales growth, 94 percent of an employee's commitment to the company, and 73 percent of distributorship productivity. Distributorships with higher levels of spiritual leadership subsequently had employees who reported higher levels of spiritual well-being through calling and membership that in turn positively impacted organizational commitment, productivity, and sales growth. The "bottom line" for this study is that we have evidence that following the Spiritual Leadership Model can be a significant source of competitive advantage. These results, while not definitive, indicate that implementation of the Spiritual Leadership Model and its sustained use would drive a significant increase in sales growth.

CONCLUSION

The Spiritual Leadership Model incorporates and extends several seemingly different approaches to leadership and motivation for implementing an intrinsically motivated learning organization that is flat, flexible, diverse, networked, and global.

Motivation in the workplace results when leaders create an environment that brings out the best in people as they achieve performance goals and receive individual, group, and system-wide rewards. Intrinsic motivation is defined as interest in and enjoyment of an activity for its own sake and is associated with active engagement in tasks that people find interesting and that, in turn, promote growth and satisfy higher-order needs.

The Spiritual Leadership Model can be applied to both personal spiritual leadership and organizational spiritual leadership. Personal spiritual leadership is about leading and leader development of individual-based knowledge, skills, and abilities associated with a formal leadership role, with an emphasis on the influence leaders have on their followers. Spiritual leaders draw on an inner-life practice and seek to develop a vision of service to others based in the values of altruistic love.

Organizational spiritual leadership focuses on a social-influence process that engages everyone and enables groups of people to work together in meaningful ways. This process involves building the capacity for better individual and collective adaptability and performance across a wide range of situations. Organizational spiritual leadership emphasizes building and using interpersonal competence to foster mutual trust and respect in pursuit of a vision of service to key stakeholders based in the values of altruistic love. In turn, spiritual leadership positively impacts spiritual well-being and, ultimately, employee well-being, sustainability, and financial performance—the Triple Bottom Line.

Norm Miller and Interstate Batteries provide excellent examples for personal and organizational spiritual leadership that maximizes personal outcomes and the Triple Bottom Line. Norm's strong inner life, based on spiritual practices, is the source of his personal values, based in altruistic love. Those values provide the foundation for hope/faith in his personal vision to love and serve others through a company that is not only a world-class provider of electrical-power-source products but also dedicated to the well-being of its employees and the communities in which they operate.

Practical Tools

For those interested in maximizing the Triple Bottom Line, the major tools introduced in this chapter include the following:

Intrinsic motivation springs from the internal satisfaction experienced when work is rewarding in and of itself through its performance and achievement. It serves as the primary source of motivation in spiritual leadership and the learning organization.

The personal Spiritual Leadership Model emphasizes leading and leader development. It provides a roadmap for strong personal leadership based on a vision of service to others through altruistic love to maximize personal commitment and productivity, psychological well-being, and life satisfaction.

The organizational Spiritual Leadership Model focuses on leadership development to build the capacity for better individual and collective adaptability and performance based on hope/faith in a vision of service to key stakeholders through altruistic love to maximize the Triple Bottom Line.

Components of the Spiritual Leadership Model provide the four basic elements (inner life, spiritual leadership, spiritual well-being, and personal and organizational outcomes) needed to understand and implement the Spiritual Leadership Model.

Chapter Three

INNER LIFE: THE SOURCE OF SPIRITUAL LEADERSHIP

The corrosion of leaders' souls is nothing new. It often occurs slowly, like a stone being hollowed out by dripping water, drop by drop. The risk of such corrosion is something all of us face in our daily journey; it comes in the form of temptations to cut corners, to be less than our best selves. At its heart, it is a result of a failure to cultivate an inner life, something that is necessary for anyone who wants to lead a productive and happy outer life.

Financier and convicted felon Bernie Madoff serves as a chilling example of how a corrupted inner life, based on satisfying one's selfish interests for fame and material gain and placing those interests over concern for the welfare of others entrusted to one's care, can lead to outward failure and disgrace. Madoff, who served as a nonexecutive chairman of the NASDAQ stock exchange, pled guilty to an eleven-count criminal complaint, admitting to defrauding thousands of investors out of billions of dollars. He was convicted of operating a Ponzi scheme that has been called the largest investor fraud ever committed by a single person. Federal prosecutors estimated client losses, which included fabricated gains, of almost $65 billion. On June 29, 2009, he was sentenced to 150 years in prison, the maximum allowed. ("Bernard Madoff" n.d.)

In 1960 Madoff founded the Wall Street firm Bernard L. Madoff Investment Securities LLC, which specialized in directly executing orders over the counter from retail brokers. According to a March 13, 2009, filing by Madoff, he and his wife were worth up to $126 million, plus another estimated $700 million for the value of his business interests in his company. By his own account, he went astray in the early 1990s when he could no longer return the high yields on which he staked his reputation to investors. He then started his Ponzi scheme, thinking that sooner or later he could invest his way out when times got better. Instead he became more and more entrenched. In spite of his stated good intentions, he ended up losing the money he promised to invest responsibly, did harm to countless people, and ended up disgraced, humiliated, and imprisoned.

Madoff gained many influential clients by posing as a prominent philanthropist, serving on boards of nonprofit institutions, many of which entrusted his firm with their endowments. He served as the chairman of the Board of Directors and as treasurer of the Board of Trustees for the Sy Syms School of Business at Yeshiva University; he also served on the board of New York City Center, a member of New York City's Cultural Institutions Group (CIG). He undertook charity work for the Gift of Life Bone Marrow Foundation and engaged in philanthropic giving through the Madoff Family Foundation, a $19 million private foundation that donated money to many educational, cultural, and health charities. Businesses, charities, and foundations around the world felt repercussions from his firm's collapse; among them were the closure of the Robert I. Lappin Charitable Foundation, the Picower Foundation, and the JEHT Foundation.

Madoff had struggled for many years to develop the inner strength, abilities, and skills needed to get to the summit of achievement. Then, just when it seemed he had reached the mountaintop and finally attained a lifetime goal of celebrity, wealth, power, and prestige . . . it happened. The inner character flaw that grew and was reinforced over the years by self-centered greed and avarice finally surfaced, to rapidly bring him and his empire down like a house of cards.

As we discussed in Chapter 2, the source of both personal and organizational spiritual leadership and ultimately the Triple Bottom Line is an inner-life practice that fuels hope/faith in a transcendent vision of service to key stakeholders through the values of altruistic love. Most leaders recognize that there is a spiritual element to life. Spirituality is giving expression to the being that is within us, manifesting the power that comes from within, and knowing our deepest selves (Conger and Kanungo 1988). Spirituality expresses the desire to find meaning in connection with others and to treat life as an offering of what we do. It acknowledges that life as lived every day is a precious gift and an endowment to become even better.

As we illustrated through the example of Cordon Bleu-Tomasso Corporation in Chapter 1, workplace spirituality acknowledges that people have both an inner and an outer life. The nourishment of the inner life can produce a more meaningful and productive outer life that can lead to beneficial individual and organizational outcomes. Because of this, organizations should nurture the inner life of their workers and create an organizational environment that facilitates inner-life development and expression for all who choose to do so.

Inner life is a process of understanding and tapping into a power greater than ourselves, along with understanding how to draw on that power to live a more satisfying and full outer life. It speaks to the feelings individuals have about the fundamental meaning of who they are, what they are doing, and the contributions they are making (Vaill 1998). Inner life as a source of spiritual leadership includes individual practices (for example, meditation, prayer, yoga, journaling, and walking in nature) and organizational contexts (such as rooms for inner silence and reflection) that help individuals be more self-aware and conscious from moment to moment.

This chapter discusses the development of an inner-life practice and the spiritual journey within the framework of the Spiritual Leadership Model. First, we describe the spiritual journey as a pilgrimage through five levels of knowing and being. We then discuss how to develop inner life through mindfulness, a key spiritual practice essential for inner life, which is the source or driver of spiritual leadership and, ultimately, the Triple Bottom Line. Finally, we offer the journey of the Fool as an allegory for the spiritual journey and the role inner life plays in it.

Inner Life, Consciousness, and the Spiritual Journey

At the heart of inner life is the quest for a spirituality that reflects a common human pursuit to draw strength from a higher power. This pursuit underlies all historic ideas of God. Walter Horton, in his book *God*, offers a general definition of God as a higher power: "The quest for God is the quest for an ideal Source of help and Object of Devotion: a Being so much greater, more enduring, and more worthy than ourselves that we may confidently lean on it for support and unreservedly give ourselves to its service" (Horton 1950).

Horton placed conceptions of God as a higher power on a continuum from atheism to pantheism, see Figure 3.1 (Horton 1950). Atheism implies that there is no higher power than one's self. According to Horton's definition of God, there are few real atheists. Unless someone believes in some higher power, whether it be family, friends, a work organization, science and technology, or a social order (for example, Communism), there is no path in life left except for death through conscious or unconscious suicide.

The first step along the continuum away from atheism lies in the absorption of nature into an orderly human social system. Examples are families and tribes, secular and religious organizations, and profit and nonprofit organizations. On the other end of the continuum lie the polytheistic religions—those that believe in several gods, often a multitude of deified natural gods. These religions often include sacred stones and mountains; ruling chiefs and kings; the sun, moon, and stars; rain and lightning; and the ancestors and heroes of the tribe. The people of ancient Egypt, who organized, managed, and led one of the greatest projects in history, the construction of the great pyramids, worshiped hundreds of gods and goddesses that ruled over all aspects of life and death. In pantheistic religions (which believe that God is everything) certain gods begin to emerge with special prominence into one supreme deity, such as Zeus in ancient Greece and Brahma in India. From this perspective, those who call themselves atheists or agnostics, who instead place trust and faith in science and

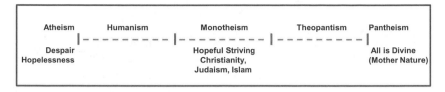

FIGURE 3.1 Conceptions of God as a Higher Power
Source: Adapted and modified from Horton, W., *God*, 9th ed., New York: Association Press, 1950.

technology, are actually worshiping an objective or nature-based pantheistic god.

According to Horton, both humanistic and pantheistic conceptions of God tend to converge toward the center of this continuum to form a unity in the thought of God called ethical monotheism, which is found with Christianity, Judaism, and Islam. The God of theism is neither the sum total of reality, as in pantheism, nor the upholder of the established order, as in humanism. The nature of the theistic God is defined in terms of ethical character, values, and purpose through principles of justice and/or redemptive love. In ethical monotheism (belief in a single God), these principles have already established the basic structure of the world at present and are still actively at work in it for its radical transformation and improvement.

An inner-life practice is central for the development of both personal and organizational spiritual leadership. Regardless of its source, inner life in spiritual leadership is the quest for a higher power as a source for hope/faith in a transcendent vision to love and serve others. For example, the Alcoholics Anonymous (AA) organization offers a Twelve Steps program to help its members experience calling and membership through love and service of others in living a life without alcohol. AA's approach is explicitly spiritual, insisting that members place their trust not in themselves but in a higher power they are free to interpret as they choose.

Levels of Knowing and Being

Inner life is also a central aspect of the spiritual journey, which is about self-transcendence—the transformation from ego-centered to other-centered

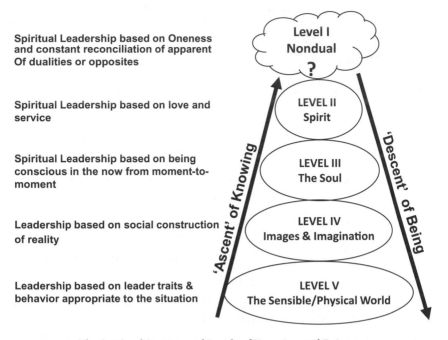

FIGURE 3.2 The Spiritual Journey and Levels of Knowing and Being
Source: Adapted and modified from Fry, L., and Kriger, M., "Towards a Theory of Being-centered Leadership: Multiple Levels of Being as Context for Effective Leadership," *Human Relations*, 62 (11) 2009: 1667–1734.

while striving to attain and maintain a state of being or consciousness from moment to moment. One way to depict the spiritual journey is shown in Figure 3.2. This figure is adapted from Mark Krieger and Yvonne Seng's article, "Leadership with Inner meaning: A Contingency Theory of Leadership Based on Worldviews of Five Religions," which examines Judaism, Islam, Christianity, Hinduism, and Buddhism as five natural experiments in sense making and social action that have evolved over the last 1,400 to 4,000 years, depending on the religious tradition. In doing so all five religions developed a model consisting of five levels of knowing and being that place development of an inner-life practice as central for spiritual development.

Everyone, in his or her own unique way, seeks knowledge about reality that they feel will allow them to attain greater fulfillment and happiness in life. These five levels of knowing and being provide different views of reality that produce different approaches to leadership. In addition, each of the five levels of being have a corresponding mode of consciousness in terms of notions such as truth, belief, justification for one's actions, and what constitutes happiness. At each level leaders find themselves concerned about questions such as these: What is knowledge? What are the processes by which knowledge is acquired? What do people seek to know? How do we become more aware of both ourselves and the world around us?'

States of being are different levels of consciousness, marked by the lower-order systems of knowledge and moving to progressively more subtle, higher-order systems in which an individual's overall level of knowing and being evolves. Such a system can be described as *holonic*: each level as a whole is embedded in a higher level of the system, creating a nested system of wholes. For example, a whole atom is part of a whole molecule; a whole molecule is part of a whole cell; a whole cell is part of a whole organism. In a holonic system of being, each successive level of existence is a stage through which individuals pass on their way to acknowledging more levels of being. When a person is at a particular level of being, he or she tends to experience psychological states that are appropriate to that level. In addition, an individual's feelings, motivations, ethics, values, learning system, and personal theories of what constitutes happiness are consistent with and appropriate to that level of knowing and being.

In the spiritual journey, each higher level of knowing and being transcends and includes each of the lower levels. Moreover, each lower level can be activated or reactivated as individuals progress and then fall back to a lower level. Thus the spiritual journey is a pilgrimage. Each level can govern a person involved in any particular activity, depending on the level of awareness and development of the individual. More important still, all individuals, independent of their current stage of development, have all of these levels potentially available. Understanding the different levels of being helps provide a roadmap for inner-life practices and the role they play in the spiritual journey and as a source of hope/faith, vision, and altruistic love in spiritual leadership.

Level V—The Sensible/Physical World

The fifth level of being is comprised of the physical, observable world that is based in the five senses, in which a leader creates and transfers knowledge through an active engagement in worldly affairs. As a state of being, individuals are born into and live within a social world where the major view of reality is based on the sensible/physical world (Burrell and Morgan 1994). Effective leadership in the sensible/physical world requires developing appropriate diagnostic skills to discern the characteristics of tasks, subordinates, and the organization, and then being flexible enough in one's leadership behavior to increase the likelihood of desired effectiveness outcomes.

Level IV—Images and Imagination

The fourth level of being is where reality is socially and personally constructed through the creation and maintenance of vision, cultural values, and images. At this level, leadership involves the use of images and imagination as part of the process of creating a compelling vision and establishing strong cultural values. The main goal of leadership at this level is to create agreement on a socially constructed reality that motivates followers to high levels of organizational commitment and performance. The primary focus at this level is on the subjective experience of individuals and groups as they relate to the development of awareness and knowledge (Almaas 2004; Burrell and Morgan 1994). Out of this level arises the legitimacy and appropriateness of a leader's vision, as well as the ethical and cultural values individuals and groups should embrace or reject. An example is Nelson Mandela's vision for South Africa:

> During my lifetime I have dedicated myself to the struggle of the African people. I have fought against white domination, and I have fought against black domination. I have cherished the ideal of a democratic and free society in which all persons live together in harmony and with equal opportunities. It is an ideal which I hope to live for and to achieve. But if needs be, it is an ideal for which I am prepared to die. (Hatang and Venter 2011)

However, at Level IV there is the possibility that the vision and values of self-serving leaders may result in deception and the exploitation of employees and stakeholders (Bass and Steidlmeier 1999). At this level there is the potential for a dark side to leadership; leaders may have a tendency toward narcissism, authoritarianism, Machiavellianism, and a strong need for personal power. This is the level of being that produced the Enron and WorldCom debacles and, more recently, the subprime financial market collapse in which greed, avarice, and unethical practices on the part of investment brokers like Bernie Madoff, mortgage lenders, and Wall Street opportunists bankrupted both individuals and huge corporations and brought the U.S. financial system to near ruin.

Level III—The Soul

The third level of knowing and being is one in which individual awareness occurs and self-transcendence begins to emerge. A. H. Almaas, in *The Inner Journey Home: Soul's Realization of the Unity of Reality,* describes the soul as "the locus of ourselves, the place where we experience ourselves . . . the locus in Reality where we experience the self" (Almaas 2004). In this context, soul refers to the whole self and self is defined as that which tends toward enhancing an individual's overall well-being. It includes both a spiritual aspect and more conventional levels of experience, such as our emotions and physical sensations. The soul is the entity where all of our experiences are integrated into a whole. It functions as the vessel that literally contains our inner events and is the place where we experience our inner life.

To awaken or become conscious at Level III involves the capacity to be aware from moment to moment of all of our experiences, thoughts, feelings, body sensations, and the mind itself; this state is sometimes called "soul awareness" (Tolle, *The Power of Now* 1999). Without an understanding of the soul as the place of felt experience in the current moment, a leader's thinking will tend to become focused on the past or the future. The leader is then trapped in an ego-centered experience, a duality in which the "experience" is separated from what is "experienced" (Osborne 1970; Tolle, *A New Earth* 2005).

All the major spiritual and religious traditions believe that without this level of awareness, individuals perceive themselves simply as the sum of their individual thoughts, feelings, emotions, and body sensations. It is thus important for leaders seeking Level III to develop and refine the ability to be present, mindful, or conscious of the present moment by withdrawing attention from past memories and future imaginings whenever they are not needed. In doing so, leaders are more able to be in touch with subtle feelings and intuitions that can result in a better understanding of the organizational context as well as the needs of followers.

At Level III's state of knowing and being, leaders facilitate ever more refined programs of change and transformation at both the individual and organizational levels. It is here that leaders cultivate such inner-life practices as contemplation, prayer, and meditation, which serve to refine the leader's individual and social identity as other-centered (Benefiel, *The Second Half of the Journey* 2005; Duschon and Plowman 2005; Kurtz and Ketcham 1992). According to Richard Rohr in *Everything Belongs* (Rohr 2003), inner life is a practice or discipline of constantly observing our thought patterns and what we pay attention to in order to get the self-centered ego out of the way. An inner-life practice asks questions like: What is my agenda? What is my predisposition? What are my prejudices? What are my fears? What are my angers? Answering these questions requires us to develop the ability to stand away from ourselves and to listen and look with a calm, nonjudgmental objectivity. This inner process can be brutal, but it is absolutely necessary for spiritual leadership. Otherwise one cannot separate from the mind's identification with thoughts and feelings.

Level II—Spirit

The spiritual aspect of a leader is concerned with finding and expressing one's calling or purpose and living in relation to others by drawing on a power greater than oneself. The second level of being seeks self-transcendence and deepening connectedness with all things in the universe. At Level II the focus is on leadership though love and service to others. Recognized examples of leadership at Level II include Mother Theresa, Gandhi, Martin Luther King, and Nelson Mandela. Very few organizational leaders exist consistently at Level II, though organizational leaders often lead from this level as a temporary state.

Level I—Nondual

Level I is the most inclusive level of being, in which there is only a transcendent unity. Underlying this level is a central theme: the goal of this world is to know the Absolute through the transcendence of all opposites and realize self-actualization. The nondual thus embraces both pure being and pure emptiness. Logically this level of being appears to involve a contradiction. However, all of the world's spiritual traditions refer in one way or another to this level of being, which is so inclusive that it includes both pure emptiness and pure fullness or completeness. Level I is the integration of all of the previous levels of being, which is beyond all distinctions, including the distinction between leader and follower. Spiritual leadership at this level is one in which the leader responds to each situation, moment to moment, as it arises within a unique context and configuration of forces. This stage is at the limits of what most individuals in the workplace can even imagine, let alone actualize in their lives or jobs. Thus, Level I leadership is a stage of being that is more to be aspired to, rather than a current reality within organizational settings.

In Figure 3.2, the nondual is identified as "?." We use the question mark to refer to that which is prior to and beyond names and uncreated, yet the source of all creation. The "?" proposed is not dependent on the meaning of what is signified by the "?" since it is the constructed and lived sense making of the "?" that infuses meaning, inner perception, and deeper values in leaders. Religious leaders that have led from Level I include the Buddha, Jesus Christ, and Mohammad.

There are some recent examples of individuals who are likely Level I leaders. Ramana Maharshi, an Indian sage of the twentieth century, emphasized in his teachings that the point where all religions converge is in the realization that God is everything and everything is God. This is the essence of the nondual. He further maintained that this realization should not be in a mystical, symbolic or allegorical sense but rather in a most literal and practical sense.

Eckhart Tolle (Tolle 1999) provides a more recent example of the Level I leader who leads by his or her vision and values for humanity. Tolle states that being at the highest level can be felt, but by its very nature it cannot be understood fully by the rational mind. To be at the level of the nondual involves abiding in a state of "feeling-realization," which is a natural state of nonseparation with Being (God) (Tolle 2005; Tolle 1999). When situations arise that need to be dealt with, appropriate actions become spontaneously clear as they arise in the now out of deep presence or moment-to-moment awareness.

In spiritual leadership, the leader dynamically resides in and responds to an ever-evolving open system of levels of knowing and being. At any level an individual, whether a leader or not, actualizes all the levels of being that reside at each of the lower levels. Leaders can aspire to and reach self-realization, a state of nonseparation from being in its most inclusive sense. At this level of being, all of the world's spiritual traditions declare that the experience of duality (that is, of separation) will dissolve. Therefore, a leader living and behaving from the nondual level would not see a distinction between the "leader" and the "led." From the nondual level of being, followership and leadership are simply labels that overly constrain the possible role sets of individuals. In the ideal, individuals have the potential to enter roles as needed to enact leadership in specific situations moment by moment.

Shifting from "Having" and "Doing" to "Being"

How does a leader activate these levels of knowing and being? The answer lies in developing the ability to shift from the "having" and "doing" to "being." "Having" and "doing" are constructs that are central to the ego-based self in Levels V and IV. The direct experience and understanding of "being" has wasted away in the world today, largely due to an overemphasis on "observables" such as bottom-line performance. Essentially, if something is not directly observable or measurable, many leaders tend to question or even deny its relevance. However, a remnant of an earlier familiarity with the concept of being is that we still call ourselves human beings—not human doings or human havings. This language reflects a direct experience and understanding of being that has existed for centuries.

Spiritual leadership development requires that a leader seek higher levels of knowing. This is illustrated by the upward arrow on the left side of Figure 3.2, which is labeled the "ascent" of knowing. This knowing begins with an awareness of leadership in the Level V physical world and an awareness of the role of vision and values in Level IV. Then comes the honesty, open-mindedness, and willingness to undertake the spiritual journey and nurture one's inner life and consciousness for moral transformation from self to other-centered in Level III. This transformation then fosters awareness of the power of leadership based on love and service of others in Level II. Ultimately, there is the desire to draw on one's inner life as the source of an ongoing effort to reside in Level I—a state of nondual awareness of knowing and being in a transcendent unity where, moment to moment, all is one.

Spiritual leadership then manifests through progressively more coarse levels of being (that is, Level I, II, III, IV, and ultimately Level V) (Wilber, *A Theory of Everything* 2000; Wilber, *Integral Psychology* 2000). This progression is illustrated by the downward arrow on the right side of Figure 3.2, labeled as the "descent" of being. Level I is the source of Level II leadership through love and service, Level II is the source of consciousness, and moral sensitivity comes in at Level III. Moral sensitivity influences the formation of leader values based in altruistic love, which in turn directly influence the development of the leader's vision (Level IV) that ultimately influences leader behavior (Level V).

Regardless of their level of inner development, leaders will always have some aspects of spiritual perception and moral sensitivity that requires further inner work. Inner life in spiritual leadership encourages leaders to understand that their inspiration and creativity, as well as their moral standards, are the product of other levels of knowing and being and are often only partially perceived or understood (Smith 1991). These levels are not like stair steps. Rather they are destinations that are resting places on the pilgrimage that is the spiritual journey. Level I is always the desired destination. However, few ever reach it and stay there for sustained periods. Rather, leaders may find that they reside at all the levels periodically.

But by committing to the spiritual journey, sojourners will find themselves knowing and leading from Levels III and II more often.

MINDFULNESS

Spiritual leadership not only requires an understanding of the spiritual journey and the levels of knowing and being. It also requires finding the honesty, open-mindedness, and willingness to undertake the journey. The spiritual journey begins when one commits to move beyond Levels V and IV into the Level III way of knowing and being, to become conscious and move from self- to other-centered. A key to this process is a program for mindfulness.

Mindfulness allows an individual to explore the often crippling emotional programs for happiness that are developed in early childhood based on needs for survival, security, affection, esteem, power, and control. It also requires exploring the over-attachment or over-identification with any particular group or culture to which one belongs.

Mindfulness is tough work, and individuals will seldom exert the effort to fundamentally change their life's vision and personal values unless they are forced to do so by some precipitating event. The "bottom line" is that the motivation to enter Level III will not emerge until the pain of change is less than the pain of staying the same.

Level III Awareness and Mindfulness

To overcome the emotional programs for happiness as part of the spiritual journey, one must personally change in fundamental ways. Figure 3.2 illustrates the essence of the kind of profound personal transformation one must seek. It is based in the realization that to the extent we can come to see others differently, we can undergo a fundamental transformation that can free us from our anguished attitudes, thoughts, and emotions. This entails a change in our being based on a change of our values and attitudes—a change of heart.

For this realization to take place, one usually has to have a conversion experience that will provide the impetus to undertake the spiritual journey.

A conversion experience—some people call it "hitting bottom," "hitting the wall," or "kissing concrete"—is awakening to the fact we are going to lose something we are not prepared to live without if we do not change. No matter what it's called, the experience is the same; the real and certain imminence of the loss is so overpowering that the cost of change just doesn't matter.

How much does someone have to lose before they hit bottom? And why do some people prefer to exist in an ongoing living hell—or die—rather than change? That is the mystery. Only the people themselves know, and no one can hit bottom for them or make the decision to change for them. But eventually they discover that they are not able to will themselves to stop debilitating habits, thoughts, or feelings. Conversion experiences are spiritual realities that aren't rooted in reason. Often the best thing a person can do to cause a conversion experience is to be patient and not beat themselves up. Then they must work to create a state of readiness by cultivating honesty, open-mindedness, and willingness to change.

Hitting bottom may occur when a person:

- Hears a spouse say it's over.
- Watches a close friend die suddenly and realizes, "My life is not forever."
- Goes to jail due to alcohol, drugs, or some other addiction.
- Has serious thoughts about how life sucks and how lovely and easy it would be to end it all.
- Sees through the rat race and accepts that it will never bring the fulfillment that power, prestige, and owning material things promise.
- Looks in the mirror and can't stand the person they see.
- Hears a doctor say, "Change your ways or you won't see another Christmas."
- Cries himself to sleep and realizes that no one cares.
- Has failed for the umpteenth time and suddenly realizes that she caused the failure because deep down she never believed she could really win.

When a conversion experience does happen, our perceptions are altered due to the impact of the collision. At that moment, we see a different possibility than that offered up by the habits we've acquired through our emotional programs for happiness and cultural conditioning. In order to explore this possibility, one must be willing to discover the Level III way of knowing and being by cultivating an inner-life practice and the capacity to be mindful and present from moment to moment.

The first stage in developing mindfulness is to learn to listen with the undivided attention of one who wants to learn from a great teacher. The operative word here is *listen*. Through prayer we speak to a higher power. Most if not all of us have prayed for something at some time in our lives. To listen involves letting go of the noise around us and in us as well as releasing our preoccupations and concerns. It is a practical attentiveness with the intention of not pursuing thoughts that might intervene from whatever source, whether they be sense perceptions, memories, or plans for the future.

Mindfulness, however, is not a magic carpet ride to bliss. Rather, it is an exercise of letting go of the ego-centered false self, which is a humbling process because it is the only self we know. A daily inner-life practice based on mindfulness gradually exposes people to an awareness of the unconscious at a rate they can handle. Mindfulness does not take away our trials, but it helps to change our attitude toward them because, in this life, happiness is rooted in one's basic attitude toward reality or what is in the present moment. Mindfulness also helps answer two fundamental questions about the reality of one's relationship with their higher power.

Where Are You?

The first question is: Where are you on the spiritual journey in relation to yourself, others, and the nondual of Level I? In answering this first question, one discovers that the spiritual journey is not about creating a career or a success story. It is a progression of humiliations of the false, ego-centered self that become more and more profound and lead to the Level III way of knowing and being. What prevents us, both consciously and unconsciously, from moving to the center of being in Level I is gradually evacuated. It is as if a veil is being lifted and the higher power of our understanding enters our awareness to call, "Here I am. Where are you? Come and join me."

Who Are You?

This is the second question. Beginning in infancy, we become identified with and believe we are our emotional programs for happiness with their resultant thoughts and feelings. The energy we put into trying to find happiness in fulfilling these emotional programs tends to increase with time. Often we place our source of happiness in external relationships and circumstances, allowing our experience of life to be dominated by external events and our emotional reactions to them. The pain that we experience due to failure and rejection and that results in seeking happiness through safety and security, power and control, affection and esteem, and group identification may be repressed into the unconscious, where it negatively affects our decisions and choices.

The beginning of freedom comes with the realization that we are not our thoughts. Mindfulness allows us to start "watching" thoughts emerge and pass, along with the resultant feelings and physical sensations produced by them.

As Eckhart Tolle states in *Practicing the Power of Now*:

> The beginning of freedom is the realization that you are not the possessing entity—the thinker. Knowing this enables you to observe the entity. The moment you start watching the thinker, a higher level of consciousness becomes activated. You then begin to realize that there is a vast realm of intelligence beyond thought, that thought is only a tiny aspect of intelligence. You also realize that all the things that really matter — beauty, love, creativity, joy, inner peace—arise from beyond the mind. (Tolle 1999)

The moment we become the "watcher," the higher level of consciousness that is the essence of Level III—the Soul—is activated and we begin to sense that thoughts are only an infinitesimal aspect of our life. We begin to awaken and become enlightened to a natural state of felt oneness with being.

Meditation as a Mindful Practice

Getting an initial sense of the watcher is simple and easy and can be experienced through a simple breathing meditation. As a mindful practice, meditation is the art of inner listening that is practiced in each of the great world religious and spiritual traditions. Each of these traditions supports a meditative practice that emphasizes the importance of daily reflection as a direct route to mindfulness and an unmediated experience of being or the true nature of reality and existence.

It does not matter which form of meditation you choose. A good meditative practice develops awareness or mindfulness of one's body and senses, mind, and heart. The most important thing is to practice it regularly. Through meditation, one takes time to quiet the mind so that one's life can be lived with greater compassion and wakefulness. Meditation supports this inner potential and allows it to come forth. It is also helpful to seek out a spiritual or religious guide, coach, or teacher as well as a fellowship, community, or group where you can be together with other people. Such guides and groups can be found through churches, temples, and Buddhist, Sufi, and Hindu organizations, as well as various secular institutions. They can reinforce your practice with the support of other people who seek spiritual awareness and consciousness. In the process of practicing regularly, you will begin to develop your capacity to remain open to the present moment and begin to nurture your patience, compassion, and openness to everything that is here and now.

Mindful Awareness

As you practice meditation you become increasingly aware when your mind strays and you become more adept at bringing the body and mind back together to the present moment. Mindful awareness is thus a process of waking up and becoming the "watcher," of being present with the breath and then a forgetting, which is your true essence or being. We cannot see clearly nor have an accurate view of reality if our emotional programs for happiness and cultural conditioning are clouding our awareness. To meditate is to discover new insights and possibilities, to awaken one's capacity to live more wisely, more lovingly, and more fully. The skill of becoming more mindful and therefore more present, compassionate, and awake may be something we learn on a mediation cushion, but this capacity for awareness helps in technical activities, sports, lovemaking, or walking by the ocean and listening to the life around you.

Mindfulness and Alleviating Suffering

There is an old saying that pain is inevitable, but suffering is optional. There is no doubt that pain is a part of life. We get sick, grow old, and die, lose loved ones, and experience catastrophic circumstances. And it is important that this pain be experienced and not suppressed into the unconscious. Happiness is a function of accepting what is. Since life is like a river, always flowing and changing, trying to hold on to "how it was" or "how it should be" will only create suffering, disappointment, and misery. This is a basic spiritual law—that things are impermanent and attachment of any kind causes suffering.

It is a mindful practice, like meditation, that teaches mindful awareness, that allows us to let go and stay centered in the midst of change. Letting go does not mean not caring about things; rather it means caring for them in a flexible and wise way in the realization that gain and loss, praise and blame, pain and pleasure are all part of the dance of life. We are no longer fearful of painful experiences; we no longer run away from them or grasp desperately for only pleasant experiences, hoping that somehow holding onto them will make them last.

Through mindfulness we come to realize that our heart has the capacity to be present for it all, that we can live more fully and freely right where we are and find composure as everything, both good and bad, manifests in the present and then passes away. We learn to listen with full awareness to all our feelings; through awareness of all the pleasant, neutral, and unpleasant aspects of experience, we can learn not to fear pain or grasp for pleasure. Becoming attached to things as they are or pushing away things we do not like leads to further suffering because this does not stop them from changing. Through mindfulness, it quickly becomes clear that fear of pain and the quest for pleasure do not lead to peace or happiness; they cause us to suffer.

Through mindfulness, we alleviate suffering and discover a natural and nonjudgmental awareness of our bodies and feelings. We begin to see and trust the world the way it is and learn to trust impermanence as a spiritual law of life. And in the midst of it all we begin to see how we can relate to all of it with compassion, kindness, and wisdom. We begin to develop a vision of love and service to others based on a universally applicable ethical system of altruistic values. These are the keys for developing spiritual leadership and entering the Level II way of knowing and being to truly love and serve others.

THREE-FOLD PATH OF SPIRITUAL TRANSFORMATION

Margaret Benefiel in her books *Soul at Work: Spiritual Leadership in Organizations* (Benefiel, *Soul at Work* 2005) and *The Soul of a Leader: Finding Your Path to Success and Fulfillment* (Benefiel 2008) identifies a threefold path that describes the spiritual journey from an initial spiritual awakening through many ups and downs of the five levels of knowing and being. The three ways—the purgative way, the illuminative way, and the unitive way—are shown in Figure 3.3 (Benefiel, *Soul at Work* 2005; Benefiel 2008).

The spiritual journey has its beginnings in the purgative way, which begins when people who are living in Levels V and IV awaken to an awareness of a spiritual reality and seek the consciousness of being in Level III. This happens when people have exhausted their own resources and sense the need for a higher power. But the seeker also discovers a higher power who gives good gifts and discovers that following a spiritual path brings an added dimension to life. In the purgative way one revels in these gifts and learns to seek a higher power for this reason. However, after a time the sojourner discovers that these abundant gifts begin to disappear. This brings confusion and a sense of distance as the prayers that once brought bounty remain unanswered. At this point, after redoubling their efforts and experiencing only more dryness, many give up the spiritual quest. Spiritual writers refer to this point as the "first dark night of the soul" (Benefiel 2008).

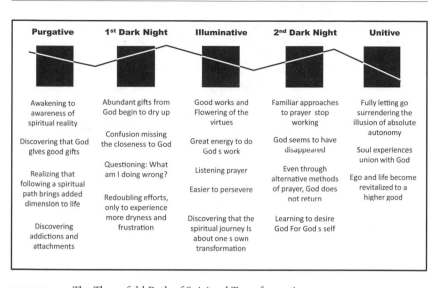

Purgative	1st Dark Night	Illuminative	2nd Dark Night	Unitive
Awakening to awareness of spiritual reality	Abundant gifts from God begin to dry up	Good works and Flowering of the virtues	Familiar approaches to prayer stop working	Fully letting go surrendering the illusion of absolute autonomy
Discovering that God gives good gifts	Confusion missing the closeness to God	Great energy to do God s work	God seems to have disappeared	Soul experiences union with God
Realizing that following a spiritual path brings added dimension to life	Questioning: What am I doing wrong? Redoubling efforts, only to experience more dryness and	Listening prayer Easier to persevere	Even through alternative methods of prayer, God does not return	Ego and life become revitalized to a higher good
Discovering addictions and attachments	frustration	Discovering that the spiritual journey Is about one s own transformation	Learning to desire God For God s self	

FIGURE 3.3 The Three-fold Path of Spiritual Transformation
Source: Benefiel, M., *The Soul of a Leader: Finding Your Path to Success and Fulfillment*, New York: Crossroads, 2008.

Those who persevere enter the illuminative way. It is at this point that we learn the spiritual journey is really about our own transformation, rather than about getting handouts from a gift-giving higher power. Instead of praying and talking to our higher power and stating what we think we need, we begin to enter silence and listen more. This is the part of the spiritual journey that marks the entrance into the illuminative way or Level III. The illuminative way in Level III is the stage of striving to transcend our self-centered ego to become more other-centered through loving and serving others. At this point, the sojourner is glimpsing the reality of Level II.

Those who continue on the illuminative way may enter the "second dark night of the soul." In this place not only does prayer no longer work, but even our higher power seems to have disappeared. There is a sense of being blocked, and no new paths open no matter how much effort is exerted. It is at this point that one learns to simply desire to be with a higher power, and not for what the higher power can give. This is hard to understand, especially if the seeker's true desire is her own transformation.

However, our higher power is still working in hidden ways during this second dark night.

Ultimately if one perseveres, the second dark night yields to the unitive way, and the hidden work that occurred during the second dark night is revealed. The seeker now fully experiences the reality of Level II and begins to experience union with a higher power or the nondual in Level I. This is the point at which one's ego and life become dedicated to a higher good. Spiritual teachers refer to this point as letting go or surrender. By far, most seekers glimpse this place and live in it briefly, then slip into a more ego-centered place. It is rare for one to arrive and stay at the unitive stage (Level II & Level 1) for long. But over time, as we continue to walk the spiritual path, as leaders we can learn to live more and more fully in this place of letting go. To the extent leaders are able to live predominantly at Levels III and above, they are more dedicated to the higher good and available to the needs of the people they serve. Because their egos are more other-centered, these leaders can use their skills and energies to serve the good of the organization as a whole rather than their own selfish interests.

Just as with individual spirituality, leaders of organizations often embrace spirituality because they need help. In doing so, they find they become more energized, more joy-filled, more productive, and more profitable because they have embraced spirituality and the spiritual journey. At the same time, if leaders and organizations are open to it, starting down a spiritual path will take both the leader and the organization to unexpected places. The organization will eventually bump into a wall that can, if the leader and organization are open, serve as an invitation to enter the Three-fold Path of Spiritual Transformation. One example of this is the spiritual journey of Robert Ouimet and his company, Cordon-Bleu Tomasso, which we covered in detail in Chapter 1.

Thus, both leaders and organizations need to understand the levels of knowing and being and the Three-fold Path of Spiritual Transformation. But how can leaders and organizations understand and articulate the first half? How can leaders become skilled practitioners, helping their organizations through the second half? To answer these questions, we will consider the journey of the Fool.

THE JOURNEY OF THE FOOL

The journey of the Fool is a developmental journey that can be used as a guide for developing personal spiritual leadership. The beginnings of this fundamental journey, which underlies many of the world's spiritual and religious traditions, including Judaism, Christianity, and Islam, can be traced back to the ancient Egyptian *Book of Life*. The journey of the Fool depicts the spiritual journey of self-transcendence and consciousness of the nondual—the journey of transformation from ego-centered to other-centered and the striving to fulfill one's ultimate purpose in love and service to others. The Three-Fold Path of Spiritual Transformation and Figure 3.3 will be used to illustrate how the Fool follows and encounters different levels of being (Figure 3.2), which produce different approaches to leadership in terms of notions of reality, truth, beliefs, and justification for actions.

The Journey Begins

The story goes that the soul of a man (or woman) begins his journey as a Fool, as a person lacking in judgment or prudence. He is totally unaware of the hardships he will face as he goes forth to learn the lessons of the world.

As an infant, the Fool is aware only of his physical senses; he is residing in a Level V way of knowing and being. At an unconscious level he begins to master the ability to bring about or satisfy his basic desires and impact the world through a concentration of individual will and power. The Fool then sets out to master his physical body. As he grows, the Fool begins to explore his surroundings through walking and talking. He begins to recognize his parental figures, who nourish, care, and provide structure and authority for him. He is discovering order and encountering rules, and he learns that his will is not paramount. He must behave in certain ways for his own well-being. And there are people in authority who will enforce these rules. He finds these restrictions frustrating but begins to understand their purpose.

Emotional Programs for Happiness

At this stage of the spiritual journey, the Fool is becoming self-aware as a being separate from a higher power. The Fool builds a universe, with himself at the center, around which these needs revolve like planets around the sun. As a result, any object entering his universe—another person or event—is judged on the basis of whether it can provide him with what he believes or demands happiness to be. At age four or five, he begins to socialize and internalize the cultural values of family, peer group, religion, ethnic group, nationality, race, and gender. He enjoys the process of learning the customs of his family and society and showing how well he can conform to them. The Fool now begins to experience the Level IV reality of being. This is the level of images and imagination, where his reality becomes socially constructed through the creation and maintenance of strong family and cultural values. The combination of these two levels of being—Level V with its physical and emotional drives and Level IV's cultural identification with the particular group and society to which he belongs—further complicates his pursuit of happiness.

The Fool has entered this world with three essential biological needs: for security and survival, for power and control, and for affection and esteem. The emotional programs for happiness based on these three instinctual needs and on cultural conditioning start to fail him and cause him pain and suffering. He finds that daily events often frustrate his emotional programs for happiness, which give rise to the destructive emotions of anger, resentment, worry, and fear. And sometimes he finds himself in the midst of an intense emotional dialogue as well as emotional turmoil. This is the beginning of a potentially addictive process based in the need to hide the pain. This pain is repressed into the unconscious in an effort to provide freedom from the pain, and he continues to pursue these programs to access worldly pleasures that temporarily offset the pain he is not yet prepared to face.

The Fool learns that he is not alone in his travels. Now he begins to feel a balancing tendency to reach out and become half of a loving partnership. In addition to family, he now yearns for relationships with friends as well as with individuals to satisfy the powerful urge for sexual union with another. In doing so the Fool needs to decide on his own beliefs. It was fine for him to conform as he grew, but at some point he must determine his own values. He becomes an adult with free will and self-control. He has a strong identity and a certain mastery over himself. Through discipline and will power, he develops an inner control that allows him to begin to triumph over his environment. He has developed a strong and vigorous self-centered ego that is, so far, his crowning achievement. For the moment the Fool's success is all he might wish, and he feels happy and satisfied.

By this stage of his journey, the Fool has developed a strong sense of personal leadership based in Levels V and IV. He has a strong self-image and the self-confident ability to crystallize his thinking and establish an exact direction for his life, to commit himself to moving in that direction and then to take determined action to acquire, accomplish, or become whatever he desires. His positive self-image gives him the self-confidence, courage, and perseverance necessary to consciously choose a course of action that leads to success as he defines it. The Fool believes he controls his destiny. His personal mission in life and the goals he pursues stem from a vision and a set of values whose ultimate purpose is to satisfy his self-centered emotional programs for happiness.

The First Spiritual Lesson

Over time, the Fool finds himself facing new challenges, some that cause suffering and disillusionment. In facing these challenges he develops the courage and resolve and finds the heart to persevere despite setbacks. The Fool soon learns that what he takes by brute strength alone is soon taken away by others who have even more strength. He begins to realize that he is not alone in his travels and finds that if he will help others, others will help him. He awakens to an awareness of a spiritual reality and has the opportunity to enter Level III—the level of soul awareness, where self-transcendence and consciousness begin to emerge.

The Fool discovers the softer power of a loving approach through patience and tolerance and realizes that his self-will must be tempered by kindness. The sensual/physical world of Level V begins to become less attractive, and he seeks moments away from the frantic activity of society. He begins an inner-life practice and starts to set aside times for rest and inner reflection, to go within himself for answers and to observe but keep silent at times. He finds himself asking the age-old question "Why?" and becomes absorbed with the search for answers out of a deeply felt need to find out why people live, if only to suffer and die. He may seek a guide or teacher who can give him direction to help him understand his feelings and emotions.

The Fool has now entered the purgative way; after much soul-searching, he finds himself awakening to an awareness of spiritual reality in which everything is connected. He has a vision of a mysterious world of wondrous design whose parts work together in harmony. As he glimpses the beauty and order of the world, he starts to find some of the answers he is seeking. Sometimes his experiences include gifts that seem to be the work of fate, perhaps in the form of a chance encounter or a miraculous occurrence. He may see his destiny in the sequence of events that have led him to a turning point. His inward reflection makes him feel ready for renewed movement and action, and he is ready to embrace the process of change. The Fool's perspective on life is wider, and he sees himself within the grander scheme of a universal plan. He has a renewed sense of purpose and meaning in life.

The First Dark Night

All is not smooth, however, and after a time the Fool discovers these abundant gifts begin to disappear. The Fool experiences the ups and downs of what some would call "Lady Luck" or "the wheel of fortune." His emotional programs for happiness that have become habits prove to be chains of bondage he finds almost impossible to break. Sometimes his efforts bear fruit and bounty, but sometimes they do not and famine results. At times his fellow travelers assist him; sometimes they deceive him and deny him aid. The Fool begins to ask himself, "Why?" Are such things fair and just? How does all this fit with his vision? He looks back over his life to trace the decisions, with their cause-and-effect relationships, that have brought him to this point. He takes responsibility for his past actions and makes amends in order to ensure a more honest course for the future. These are the demands of justice so he can wipe the slate clean. This is a key time of decision for the Fool. He must make these important choices and remain true to his insights. If he does not, he will slip back into his old habits and emotional programs and a seemingly easier, more unaware existence that closes off further growth and brings his spiritual journey to a halt.

In asking these questions and making these decisions, the Fool discovers he has entered the first dark night of the soul. He begins to develop a moral code and starts to realize the sacrifices his soul has made to experience the human senses and satisfy the desires of the flesh. Undaunted, he pushes on, determined to realize his vision. Sooner or later he finds out that life is not so easily tamed, and he encounters his personal cross—an experience that is too difficult to endure. It is an overwhelming challenge that humbles him until he has no choice but to let go. In desperation, he cries out to a higher power, "Teach me and I will hold my tongue, and cause me to understand where I have erred." He no longer views his sacrifice and suffering as having been sent as a form of punishment or trial. He cries out "Teach me . . ." in the realization that man makes his own happiness or unhappiness through obeying not only physical laws, but also through obeying or not obeying spiritual laws as well.

Illumination

At first, the Fool feels he has sacrificed everything. He feels defeated and lost. But from the depths of this bottom and in the midst of despair he learns an amazing truth: that when he relinquishes his struggle for control, everything begins to work out as it should. The Fool has now entered the illuminative way; he begins to discover that the spiritual journey is about his own transformation. By surrendering and becoming open and vulnerable, the Fool discovers miraculous support from his inner-life practice. He surrenders to his experiences rather than fighting them and finds a surprising sense of joy, peace, and serenity. He begins to flow with life free of urgency and pressure. Having experienced the death of his former values and beliefs, he is now ready to begin a new set of lessons, those of the spiritual laws based on love and service of others. Although this may seem a burden that is crushing at times, he eventually discovers that this death is not a permanent state. It is simply a transition to a new, more fulfilling way of life. The Fool begins to work on eliminating old habits, addictions, and failed approaches. He appreciates the basics of life and cuts out nonessentials.

The Second Dark Night

What more could the Fool need? In terms of physical wants and needs, not much, but the Fool is courageous and continues to pursue the deepest levels of his being. There are always temptations to return to the old emotional programs and satisfy the desires of the body and flesh to the fullest extent. In confronting these temptations the Fool enters the second dark night of the soul. Here there is a knot of ignorance and hopelessness lodged deep within the unconscious—the idea that man is bound by his carnal desires and by material conditions, and is a slave to fate. As such, there is a spiritual blindness or physical sensations divorced from understanding. The seductive attractions of Levels V and IV, based on a self-serving image and satisfying emotional programs for happiness, may be so compelling that the Fool may not realize he is a slave to them. This is the chain and fatality of the material life based on having and doing rather than on being and consciousness. It is a negative polarity. But where is the opposite pole? Without both, neither can exist. The Fool is gaining powers. His dilemma is whether he uses them for good or evil. Will he remain chained by the temptations of living in a world driven by materialism, power, and prestige? By confronting this devil he begins to see that he may be caught up in anger and resentments rooted in the past and have a victim mentality and blame others for what happens to him, instead of learning from his experiences. Or he may be trapped in the future through worry and fear over losing something he holds dear or not getting something he feels he needs badly.

As part of the second dark night, and to generate enough power to smash the walls of this fortress and have a conversion experience, the Fool must encounter a major setback—an illness, a natural disaster, the loss of integrity, trust, or honor, or overwhelming circumstances in life. Sometimes the Fool achieves cosmic consciousness in a blinding flash, but more often enlightenment comes in gradual stages of realization. Regardless of how that realization comes, after the Fool has experienced even a glimpse of truth, his life is never the same. The truth has set him free from the secure and protective prison of materialism. This revelation makes the painful experience worthwhile. His dark despair is blasted away in an instant, and the light of truth is freed to shine from within. He can now either choose to exert the strenuous effort necessary to follow that light into Levels II and I, entering the unitive way on the Three-Fold Path. Or he can continue to stay in the second dark night of the soul and feel powerless at the mercy of his emotional programs for happiness and cultural conditioning.

If he continues on, the Fool discovers hope, for he is now attuned to guidance he receives through divine inspiration, rather than material things and the desires of the flesh. He experiences a serene calm and is filled with joy. He feels blessed with trust and faith in the future that replaces the negative energies. His heart is open, and love pours out freely. His one wish is to share his heart generously with the rest of the world. For the Fool, this is a magical moment of peace after the storm. He is learning to first communicate with himself and thus bring the first pinprick of light to this second dark night. As the Fool learns more and more, the faint light grows. He is beginning to properly use and control his will, emotions, intuition, and psychic powers.

The Unitive Way

With perseverance, at last comes the dawn of clarity and understanding that dispels the clouds of confusion and fear. Through this enlightenment, the Fool both feels and understands the inherent goodness and unity of all things in the world. And with this dawn comes full consciousness or realization in Levels II and I of the unitive way. Obstacles have been overcome, confidence is restored, lessons have been learned and, ultimately, new wisdom arises. He has the victory and achievement of balance between self-consciousness and sub-consciousness, as well as the balance between will, power, and intellect. Within the Fool a sense of pure spirit has dawned and has risen above the egocentric, self-conscious mind. Now he enjoys a vibrant energy, enthusiasm, and assurance. No challenge seems too daunting. He becomes involved in a grand vision, purpose, and mission based on love and on service of others. He is able to realize his greatness as he draws to himself everything he needs.

The Fool has been reborn and, if only for a time, finds himself experiencing the reality of Levels II and I. He finally realizes that joy, not resentment or fear, is at life's center. The real tomb is the material world and the physical body, which contains the soul with its pure spirit. The world is the vehicle he must use as he evolves through the levels of knowing and being along the Three-Fold Path. With this realization comes absolution, in which he forgives himself and others through the knowledge that his real self is pure and good. Past mistakes are regrettable, but he now knows that they were due to his ignorance of his true nature. He is cleansed and refreshed, ready to start anew.

The Fool recognizes it is time to make a deeper judgment about his life as his own personal day of reckoning has arrived. Because he sees himself truly, he can make necessary decisions about the future and wisely choose which values to cherish and which to discard. The Fool reassesses his life to find his life's purpose and brings everything he has learned thus far into a philosophy that allows his spirit to grow. He has a sense of calling and discovers that his true vocation must be practiced through love and service—his reason for entering this life. His doubts and hesitations vanish. He is ready to pursue his vision.

The Fool reenters the world, but this time he is conscious and has integrated the disparate parts of himself and achieved wholeness. He has reached a new level of happiness, peace, and fulfillment that is not based on his physical circumstances or personal situation. Life is full, meaningful, and full of promise. He becomes actively involved in the world in pursuit of his calling by sharing his unique gifts and talents; he finds that he accomplishes much and prospers at whatever he attempts. Because he acts with inner clarity and certainty, the whole world seems to conspire to see that his efforts are rewarded.

So the Fool's journey was, ultimately, not so foolish after all. By being honest, open-minded, willing, and perseverant, he completed the journey in his search for his true self. Paradoxically, in the search for self, he discovered he could find it only by shedding it and embracing the all-knowing and encompassing pure spirit from which he came. He perceives the underlying unity of pure spirit in all things. Now he is fully aware of his place in the world. This cycle is over. He has learned the lessons of life and the world. He has learned to balance his body, mind, emotions, and spirit and to love and appreciate the life he has been given.

But this is not the final destination. The spiritual journey is not over because, like the peeling of an onion, new layers of the unconscious and the evils that lurk there will continue to emerge. Soon a new spiritual journey must begin to uncover more of the Fool's worldly attachments and identifications. Like the Fool, we may get stuck and refuse to surrender to the spiritual lessons inherent in our circumstances and stay there for a lifetime. For example, 95 percent of alcoholics who attend AA meetings never work the Twelve Steps (AA's spiritual path) and wind up suffering the practicing alcoholic's progressive and terminal fate of jails, institutions, or death ("What is the Success Rate of Recovery in AA?" 2008). They never hit bottom, become honest, open-minded, and willing enough to traverse the dark nights of the soul. Those who do and work the steps find that work to be a lifelong spiritual journey as they continue to confront character defects based in pride, anger, lust, greed, envy, gluttony, and sloth (the seven deadly sins) after the obsession to drink has been lifted by their higher power.

CONCLUSION

Leaders who desire to maximize the Triple Bottom Line through spiritual leadership must first look inward. The source of personal and organizational spiritual leadership and, ultimately, the Triple Bottom Line is an inner-life practice based in the spiritual journey that reflects the quest to find and draw strength from a higher power. Horton's conception of God as a higher power offers leaders a continuum of choices for a source of power beyond self-sufficiency that they may confidently lean on for comfort, support, and strength.

Viewing the spiritual journey as a quest of transformation through the five levels of knowing and being gives a more complete understanding of the role of inner life in spiritual leadership and the importance of embarking on the spiritual journey. It also requires the realization that no state or level of knowing and being is permanent and that even the most seasoned spiritual travelers can find themselves at any level.

Mindfulness is key to inner life as a source of spiritual leadership and requires a mindful practice to foster mindful awareness. A daily inner-life practice focused on moment-to-moment mindfulness gradually exposes one to an awareness of the unconscious at a rate one can handle.

The journey of the Fool illustrates that the spiritual journey requires taking the three-fold path of spiritual leadership and facing the dark side of our personality and the investments we have in our emotional programs of happiness and cultural conditioning.

Practical Tools

For those interested in maximizing the Triple Bottom Line, the major tools introduced in this chapter include the following:

Horton's definition and continuum of God as a higher power offers a range of humanistic, monotheistic, and pantheistic conceptions of a Being, higher power, or God on which a leader may confidently draw on for support.

The five levels of knowing and being are the stages of the spiritual journey toward personal transformation to love and serve others in the quest for the nondual or sense of oneness with all.

Mindfulness provides the foundation for inner life, the spiritual journey, and maintaining a state of being or consciousness from moment to moment.

The Three-Fold Path of Spiritual Transformation describes the spiritual journey as a spiritual awakening through the purgative way,

personal transformation through the illuminative way, and ultimately dedication to a higher good based on love and service through
the unitive way.

The Journey of the Fool is an allegory that illustrates the spiritual
journey through the levels of knowing and being and the Three-Fold
Path of Spiritual Transformation.

Chapter Four

Spiritual Leadership and the Values of Altruistic Love

Since 2005 Earl Maxwell and his organization, Maxwell, Locke, and Ritter LLP (MLR), have been part of an ongoing study for organizational spiritual leadership. MLR is an accounting, tax, and consulting firm whose vision is to help dynamic companies and people achieve their dreams. The company is the largest locally owned and managed CPA firm in the greater Austin, Texas, area. Their extensive experience runs through all facets of business and personal tax and financial planning matters. MLR represents an excellent example of a company that has embraced spiritual leadership and the values of altruistic love, and that has shown dedication to the spiritual well-being of its workers and the Triple Bottom Line (Maxwell 1998).

Since the firm's inception in 1991, the managing partners believed that MLR should focus on three things: their clients, their people, and the community. They created a philosophy and mission based on core values that remain the basis of MLR's culture today and that provide the foundation for the niches and industries they serve. As part of the company's mission, employees focus on providing compassion and courtesy to customers, treating others as they want to be treated. MLR says it accomplishes this by selecting and retaining *great people*, serving *great clients*, and focusing on *great execution*. Central to MLR's mission is a focus on spiritual leadership based on hope/faith in a vision of service to key stakeholders; the company nurtures an organizational culture grounded in the values of altruistic love (Maxwell 1998).

Even though love is considered to be the most important human experience by all major spiritual and religious teaching, the words *love* and *leadership* are rarely linked. No business school in the country offers a course on leading through love. Tina Turner's famous lyric "What's love got to do, got to do with it. What's love but a secondhand emotion?" certainly has been the view of most organizations that obsessively focus on performance and short-term profit.

Ken Blanchard claims that a key to effective leadership is to be madly in love with all the people you are leading. Rudy Giuliani, the former mayor of New York, in speaking of leadership says flatly, "if you don't love people, do something else." When Warren Buffet, one of the richest men in the world and the primary shareholder, chairman and CEO of Berkshire Hathaway, was asked how he would define success, he said:

> For me, if the people who you hope love you, do, that's success. Wouldn't it be great if you could buy love for $1 million? But the only way to be loved is to be lovable. You always get back more than you give away. . . . There's nobody I know who commands the love of others who doesn't feel like a success. And I can't imagine people who aren't loved feel very successful. (Openshaw 2007)

In the global Internet age, successful organizations depend on the knowledge, commitment, and enthusiasm of everyone. Leadership through love is about allowing people to be at their best while allowing them to make mistakes as they make a difference in their own and others' lives. If you think love, leadership, and performance don't go together, just look at Southwest Airlines. Herb Kelleher, legendary leader of Southwest, stated, "I would far rather have a business led by love than by fear." Southwest is a company he declared from the start would be "led by love"; it is headquartered at Love Field Airport, and its stock market listing is LUV. It is currently the most profitable airline in U.S. history; its stock market valuation is consistently higher than that of any other U.S. airline.

Tim Collins is a career soldier who rose to prominence and ended up in newspapers worldwide because of an impromptu speech on leadership and love he gave to the Irish regiment he commanded in Iraq. Like Kelleher, Guiliani, and Blanchard, he believes that you have to love your people to lead effectively. He explains that the foundation of leadership and love is knowing and caring about what motivates people, what is important to them, and helping them grow and fill those aspirations at work. Therefore, for a leader, love in the workplace means genuinely caring for one's people and sharing one's knowledge, understanding, and compassion to enable them to grow and succeed.

Regardless of whether one is concentrating on developing spiritual leadership personally or for an organization, the values and foundations remain the same. The previous chapter focused on the importance of inner life as key to developing spiritual leadership. This chapter further details the qualities of spiritual leadership through hope/faith, vision, and altruistic love. Then we explore the values of altruistic love in depth. Finally, we look in detail at Maxwell, Locke, and Ritter LLP and how the company employs spiritual leadership through hope/faith, vision, and the values of altruistic love.

The Qualities of Spiritual Leadership

Spiritual leaders are responsible for creating vision and value congruence across all organizational levels as well as for developing effective relationships between the organization and environmental stakeholders (Maghroori and Rolland 1997; Fry 2003). People need something to believe in, someone to believe in, and someone to believe in them. A spiritual leader is someone who walks in front of you when you need someone to follow, behind you when you need encouragement, and beside you when you need a friend. A spiritual leader believes that people, when they are involved and properly informed, can make intelligent decisions and, with appropriate information, assume responsibility for decisions that affect their lives.

As discussed in Chapters 1 and 2, organizational spiritual leadership is an intrinsic motivation process based on vision (performance), altruistic

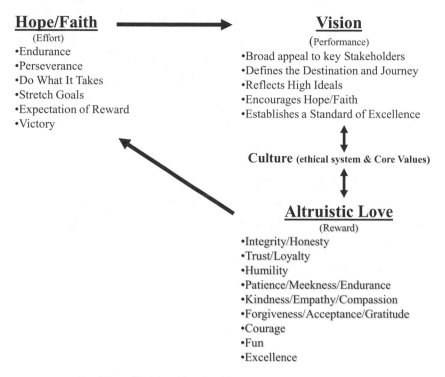

FIGURE 4.1 Qualities of Spiritual Leadership
Source: International Institute for Spiritual Leadership

love (reward), and hope/faith (effort). The qualities of organizational spiritual leadership are shown in Figure 4.1 in terms of the values, attitudes, and behaviors necessary for such leadership.

Hope/Faith

Fundamental to organizational spiritual leadership is hope/faith. Hope is a desire with expectation of fulfillment. Faith adds certainty to hope. Faith is more than merely wishing for something. It is based on absolute certainty and trust that what is desired and expected will come to pass. People with hope/faith have a vision of where they are going, and how to get there; they are willing to face opposition and endure hardships and suffering in order to achieve their goals.

True faith in something or someone is demonstrated through action or work. Often the metaphor of a race is used to describe faith working or in action. There are two essential components to every race: the vision and expectation of reward or victory, and the joy of the journey of preparing for and running the race itself. Both components are necessary and essential elements of any vision that can generate hope and faith.

In running the race of faith, one must run to win, exercise self-control, and strive for excellence to exceed one's personal best. The race of faith is a marathon, not a sprint; it requires endurance, perseverance, and a willingness to "do what it takes" to maximize one's potential. It requires setting goals that are challenging—a "stretch," yet achievable—and laying aside encumbrances and distractions in pursuing the vision of the preparation, running, and ultimate victory of the race

Vision

Of paramount importance in organizational spiritual leadership is a clear, compelling vision. An effective vision provides a picture of a desired future along with some implicit or explicit commentary on why people should strive to create that future. A vision should vividly portray a journey that when undertaken will give one a sense of calling, of lending one's life having meaning and making a difference. It describes the organization's journey and why the leaders and followers are taking it. Vision energizes people, gives meaning to work, and garners commitment. It also establishes a standard of excellence. Because it mobilizes people, it has broad appeal; it reflects high ideals and encourages hope/faith. In motivating change, vision serves three important functions: it clarifies the general direction of change, simplifies hundreds or thousands of more detailed decisions, and helps to quickly and efficiently coordinate the actions of many different people.

Culture

An effective vision forms the basis for the organization's culture and the ethical system and core values underlying it. Culture influences the range of behaviors that members view as appropriate and provides them with a framework that influences their thinking and behavior. It is primarily implemented through a process of organizational socialization or "learning the ropes." This includes indoctrination and training to teach new members and reinforce for existing employees what is important and "how we do things around here" (Schein 1990).

Culture is comprised of visible artifacts such as dress, office layout, ritual, symbols, and ceremonies. At a hidden or more subjective level are the beliefs and values that people use to justify and explain what they do. However, the essence of culture is its pattern of shared, basic assumptions. These assumptions define the key understandings and norms that are shared by members of the organization and taught to new members as correct. Culture often operates at an unconscious level, tends to be taken for granted by organizational members, and is treated as nonnegotiable. Basic assumptions are so taken for granted that someone who does not hold them is viewed as a "foreigner" or "crazy" and is automatically discounted and dismissed as an undesirable deviate (Schein 2004).

Values, Attitudes, and Behavior

The qualities of spiritual leadership include core values that an individual considers to be important. People bring to work values that are stable over time and difficult to change. Values affect one's perception of the situation or problems, how one relates to others, and act as guides for choices and actions. They determine a person's preferences about what they consider to be good or bad and form the foundation of moral principles for an individual's, team's, or organization's ethical system. For example, honesty is a value that is considered to be good and desirable in all cultures and across all religious and spiritual traditions (Smith 1991).

Values then determine attitudes. An attitude is an evaluation that predisposes a person to act in a certain way. Attitudes are relatively lasting thoughts, feelings, and behavioral tendencies toward specific people, groups, ideas, issues, events, or objects. The values of spiritual leadership form the foundation for an organization culture based on altruistic love and therefore provide the basis for consistency in employee attitudes and behavior. For example, leaders who highly value altruistic love and have true care and concern for both themselves and their fellow workers would have different attitudes and behave very differently than self-serving leaders driven by personal ambition.

The Values of Altruistic Love

According to Richard Daft in *The Leadership Experience*, successful leaders recognize that cultural values are central to helping the organization attain its vision and ultimately achieve its strategic goals (Daft 2008). In spiritual leadership this means emphasizing the values of altruistic love that promote an employee's sense of being connected to others in a way that provides feelings of completeness and joy (Giacalone and Jurkiewicz 2003). Moreover, spirituality in the workplace is linked to the organization's ethical system in a way that allows for people to align organizational values to their own philosophical and spiritual roots so that the values of altruistic love become an integral part of the organization's day-to-day functioning.

Altruistic love in spiritual leadership is defined with implications for spiritual well-being. It is "a sense of wholeness, harmony, and well-being produced through care, concern, and appreciation for both self and others" (Fry 2003). Spiritual leaders living the values of altruistic love truly care for the well-being of their workers. They say what they'll do and do what they say, and if for some reason they can't and someone else is affected, they let them know as soon as possible. The values of altruistic love provide a positive influence not only within the firm but outside it as well. That influence goes beyond leader-follower relationships to encompass customers, the community, and other key stakeholders.

Charles Allen, in *The Miracle of Love*, discusses the values underlying altruistic love using 1 Corinthians 13, 4–8, 13, which is perhaps the most widely quoted illumination of altruistic love (Allen 1972):

Love
Is patient and kind;
Is not jealous or boastful;

Is not arrogant or rude.
Love
Does not insist on its own way;
Is not irritable or resentful;
Does not rejoice in wrong,
But rejoices in the truth.
Love
Never gives up;
Never loses faith;
Is always hopeful;
Endures through every circumstance;
Love
Never ends;
So in faith, hope, and love abide, these three;
But the greatest of these is love.

Spiritual leaders, by "walking the walk" as well as "talking the talk" in the values of altruistic love, work to transfer their attitudes and behaviors to the larger organization. While the positive values a leader and organization can adopt are endless, spiritual leadership focuses on a few essential ones: integrity/honesty, trust/loyalty, humility, patience, kindness, forgiveness, courage, fun. People who successfully lead through spiritual leadership would typically be able to make the following statements about themselves and the way they lead.

Integrity and Honesty. *I walk the walk as well as talk the talk. I say what I do and I do what I say. I seek and rejoice in truth and base my actions on it.*

Laura Reave, in "Spiritual Values and Practices Related to Leadership Effectiveness," notes that integrity and honesty are essential to leadership success and the most frequently mentioned values for business leaders. Integrity and honesty affect the ethical climate in an organization, influencing the ethical choices that workers make. Lapses in integrity and honesty can severely damage leader effectiveness and ultimately lead to organizational failure. Ken Lay and Jeff Skilling, for example, were widely admired leaders whose lack of integrity and honesty destroyed Enron.

Spiritual leadership begins with personal integrity, which is reflected in ethical behavior (Reave 2005). It is through integrity that employees and other stakeholders look for alignment in leaders' values, attitudes, and behavior. They look at not only what leaders do but also the motivations and beliefs that underlie that behavior. Often leaders become so involved in crafting images of themselves and seeking the approval of followers that their inner moral compass is undermined. However, over time those who become familiar with such leaders are able to carefully examine consistency between a leader's values, attitudes, and behavior to assess whether they are credible and worthy of trust.

Integrity requires honesty with oneself and others to promote internal and external consistency with truth, because honesty in keeping a promise provides consistency and evidence that the promise was a "true" statement. Honesty also means being honest with oneself, which involves self-awareness, a critical component of emotional intelligence that allows people to know their strengths and limitations. Self-aware people can gauge themselves and know how they affect others. Jim Collins, in *Good to Great*, looked at the performance of companies that had out-performed the Dow Jones average for thirty years and found self-honesty to be crucial. In particular, the leaders of these companies were able to face the hard facts of a bad situation. They also honestly and proactively communicated the truth in times of crisis, explaining the reasons for change while listening sensitively to employee responses (Collins 2001).

Gary Loveman, CEO of Harrah's Entertainment, the world's largest casino gaming company, practices as well as preaches that telling the truth and admitting mistakes is the best road to success. As recounted in Jeffery Pfeffer's "The Whole Truth and Nothing But: The Value of Honesty in Organizations," Loveman noted that you can't bring to bear corporate resources and expertise to help an underperforming area unless you know there's a problem. This requires having people in the company who are willing and comfortable enough to tell the truth. When Loveman made a decision about Harrah's health-care plans, which were proving costly and inconvenient to employees, he faced the facts. He got in front of as many people as he could and not only apologized but also admitted the mistake was his; then he outlined what he was doing to fix it. Loveman maintains that the only way to run an organization is to build a culture based on honesty and truth-telling—and that this behavior has to start at the top (Pfeffer 2007). Admitting errors also helps mobilize effort and improve morale. Covering up mistakes or blaming them on outside forces fuels a culture of helplessness. Everyone makes mistakes. No one can know everything.

Spiritual leadership requires integrity and honesty in telling the truth, asking for help, listening, and learning. No major problem will be fixed until leaders identify and describe it. No one will be likely to take responsibility for his or her own mistakes unless they see the company's leaders doing the same.

Trust and Loyalty. *In my chosen relationships, I am faithful and have faith in and rely on the character, ability, strength, and truth of others.*

Trust is a willingness to rely on or be vulnerable to another party in a situation that involves risk and uncertainty. People place their loyalty and are unswerving in allegiance and faithful to the cause, ideal, custom, institution, or product in which they place their trust. Followers and key stakeholders especially look for consistency between a leader's values, attitudes, and behavior to assess whether the leader is credible and trustworthy. Furthermore, trust has been shown to be important to many measures of organizational performance, such as job satisfaction, job commitment, job performance, and reduced turnover.

When workers and leaders trust each other, they believe they are professional, dedicated, knowledgeable, and capable. They are trusted because of their expertise and because they can be counted on to act responsibly. When employees trust their leaders they are willing to take the risks inherent in creativity and are confident that the leader will have the competence and knowledge to evaluate their ideas and that they possess the dedication to implement them. Trust and loyalty act to reduce or eliminate distractions such as rumors, political infighting, lack of focus, and conflict. Problems like these fade into the background as workers focus more energy on serving customers.

Spiritual leadership creates high-trust organizations where problems are easily and efficiently dealt with. Problems are solved instead of becoming huge obstacles; leaders are spared the need to first unscramble the mess to find who said what or who caused the problem to spiral out of control.

Instead, the energies of the leader and workers are directed to the customer and against the competition. Leaders freely share valuable insights through solid, reliable communication about the business. Workers are aligned under a common vision with goals that permeate all activities. They have a passion for their work; they have respect for the good deeds done by fellow workers and support and reinforce them.

Humility. *I am modest, courteous, and without false pride. I am not jealous, rude, or arrogant. I do not brag.*

Humility is often equated with a sense of unworthiness and low self-regard. However, true humility is characterized by being able to accurately assess one's strengths and weaknesses, an ability to acknowledge limitations, and a "forgetting of the self." Humility represents wisdom in knowing one has talents and abilities to share with the world. To be humble is to have an accurate opinion of oneself, not a low opinion.

Inherent in humility is honesty, open-mindedness, and a willingness to admit and learn from mistakes and seek advice. Humility is one result of an inner life and the spiritual journey—the realization that, despite one's personal power, one is not omnipotent. It's an admission that there is more we can learn about ourselves, others, and a being, higher power, or God from which we can draw strength and insight to become more other-centered. A remarkable result of becoming more other-centered is that the more humility we exhibit, the more we focus on other people and their needs, the more we receive.

Humble leaders also do not seek to develop a personal cult with public attention and devoted followers. Instead they focus their attention on the vision and values of the organization, creating both a strong organizational culture and sustained excellence. According to *Chief Executive*, the success of the twenty-five top market value-added companies was attributed to their CEO's personal humility, dependability, and consistency. Stephen Covey, who wrote the best-selling *Seven Habits of Highly Effective People* (Covey 1989), asserts that humility is one of the characteristics of people at the top. He found that they are more teachable and open and that they more often show reverence and respect for other people.

Jim Collins, in *Good-to-Great* (Collins 2001), found similar results: leaders who led their business, often through wrenching change, had "the triumph of humility and fierce resolve." Collins describes how, during interviews, such people would modestly describe the contributions of others in the company at length but instinctively deflect discussion about their own role. Many had gone though significant life experiences and at some point—through self-reflection, conscious personal development, a mentor, a great teacher, loving parents or a significant life experience—embarked upon the spiritual journey and gained humility in the process. Collins also found that in more than two-thirds of 1,400 companies the presence of a gargantuan ego contributed to the demise or continued mediocrity of the company. This pattern was particularly strong in companies that showed superior performance under a talented, yet egocentric leader, only to decline in the years after the leader's departure.

Courage. I have the firmness of mind and will, as well as the mental and moral strength, to maintain my morale and prevail in the face of extreme difficulty, opposition, threat, danger, hardship, and fear.

Spiritual leadership requires courage if one's attitudes and behaviors are to reflect the core values of altruistic love. Leaders often have to reach deep within themselves for the strength and courage to resist temptations or stay true to their values when others may ridicule them. This is especially true for leaders working in large organizations in which there is tremendous pressure to get along, fit in, and do whatever brings promotions and an increase in pay. A critical facet of courage is that it is under voluntary control and not something someone is born with. Everyone is therefore capable of choosing the path of courage or succumbing to inaction or flight or of surrendering to fear. Aristotle wrote a great deal about courage. According to him it is the first human virtue because it makes all the other virtues possible. Without courage, all virtue is fleeting, however admired and sought-after it may be; without the courage of our convictions, virtue can be surrendered easily and without a fight.

Courage is having the ability to step forward through fear. Courage does not mean the absence of fear, but the ability to act in the face of it. At the heart of all fear is an expectation of losing something we hold dear or not getting something to which we are highly attached. Courage enables one to proceed in spite of fears and failure—to live based on one's core values in the face of adversity, dissent, and criticism. It is only natural for people to feel fear when real risk is involved. The workplace can harbor many kinds of fear, including fear of failure, fear of change, fear of the boss, fear of losing one's job, fear of losing the respect of one's peers, or fear of losing one's reputation. Courage in the face of fear means accepting responsibility for mistakes and taking action when action is called for. It means taking risks, speaking one's mind, and fighting for one's beliefs.

When we shrink from difficulties through lack of courage, ineptitude creeps in, followed by loss of self-esteem. However, through courage one can regain one's dignity and self-esteem. Witnessing ourselves perform even small acts of courage motivates further courageous acts. Courage calls for nonconformity, pushing beyond one's comfort zone, going against the grain, and breaking tradition. Often one must initiate change even though taking the chance on change may lead to mistakes, enduring ridicule or scorn, being out voted by opponents, and sometimes failing miserably. Leaders must also have the courage to set boundaries, stick to them, and be honest. This means saying what you think, asking for what you want, and fighting for causes that benefit the whole. Courage is a powerful antidote to loss of hope, loss of meaning, and a sense of incompetence and impotence. Courage helps thwart demoralization, and it is a critical component to facing loss (for example, of prestige, a job, a marriage, or loved ones) or the terror of dying.

There are several key sources of courage. Courage is sustained by one's inner life through hope/faith, relationships, and pride in past achievements. Spiritual leaders are willing to take risks for a larger calling or purpose, and they encourage their people to do the same. Accepting or even welcoming failure enables courage. Failure can be beneficial since both people and organizations can learn valuable lessons when things go wrong, as failure can often be a source of strength and an important first step toward success. Through courage, failure is more easily accepted, as is the determination to move forward. Anger, when harnessed and exercised appropriately, can be used to find the courage to deal with difficult situations. In moderate amounts, anger is a healthy emotion that provides motivation to move forward. Outrage over a perceived injustice can also provide the courage to step through fear and to act. Getting mad at yourself may fuel your courage to face a daunting challenge.

Finally, love is a strong aspect of courage because it makes us willing to sacrifice. Leaders who have genuine care and concern for their workers will take risks to help them grow and succeed. Having the support of others is also a source of courage. People will take risks they otherwise wouldn't take and have less fear of failure when they are part of a supportive and caring team. One gets courage by loving something more than one's own well-being. Courage is the springboard for transcending the selfish ego and serving others. When you love a higher power, when you love freedom, when you love other people, you find the strength to demand courage of yourself and of those you aspire to lead. Then it is possible to find the courage, as Eleanor Roosevelt put it, "to do the thing you cannot do."

Unfortunately, most leaders don't consider courage to be a key cultural value. They mistakenly believe that courage is called for only during times of crisis. However, courage is crucial in a wide range of work situations, and anyone can demonstrate courage. Opportunities for courage at work occur nearly every day, and these situations are often the defining moments of a person's career. Examples include speaking up at a meeting for one's position, confronting gossip, making the transition to a new position, and revealing vulnerability. People with courage state their goals and then "do what it takes" to achieve them. They develop new models and approaches when the old ways no longer work. They take risks to reinvent themselves and never quit. It is this drive for constant learning and improved performance that builds courage and is why courage is a key value for altruistic love.

Patience, Meekness, and Endurance. I bear trials and/or pain calmly and without complaint. I persist in or remain constant to any purpose, idea, or task in the face of obstacles or discouragement. I pursue steadily any course or project I begin. I never quit in spite of counter-influences, opposition, discouragement, suffering, or misfortune.

Patience is not easy in a world of instant messages that can be sent anywhere at any time or when desired wants are available for purchase with a few clicks of a mouse. Instant gratification is the cornerstone of our consumer-based world economy. However, we don't always get instant gratification; some of the best things in life require years of hard work and waiting. Steven Covey, in *Seven Habits of Highly Effective People* (Covey 1989), speaks of this as the law of the harvest. Some things, such as developing patience, that are key to a happy and effective life take time and can't be hurried. There are no shortcuts.

Patience is the state of endurance under trying circumstances, having the ability to bear pains or trials calmly without complaint. A person who has patience can exercise restraint under provocation or strain. The great saint Thomas Aquinas spoke of patience as acting in a praiseworthy manner by enduring things that hurt in the here and now, but, at the same time, not being unduly saddened by them.

Patience, a virtue we are all called upon to exercise frequently, helps one deal with frustrations, disappointments, contradictions, privations, sickness, and hardships (all of which cause pain) without becoming irritated or despondent. To exercise patience, one must develop the ability to keep control over the impulses that arise suddenly when something disagreeable happens. Having patience does not mean we condone injustice or any wrongs we may suffer. Nor does it mean one should not speak up or defend oneself or others against some unjust action. It does mean, though, that we must be patient with the weaknesses and frailties of others and not let emotion and hurt pride cause us to respond in ways that we will regret and that might cause others to retaliate.

The cultivation of patience requires consciousness of one's thoughts, emotions, and impulses. Patience is difficult to cultivate without an inner life and faith in a higher power, which helps one endure with serenity the pain and sorrow from our human conflicts, frustrations, irritations, setbacks, illness, and death. A natural fruit of patience is peace of mind. Like the other values of altruistic love, patience is nurtured by one's inner life. It is acquired by continual attempts—in spite of many failures—to access and maintain Level III awareness, as was discussed in the previous chapter. This helps us develop patience so that we are not upset by trivial incidents, no matter how unpleasant, and so that we do not lose peace of mind or serenity.

Meekness is a key component of patience. A defining characteristic of meekness is self-restraint. Meekness is an expression of altruistic love that is controlled and patient; a meek person is willing to forgive when forgiveness will earn no reward. Meekness is enduring injury with patience without resentment. It is "controlled power"—the willingness to suppress the urge to lash out at the wrong time. According to Mark Rutland in *Take the WEAK Out of Meek*, true leadership is defined by those who embrace the service of their followers and relinquish their need for control. He argues that few leaders exemplify meekness in leadership more than Abraham Lincoln did in his approach to the Confederacy after the Civil War. The South was smashed, with more than 250,000 of its young men dead, its heartland in shambles, its agriculture and industry destroyed. But the Union Army and Congress wanted the rebel states occupied, gutted, and forever stripped of full participation in the Republic (Rutland 2004). Lincoln would have none of it. Instead he longed to return the wayward to the fold, and he refused to use his power in unrestrained vengeance. In doing so, he proved the depth of his spiritual leadership through meekness. In his Second Inaugural Address he boldly called for healing love "with malice toward none, with charity toward all." Spiritual leadership is made manifest through patience and meekness.

Kindness, Empathy, and Compassion. *I am warm-hearted, considerate, humane, and sympathetic to the feelings and needs of others. When people are suffering, I understand and want to do something about it.*

Kindness, empathy, and compassion form the essence of other-centeredness. Kindness is an act of charity, generosity, or helpfulness without expectation of receiving anything in return, especially toward those who are suffering or needy. A study of thirty-seven world cultures asked 16,000 subjects about their most desired trait in a mate. Both sexes responded that their first preference was kindness (the second was intelligence). To be kind requires sympathy, which implies feelings shared with a sufferer as if the pain belonged to both persons. In sympathy, one does not actually experience the other's painful feelings (for example, their loss of a loved one in an accident) but still shares the other's feelings through an attempt to imagine and identify with the other's situation.

Empathy goes beyond sympathy in that empathy requires a deeper sense of emotion and understanding of another's feelings. Empathy—through engaged detachment—is a higher level of intellectual and emotional awareness, of being sensitive to and vicariously experiencing the feelings, thoughts, and experience of another. In empathy, one is actually able to comprehend another's feelings and experience them. In effect, one "borrows" another's feelings to imagine and understand the other's feelings, desires, ideas, and actions. The effective empathizer is one who is able to balance involvement with appropriate detachment. Traditionally, organizations view the experience of emotions, such as sympathy, in the workplace as burdensome, emotionally exhausting, and something that could lead to burnout (such as when a physician shares a patient's suffering). However, recent research suggests that a leader's ability to understand another's emotions and to empathize results in more intelligent and effective decisions and relationships.

Empathy, as a key component of emotional intelligence, is important for effective leadership due to the increasing use of teams, the rapid pace of globalization, and the growing need to retain scarce and highly trained talent. Teams are often charged with reaching consensus in the face of charged emotions based in conflict or in clashing alliances and agendas. Globalization requires cross-cultural dialogue and an understanding of cultural and ethnic differences in expressing feelings and emotions that can lead to miscues and misunderstandings. Leaders' empathy in understanding the feelings of their key people plays a vital role in retention of talent; the stakes are even higher in today's information economy because when good people leave they take the organization's knowledge with them.

Central to compassion is the process of identifying with others and bringing people closer. Compassion has three components: empathy, caring for the other person, and willingness to act in response to that person's feelings. Compassion is more vigorous and broader than empathy in that it gives rise to an active desire to alleviate another's suffering. Compassion requires knowledge of another's suffering and moves us to act. It testifies to the inherent closeness possible between people, whether it is the suffering of strangers, associates, or loved ones. This feeling of closeness toward others can be developed based on the simple recognition that all human beings wish to be happy and avoid suffering.

The effects of injury, illness, or the death of loved ones can spill over into the workplace. Suffering is inevitable in organizational life and springs from many sources both inside and outside the organization. Suffering can also arise as a result of toxic interactions with bosses, coworkers, or customers or from organizational processes like downsizing. These painful experiences have a significant negative impact on employees, the organization, and its stakeholders. A recent survey from the Grief Recovery Institute found firms lose more than $75 billion dollars annually from employees' grief-related incidents.

Compassion can strengthen emotional connections at work and boost one's ability to function as a productive employee. Unfortunately, kindness, empathy, and compassion don't get much respect in most organizations. How can leaders make hard decisions if they are "feeling" for all the people who will be affected? However, evidence is emerging that compassion aids in making and implementing tough decisions. Compassion is not about being soft; it is not somehow about "bleeding hearts." Leaders must sometimes fire or let people go, even loved ones. Compassion is a form of disinterested love with the potential for a healed outcome that changes the context of the situation and the quality of the experience of those involved.

Compassion may take a wide range of forms, including gestures of emotional support, giving of material goods, or providing the sufferer with work flexibility. Giving emotional support could be offering words or gestures designed to extend comfort, such as hugs, listening, and questions about well-being. Giving material goods can be things like small tokens to coordinated collections of money, cards, flowers, or food. Providing work flexibility could be time off for a sufferer to recover or coworkers being allowed to cover a shift, deliver food, attend funeral services, or go out of their way to attend to a coworker's suffering.

Leaders who are kind, empathetic, and compassionate do more than just sympathize: they act in ways that foster improvement in their companies that endures in subtle but important ways. Noticing another's suffering, empathetically feeling that person's pain, and responding or acting in a manner intended to ease the suffering are three key elements of compassion. Leaders with compassion will work to implement organizational policies and a shared value of compassion that heighten workers' vigilance for pain and make workers accessible to one another. Through this noticing, workers can collectively feel concern and compassionately share in the distress of a suffering employee.

Compassionate responding, however, may or may not erase the cause of one's suffering. For example, giving a hug and listening empathetically as someone discusses the painful process of caring for their mother with Alzheimer's disease or being passed over for a much desired promotion may aim to make the suffering more bearable but may not have a dramatic effect. Yet regardless of the extent the sufferer's pain is alleviated, compassionate leaders who foster and support this process of noticing, feeling, and responding will have employees who feel a heightened sense of membership and belonging—a key component of spiritual well-being in the spiritual leadership model.

Forgiveness, Acceptance, and Gratitude. I suffer not the burden of failed expectations, gossip, jealousy, hatred, or revenge. Instead I choose the power of forgiveness through acceptance and gratitude. This frees me from the evils of self-will, judging others, resentment, self-pity, and anger and gives me serenity, joy, and peace.

A powerful example of the power of forgiveness is illustrated by Desmond Tutu's explanation of the peaceful transition in South Africa from conditions of inhumane oppression to freely offered forgiveness. The following excerpt explains the meaning and power of forgiveness.

> Forgiving and being reconciled are not about pretending that things are other than they are. It is not patting one another on the back and turning a blind eye to the wrong. True reconciliation exposes the awfulness, the abuse, the pain, the degradation, the truth. It could even sometimes make things worse. . . . In forgiving, people are not asked to forget. On the con-

trary, it is important to remember, so that we should not let such atrocities happen again. Forgiveness does not mean condoning what has been done. It means taking what happened seriously and not minimizing it; drawing out the sting in the memory that threatens to poison our entire existence. It involves trying to understand the perpetrators and so have empathy, to try to stand in their shoes and appreciate the sort of pressures and influences that might have conditioned them. . . . Forgiving means abandoning your right to pay back the perpetrator in his own coin, but it is a loss that liberates the victim. . . . We will always need a process of forgiveness and reconciliation to deal with those unfortunate yet all too human breaches in relationships. They are an inescapable characteristic of the human condition. (Tutu 1999)

The need for forgiveness is triggered when a transgressor violates a person's expectations concerning a situation or event. Such situations could include being insulted, forsaken by a lover, attacked by an enemy, or some manner of disrespect displayed at work. Seeking revenge against a transgressor is deeply ingrained in the biological, psychological, and cultural levels of human nature. It is typical for the offending party to literally "rent space in our head," which over time wears us out spiritually and psychologically. At work these resentments can lead to workplace conflict, avoidance behavior, gossip, overt arguments, and retaliation. While these common responses may yield some benefit—such as the release of negative emotions, decreased contact, or feelings of self-righteousness and empowerment—they ultimately perpetuate or even escalate the conflict. This can lead to negative personal outcomes, such as anxiety, stress, anger, hostility, and embarrassment, as well as ineffective problem-solving on the job and lower organizational effectiveness.

Forgiving does not mean we must like the people we forgive or condone the harm they may have done. An important aspect of forgiveness is that it is for the real benefit of the forgiver, not the forgiven. Forgiveness may not restore a relationship to what it was previously. Forgiveness is also not about forgetting. It is not a suit of armor that shields one from injury, nor does it give others permission to do whatever they want to do to us in the future. Although forgiving releases us from any claim to administer justice to the offender, it doesn't release them from their conscience or from the consequences (legal or otherwise) of their actions.

Forgiveness is essential to spiritual well-being. It frees us from the need for retribution and revenge as well as resentment and other negative emotions resulting from past hurts. Research indicates that forgiveness enhances physical health, psychological well-being, hope, job satisfaction, and satisfaction with life. Forgiveness is a key value of altruistic love that benefits workers and the organization because it requires us to develop and implement skills used in effective problem-solving and conflict resolution. Forgiving leaders are also more productive and relate to coworkers in a more positive and effective manner.

Acceptance is necessary for both the personal transformation in forgiveness and for spiritual growth. Acceptance recognizes that one has little, if any, control over the things that contribute to or detract from one's happiness—spouse, children, physical or mental health, coworkers, money, random events, violence, and harmful situations. This is perhaps best expressed in Reinhold Niebuhr's well-known serenity prayer, which is the cornerstone of twelve-step programs such as Alcoholics Anonymous: "God [or higher power], grant me the serenity to accept the things I cannot change, courage to change the things I can, and the wisdom to know the difference" (Niebuhr n.d.).

Most frustrations in life come from one's unwillingness to accept the things we should change in ourselves and our futile attempts to change things we should accept as beyond our control. Acknowledging that some troubling aspect of our lives can't be changed—such as no sign of remorse from a transgressor—is the hardest part of acceptance. However, the alternative to doing so is often hopelessness, despair, and other debilitating emotions that will only add to one's burden. Negative attitudes and emotions only aggravate the problem, increasing the pain and adding more fuel to the fire of resentment. Failure to accept "what is" leads to blaming something or someone else and a sense of powerlessness. Acceptance of what is in the now moment allows one to take responsibility for one's circumstances and to draw on one's resources and higher power to change them in the future.

However, acceptance does not mean endorsement of inappropriate or wrong behavior. Rather, it refers to a state of mind that views everything as a gift, that allows one to be peaceful in this moment and know the difference between what can be changed or improved and what can't. Ultimately, acceptance embraces all things, good and bad, as a gift or invitation for spiritual growth and transformation. The degree to which one is aware or conscious of this spiritual truth is a measure of one's gratefulness or gratitude. Therefore, acceptance is not indifference or detachment. Rather it involves gratitude and receptivity.

Along with acceptance, gratitude is important for forgiveness because it is a process through which people positively interpret everyday experiences and as such is a crucial determinant of well-being. Research reports higher levels of alertness, enthusiasm, attentiveness, energy, and prosocial behavior (for example, helping someone, offering emotional support) on the part of grateful people versus less grateful people. Once we have accepted a situation, gratitude provides an emotional process whereby self-destructive emotions are transformed into attitudes that permit healing and restoration. Feeling grateful also inhibits one from engaging in destructive interpersonal behavior.

Gratitude provides meaning in life by embracing life itself as the ultimate gift. It provides a path to the nondual on the spiritual journey in helping us recognize that all humans are connected to one another in a mysterious and miraculous way. It is a means by which tragedies are transformed into opportunities for forgiveness and growth. A grateful focus helps us confront and overcome obstacles and avoid disillusionment through giving thanks for newfound strength and resources that result from challenges, affronts, and setbacks. Grateful people are not naively optimistic, nor are they under some false illusion that pain and suffering is nonexistent. Rather, they consciously choose to extract benefits from adversity; one of the major benefits of such a choice is the perception that life, in and of itself, is a gift.

Gratitude is thus a central value in altruistic love and has important implications for organizational functioning and worker well-being. As a vital cultural value, gratitude stimulates moral behavior that is motivated out of concern for others. By experiencing and expressing gratitude, leaders can transform themselves and, by extension, the larger units within which they are embedded. Gratitude acts to reinforce a culture that can improve worker well-being and lower toxic emotions in the workplace.

A striking example of organizational forgiveness, acceptance, and gratitude is illustrated by the Amish community's response to the Amish school shooting on October 2, 2006. On that day, gunman Charles Carl Roberts IV took hostages and eventually shot and killed five girls (ages six through thirteen) before committing suicide in the West Nickel Mines School, an Amish one-room schoolhouse in the Old Order Amish community of Nickel Mines. On the day of the shooting, a grandfather of one of the murdered Amish girls was heard warning some young relatives not to hate the killer, saying, "We must not think evil of this man." Another Amish father noted, "He had a mother and a wife and a soul and now he's standing before a just God" ("Amish School Shooting" n.d.). Jack Meyer, a member of the Brethren community who lives near the Amish in Lancaster County, explained: "I don't think there's anybody here that wants to do anything but forgive and not only reach out to those who have suffered a loss in that way but to reach out to the family of the man who committed these acts." Amish community members visited and comforted Roberts' widow, parents, and parents-in-law. An Amish neighbor comforted the Roberts family hours after the shooting and extended forgiveness to them.

One Amish man held Roberts' sobbing father in his arms, reportedly for as long as an hour, to comfort him. About thirty members of the Amish community attended Roberts' funeral, and Marie Roberts, the widow of the killer, was one of the few outsiders invited to the funeral of one of the victims. She wrote an open letter to her Amish neighbors, thanking them for their forgiveness, grace, and mercy. She wrote, "Your love for our family has helped to provide the healing we so desperately need. Gifts you've given have touched our hearts in a way no words can describe. Your compassion has reached beyond our family, beyond our community, and is changing our world, and for this we sincerely thank you" ("Amish School Shooting" n.d.).

Scholars of Amish life note that "letting go of grudges" through forgiveness, acceptance, and gratitude are deeply rooted values in Amish culture. Amish willingness to forgo vengeance does not undo the tragedy or pardon the wrong, but rather constitutes a first step toward a future that is more hopeful. The Amish have also set up a charitable fund for the family of the shooter. Ultimately, the West Nickel Mines School was torn down, and a new one-room schoolhouse, the New Hope School, was built at another location.

Excellence. I do my best and recognize, rejoice in, and celebrate the noble efforts of my fellows.

Excellence as a cultural value supports altruistic love requiring leaders to help employees do their best. In *Encouraging the Heart*, Kouzes and Posner explore the principles and practices that support the basic human need to be loved for what we do and who we are, and how leaders can apply these principles and practices for excellence in daily work. At its core, *Encouraging the Heart* is about getting extraordinary things done in organizations by recognizing and celebrating the achievements of others. Underlying the practice of encouraging the heart is a set of recognizable, learnable, and repeatable actions leaders take that both make people feel loved and reinforce performance excellence. These include setting clear standards, expecting the best, setting an example, paying attention, personalizing recognition, telling a story, and celebrating together.

To encourage the heart is to first set clear standards. Standards in this context can mean goals, principles, or values, but regardless of the precise meaning of the term, it is absolutely critical that everyone identify with a common set of standards. There must be standards of excellence that are tied to the organization's vision and that are inspirational in bringing out the best in workers and making them feel like winners when they have achieved something. In addition, leaders must have faith and believe that their people can achieve the high standards that have been set. This faith in others is fundamental both to encouraging the heart and to organizational spiritual leadership. Also known as the Pygmalion effect, it is a belief on the part of the leader that, even if followers don't believe in themselves initially, instills self-confidence and creates a self-fulfilling prophecy that "Yes! We can do it!"

Leaders can't delegate encouraging the heart. Every leader must set the example and embody the standards they expect their people to measure up to. If you want others to encourage the heart, you start by modeling it yourself. It's not something one waits around for others to do. However, do not confuse positive role modeling with being soft. Leaders must always be on the lookout for examples of excellence in meeting or exceeding values and standards by paying attention and understanding the significance of peoples' actions. Kouzes and Posner call this CBWA or *caring by walking around* (a takeoff on MBWA or *managing by walking around*) and observing workers in their own settings. Leaders actively look for those people who embody desired values and standards wherever they are. Once found and before recognizing them publicly, the best leaders get to know these employees personally in terms of their likes and dislikes, their needs and interests (Kouzes and Posner, *Encourage the Heart* 1999). Then when it comes time to recognize them, they know a way to make the recognition special, meaningful, and memorable (but not necessarily formal, costly, and time-consuming).

Throughout human history, storytelling has been a key way to establish and reinforce culture and standards of behavior. Other ways to publicize what people do is to exemplify and reinforce cultural values through such vehicles as newsletters, annual reports, advertisements, voice mail, e-mail, and Web-based video. However, part of making recognition special and personal is to make sure an appropriate audience hears the story that exemplifies excellence in achieving. A story captures our attention and excites and entertains us. But even more important, the narration of what happened provides a behavioral map that employees can easily visualize and store in their minds. Good stories enable workers to see themselves being able to achieve excellence; people remember the particulars of how to do something far longer after hearing a story than after sitting through a lecture.

Celebration is a vital aspect of excellence that reinforces a sense of community, which is a key to the expression of altruistic love. Celebrations, such as stopping work for a few minutes or gathering at a designated time to honor a personal or group accomplishment, provide the social space where people can experience a sense of connection. Many of these occasions follow the tradition of using meals or eating together as a way to celebrate important occasions and signify friendship and fellowship. These types of celebrations allow workers to positively appraise their situation and to experience the positive emotions of care and concern that are important in coping with job stress. They also reinforce fun as a key cultural value by tangibly and publically showing care and concern for the person or group, their achievements and worth, and reinforce the belief that the organization is a good place to be.

MathWorks is a great example of a celebration culture. Founded in 1984, it's now a leading developer and supplier of software for technical computing and model-based design that employs more than 2,000 people. At the end of a weeklong orientation, new employees play a Jeopardy-like game about the company. For specific events like a new product launch or company anniversaries, they have designed elaborate scavenger hunts and even a nine-hole miniature golf course on two floors of their building. Then there are summer outings during which employees and their families enjoy a weekend of golf, hang gliding, mountain biking, parties, and the like. On a smaller scale are events like the Dove Bar celebrations. Whenever a group successfully finishes a new product, an e-mail message invites everyone who had anything to do with the project to celebrate around an ice-cream cooler right outside the project manager's door. Employees get a tasty treat, while the project team members receive congratulations from their colleagues and leaders.

The critical ingredient in the celebration of excellence is togetherness in care and concern for one another—the essence of altruistic love. It is an integral part of culture that serves as an organization's heart and welds the organization together. The key is to link a high level of participation and play not just in the work itself but in the celebration of achievements. The more people feel included and encouraged through well-designed and participatory celebrations, the more vital will be the sense of vision, purpose, meaning, belonging, and espirt de corps. When leaders do this they reinforce people's common stake in reaching their goals. In addition, information can be exchanged, relationships nourished, and a sense of shared destiny can be sustained.

Fun – Enjoyment and playfulness must exist at work in order to stimulate minds and bring happiness to the workplace. I therefore view my daily activities and work as not to be dreaded but, instead, as reasons for smiling and having a terrific day in serving others.

There is increasing evidence that a fun work culture provides valuable benefits for workers and their organizations. Leaders who adopt fun programs for employees claim that the payoff is high morale and productivity, low turnover, and exceptional products and services. Crown Point Cabinetry, A New Hampshire–based manufacturer of custom cabinets, significantly increased productivity and reduced turnover by offering fun food, celebrations, and projects. Industry leaders such as Southwest Airlines and Outback Steakhouse have become well-known for their success in promoting a culture of fun. In fact, many of the companies recognized as among the best companies to work for in America have made having fun a part of their mission and culture. Many organizations are recognizing the value of creating a fun workplace in terms of the positive impact it can have on the organization's quality of work life, recruiting, absenteeism, turnover, increased customer satisfaction, and financial performance.

Fun activities are intrinsically rewarding experiences that are intensely absorbing and provide joy and amusement. Fun at work can take two forms—through the work itself and in celebration and coming together in a festive atmosphere to honor and observe notable occasions or achievements. As we discussed in Chapter 2, intrinsic motivation is interest and enjoyment of an activity for its own sake and, at work, is associated with active engagement in tasks that people find interesting and fun. Fun is therefore central for organizational spiritual leadership, since it is an intrinsic motivation process based on vision, hope/faith, and altruistic love.

A national survey of more than 500 human resource managers concluded that having fun at work means an environment that makes people smile. These managers believe that there are many advantages and few disadvantages to a fun work environment. A fun work strategy intentionally encourages, initiates, and supports a variety of enjoyable and pleasurable activities and that such activities positively impact the attitude and productivity of individuals and groups. Fun work settings are created through funny, humorous, or playful activities that publically communicate the leaders' belief that personal or group achievements are valued by the organization. Kouzes and Posner in their best seller, *The Leadership Challenge* (Kouzes and Posner 2003), profiles leaders who have concluded that if your workers aren't having fun doing what they're doing, chances are that people aren't doing the best they can do. Examples include Chili's former CEO, Norm Brinker, who acknowledges the importance of creating a fun workplace. He believes that if you're having fun, you'll never work a day in your life. Another is Southwest Airlines, which first and foremost looks for people with other-directed outgoing personalities and a sense of humor—people who don't take themselves too seriously. They recruit people who want to be part of an extended family of people who work hard and have fun at the same time. Southwest knows that the only way to achieve its core principle of making flying fun for its customers is to make its employees' jobs fun first.

Play is a key aspect of fun, it allows us the freedom to tap into our inner, creative being. Play speaks to the kid still inside us that never hesitated to ask "Why?" or "How come?" It reinforces unconventional behavior and offers the opportunity to be uninhibited and to engage in activities that are at least in part free from the shackles of conventions and rules. People who incorporate play and have fun at work also approach their responsibilities and challenges with more energy and enthusiasm. Intellectual playfulness, for example, is necessary to free one from external constraints and is essential for creativity and innovation. The best innovations are usually the result of playing with ideas.

Top companies like Yahoo, Google, Microsoft, Cisco, and Sun Microsystems recognize this and have incorporated play as a key aspect of their cultures. They are even gearing their recruitment to come up with new ways to spread the word about the coolest, hottest jobs they have that incorporate a sense of freedom, a sense of ownership, and a very noncorporate attitude where work and play can be amalgamated to form *woly*. *Fortune* magazine placed Google at the top of its list of the hundred best places to work. Google's corporate philosophy embodies such principles as "you can make money without doing evil," "you can be serious without a suit," and "work should be challenging and the challenge should be fun."

In sum, the values of altruistic love create a strong and positive force for intrinsic motivation when combined with hope/faith in a vision of service to key stakeholders. This force then works to satisfy the fundamental needs of both leader and follower for spiritual well-being through calling and membership; and, ultimately, to foster higher levels of employee well-being, organizational commitment, financial performance, and social responsibility—the Triple Bottom Line. We've shared many small examples of how organizations address values related to altruistic love. Let's now return to Maxwell, Locke, and Ritter to see how they have created an organizational culture based on the values of altruistic love.

THE VALUES OF ALTRUISTIC LOVE: MAXWELL, LOCKE, AND RITTER LLP

Although the roots of their practice extend back to the 1960s, MLR was established on a Saturday morning in 1991 by Earl Maxwell, Tom Locke, and Mark Ritter, who had been partners together in a local "Big Six" accounting firm. Over breakfast at a restaurant in Austin, Texas, they pulled out a pencil and made jottings on a napkin. All they knew was that they were committed to creating something quite different from the traditional, highly bureaucratic (and often workaholic), fear-led CPA firm culture, where the time commitment necessary for success left little room for a family life. In particular, they wanted to provide the highest-quality solutions and services for their clients established in an environment that promotes personal goals, self-esteem, and professionalism. They asked, "How much money do we need? How much do each of us need to contribute? Do you think anyone will loan us the difference?" They wrote the answers on the back of that napkin. That's how the firm started and how they operated for eight years, on the basis of trust, without a written partnership agreement.

The founding partners believed that MLR should focus on three things: their clients, their people, and the community. They created a philosophy and mission based on core values that remain the basis of MLR's culture today and that provide the foundation for the niches and industries they serve.

MLR's Purpose

To help dynamic companies and people achieve their dreams (Maxwell 1998).

MLR's Mission

MLR is dedicated to serving our clients with the highest regard for competency, compassion, and courtesy. We strive to provide solutions and value to companies (from start-ups to 100-year-old businesses, family-owned and Fortune 500), their executives and professionals. We believe this dedication allows us to treat others as they would like to be treated rather than how we feel we should treat them. As an employer, we have created an environment where people do things because they want to, instead of being afraid not to. Our people actively participate in the community, and we maintain our reputation by committing ourselves and living up to our commitments. This collaborative environment allows us to treat each other with honesty, dignity, and respect (Maxwell 1998).

MLR's Core Values

We are dedicated to:

- Creating an environment where people do things because they want to, instead of being afraid not to.
- Encouraging open communication.
- Committing ourselves and living up to our commitments.
- Treating everyone with honesty, dignity, and respect.
- Serving our clients with the highest regard for competency, compassion, and courtesy.

- Actively participating in the community.
- Treating others as they would like to be treated. (Maxwell 1998)

With 16 partners and more than 100 employees MLR has been voted one of the best places to work in Central Texas for the last eight years. MLR's employees enjoy a competitive compensation and benefits package, which includes medical, dental, life, long- and short-term disability, flexible benefits plan, a 401(k) plan with employer contributions, profit-sharing, and paid holidays, as well as vacation and sick leave in the form of a Paid Time Off (PTO) bank. Because MLR is dedicated to helping their people achieve their dreams, they provide two additional key benefits. (1) Flexible work arrangements include flex-time, flex-space, and reduced-hour arrangements so people have every opportunity to balance personal and professional priorities. (2) Outstanding programs of training and professional development available to all employees.

MLR's core values are built on a foundation of people dedicated to sustainability through actively participating in the community. One of the first things a visitor notices upon entering MLR's office is the community wall, which is covered with certificates and plaques from various community organizations. MLR has won numerous community awards over the years, including:

- Austin Independent School District— Austin Works
- *Austin Business Journal*'s Best Places to Work
- Quality Supplier Service Award from Austin White Lime Company
- San Juan Diego Catholic High School Recognition
- *Austin Business Journal*'s Health Care Heroes
- The Arts Education League of Austin Lyric Opera's Perfect 10 Award
- Ballet Austin Corporate Balletomane Award
- St. Edward's University Kauffman Entrepreneur Internship Program
- Fund for Childcare Excellence—Family-Friendly Business Designation

- Samaritan Center—Ethics in Business Award
- Austin Mayor and City Council—Distinguished Service Award
- Texas Society of CPAs Lone Star Pathfinder Award
- Austin Chapter of Texas Society of CPAs—President's Award / CPA of the Year award
- Austin Chapter of Texas Society of CPAs—Firm Special Recognition
- F.E.M.A.L.E. (Formerly Employed Mothers at the Leading Edge) Family-Friendly Business Award
- Austin Partners in Education Employers Support Parenting Award
- Austin Partners in Education Hall of Fame

MLR works hard to attract people who share their core values. MLR encourages participation in volunteering to serve within the community. The organization recognizes that there is no better training ground for acquiring and practicing the values of altruistic love so central to MLR's culture than service to the greater Austin community,

The Spiritual Journey of Earl Maxwell and MLR

However, it has been far from smooth sailing for MLR during the transformation from traditional CPA culture to one based on organizational spiritual leadership. Earl Maxwell was an early pioneer who argued for spirituality in the workplace; in his vision, people do not just look for a job in order to get by but, instead, look for purpose in their lives in a workplace that provides a sense of community. The first seven years of MRL's journey are chronicled in Earl's 1998 book, *Service, Prosperity, and Sanity: Positioning the Professional Service Firm for the Future* (Maxwell 1998). Initially, Maxwell wrote the book to provide an orientation for employees who had just joined or would soon join MLR. But the book became one of the first to advocate organizational spiritual leadership and, in particular, the values of altruistic love. It is also one of the first books to advocate these values as necessary for spiritual well-being and a Triple Bottom Line that simultaneously meets the needs of the workforce of the twenty-first century, addresses the sustainability of the community, and achieves adequate financial returns.

For fourteen years, Maxwell had been on the "fast track" of an international "Big Six" accounting firm, and he ultimately became the managing partner of the firm's Austin office. The power in these organizations rested at the top, where information was closely guarded by those entitled to do so based on years of dedicated service, huge personal sacrifice in terms of hours worked and time away from family, and other rites of passage. The system was driven by the assumption that the younger professionals would work hard, go anywhere, and do anything required to ultimately achieve the money, perks, recognition, and security offered to partners (Maxwell 1998).

For Maxwell, being head of this highly bureaucratic, top-down organization was exhausting work; he found that his job was to approve or make all the decisions. Information regarding financial performance and the firm's strategies were closely guarded secrets. Partners met behind closed doors, while everyone else in the firm wasted much time speculating about what was decided in those meetings, how the decisions would affect them, and who the next victims would be. Once a year the partners went to a national meeting in which the same process was repeated to determine what the national office was going to do to them the next year. There the partners received marching orders and information about how the Austin office's strategies should be communicated to their troops. This organizational paradigm worked for decades, even though only a small percentage of the people who joined these firms eventually became partners. Most people burned out and left the firm due to the excessively long hours; they were not willing to put in the ten to fourteen workaholic years required to become a partner.

Fear was by far the main motivational force in the organization. The opinions of employees were not important, and they were afraid to express them for fear of offending superiors. Multiple fears—fear of setting realistic goals and not living up to expectations, fear of looking bad, fear of going over budget, fear of offending a client, fear of not getting promoted, fear of the consequences of refusing a transfer, and the ultimate fear of being "counseled out"—drove and adversely affected many decisions. The activities and behaviors surrounding these fears could involve CLMs (career-limiting moves) or, even worse, CEMs (career-ending moves).

Maxwell and his partners recognized that while many firms demand that their people treat clients with care and compassion, these same firms abuse their own people. The partners believed that the definition of prosperity should be more than a simple focus on money and that they could bring better balance to all their lives and restore sanity to the workplace. This meant certain values must be of paramount importance if they were to achieve their new radical vision (for a CPA firm) of truly caring for their clients *and* caring for one another. First and foremost, integrity, openness, and honesty from all was expected and demanded. This would be the foundation for people doing things because they wanted to, not because they were afraid not to—a workplace where people looked forward to spending their time.

Several changes were initiated to signal the beginning of this transformation. To indicate a more egalitarian environment, MLR stopped referring to their people as two classes—professional and nonprofessionals. They changed their titles from six levels (partner, senior manager, manager, senior, senior assistant, and assistant) to three (shareholder, senior associate, and associate). The new system meant that shareholders roll up their sleeves, relinquish parking spaces, move from window offices, and fly coach with their people. MLR instituted a casual day on Friday long before it became vogue. As a first step to a family-friendly workplace they allowed challenged parents to bring their children to work on school holidays and in-service training days for teachers. Perhaps most important, to break the mold of secrecy MLR began a move to transparency and open-book management by opening their financial statements.

These changes coincided with a dismal financial year in 1992. The shareholders remained true to their value of caring for their own people. In addition to painful cost cutting, the shareholders agreed to forfeit two months' salary since MLR, at that time, had no money and they had exhausted their line of credit. Some people had to be let go. At traditional firms these people just disappeared and ceased to exist. However, MLR took great care to help the people leaving the firm by giving them access to their offices and the resources of the firm until they found another job. This approach was shared in an office-wide meeting, where everyone in the room was asked to do what they could to assist in these job searches.

Initiatives were started over the next eighteen months as MLR dug themselves out of their hole. When the shareholders realized they did not have the knowledge or experience to effectively proceed on their own, they brought in an outside consultant to help further the transformation. With the consultant's help, the firm decided to move from performance-based bonuses to firm-wide profit sharing. At the end of each year, 50 percent of net income would be distributed according to a percentage applied to everyone's base salary. This would require that all people join in the development of the annual operating plan. To facilitate this process, the firm has created four process teams and a leadership team:

The Common Area Team is responsible for the processes in the reception area, library, conference rooms, file rooms, kitchen, and hallways.

The Technology Team make decisions concerning computer hardware, software, networks, the Internet, remote processing, voice mail, e-mail, faxing, copy machines, etc.

The Marketing and Client Services Team Focuses on improving processes related to client service, including cycle time—starting with a prospect's first contact with MLR; to proposal delivery and contract award; through planning, execution, and delivery of the work product/service; to billing and collection; and finally to follow-up and rehire for the next project.

The Human Resource Team handles fringe benefits, the evaluation and counseling system, firm social events, bonus and compensation systems, and continuing professional education

The Leadership Team is responsible for community contributions, revenue estimates, and compiling and approving the operating plan. This team is comprised of select shareholders, the four process team leaders, and, on a rotational basis, three people who are not regular members. (Maxwell 1998)

Each team is furnished with basic assumptions for the operating plan. Although participation on these teams is voluntary, it is rare that not everyone participates. Shareholder meetings are held to discuss raises, confidential recruiting decisions, negotiations (for example, to acquire other practices), and sensitive client matters.

In 1996, Earl had a transformational experience during a three day spiritual journey called the Walk to Emmaus. In the months that followed this experience, he felt a strong calling to either enter the ministry or to become a teacher. During this period of discernment, MLR's marketing director (now a pastor) was attending the Lutheran Seminary in Austin. He served as Earl's spiritual advisor during this period. After much thought, discussion, and prayer, he decided to not enter seminary, or to become a teacher. Instead, Earl decided to begin approaching the workplace of Maxwell Locke & Ritter LLP as his ministry. Later, in the early 2000s, Earl served as President of a large church congregation during a very difficult time in the life of the church. By the end of this two year experience, he knew he had made the right decision to not enter the ministry. He was simply not meant to be a senior pastor in a church.

After Earl went through his crisis of personal spiritual leadership, MLR faced its first dark night of the soul. MLR experienced its best year in 2000; however, that was followed by its worst year in 2001. Due to the downturn in the semi-conductor industry, MLR lost 40 percent of their revenues. Forty-three people who had lived off $5 million suddenly found it necessary to survive on $3 million overnight. The numbers said MLR needed to reduce the number of their people by fifteen. For three meetings MLR's nine partners debated the problem. At the end of the third meeting, Mark Ritter had the wisdom to point to one of the framed values on the wall: "We care for our clients and we care for each other." He suggested that the statement be blown up to poster size and placed in the middle of the conference room table before they met again.

At the next meeting, a poster stood in the middle of the table that read, "We care for our clients and we care for each other." This completely changed the nature of conversation. Instead of dismantling the firm, the partners decided to live off the previous year's undistributed earnings; everyone would go a couple of years without profit sharing, and they would cut other expenses. Through clarifying that MLR's culture would continue to be based on altruistic love, the partners realized that values had won out, and that money and everything else would be revitalized if they kept their focus on a higher good. Continuing to stay in business was not an option if that meant MLR would lose its spiritual values. Their values were the greatest good. Firm revenues are now a multiple of those in 2001, and Earl Maxwell believes if they had not stayed true to their values based on altruistic love and revitalized everything else to a higher good, MLR would not be nearly as successful as it is today.

CONCLUSION

Underlying the foundation for altruistic love are the values of integrity/honesty, trust/loyalty, humility, courage, patience, kindness, forgiveness, excellence, and fun. The fields of medical research and positive psychology have begun to confirm that the values inherent in altruistic love have the power to overcome the negative influence of destructive emotions such as anger, resentment, worry, and fear. As a key component of organizational culture, altruistic love defines the set of values, attitudes, and behaviors considered to be morally right. These are shared by current group members and taught to new members.

There are great emotional and psychological benefits to be gained from separating love, or care and concern for others, from need, which is the essence of giving and receiving unconditionally. Spiritual leaders are dedicated to the selfless promotion of the growth of their people and are willing to extend themselves for the purpose of nurturing their own or another's spiritual growth. They recognize that when leaders are able to help others grow to become the best people they can be, the leaders are being loving and they too grow.

Spiritual leadership has enabled Maxwell, Locke, and Ritter, even in the stodgy CPA industry, to create and sustain a fun, caring, family-sensitive, performance-driven organization dedicated to sustainability through in community service. MLR's vision, purpose, and mission have broad appeal to their clients and other key community stakeholders. They reflect high ideals and establish a standard of excellence that encourages hope/faith in its people to persevere and "do what it takes" to jointly set and achieve challenging, stretch goals. MLR's ethical system and its core cultural values based in altruistic love encourage integrity, honesty, and trust in its business conduct.

MLR has a culture focused on employee well-being, one based in compassion, forgiveness, and acceptance—altruistic love—that not only gives permission for people to leave but offers them blessings and assistance in finding them a better place to prosper. It is also a culture of excellence that results in the organization being one of the most profitable CPA firms of its size in the United States. Moreover, MLR encourages people to hit numbers that are very black and white in a workplace where people celebrate, have fun, and relax to a much greater extent than is the industry norm.

There is no better example of maximizing the Triple Bottom Line through spiritual leadership than Maxwell, Locke, and Ritter LLP. Through living their core values based in altruistic love, the people of MLR have created a healthy and balanced organization focused on long-term client relationships. By striving to keep their family life foremost, their employees' spiritual well-being is reinforced and performance is enhanced. By giving unselfishly to the community, employees become infused with a deep sense of satisfaction and gratitude.

Practical Tools

For those interested in maximize the Triple Bottom Line, the major tools introduced in this chapter include the following:

The Qualities of spiritual leadership detail the underlying values, attitudes, and behaviors necessary for spiritual leadership through hope/faith, vision, and altruistic love.

The values of altruistic love (integrity and honesty; trust and loyalty; humility; courage; patience, meekness, and endurance; kindness, empathy, and compassion; forgiveness, acceptance, and gratitude; excellence; and fun) provide the foundation for the organizational culture and ethical system that is essential for spiritual leadership.

Chapter Five

SPIRITUAL LEADERSHIP AND SPIRITUAL WELL-BEING

In early 2007, Maxwell, Locke and Ritter LLP (MLR) formalized their commitment to employee wellness and spiritual well-being by establishing a Wellness Team to ensure that all employees have the opportunity to take advantage of activities that promote healthy behaviors and positive attitudes. Although support for physical, intellectual, and spiritual wellness has been a part of the firm's culture since its inception, the Wellness Team and its leaders are responsible for making sure these efforts continue to develop and grow in an organized way. For the mind and spirit, there's the "brown bag book club," at whose lunchtime meeting employees can share ideas while discussing literature and social issues. The whole firm is involved to some extent in such firm-wide activities, whether it is simply getting a flu shot each winter, playing on an interoffice kickball team, or participating in a group weight-loss program.

MLR regularly brings in inspirational and educational speakers. It provides employees with coaching and mentoring opportunities, from technical and leadership development to personal vision statements. It is part of the team's mission to be not just well, but to have a great firm that lives up to its cultural values. MLR also added a wellness room to the office as a retreat for workers who want to take a break and mediate or relax during the work day. The room features calming music, soft lighting, and a fountain.

Community service is a key part of the wellness initiative as well. Throughout the year MLR employees take part in blood drives and fundraising walks. Every Monday a few employees deliver Meals on Wheels. The firm also sponsors 5K and 10k running teams, CPR training, subsidized gym memberships, team volleyball, free healthy snacks, massage sessions, and bowling. MLR believes businesses should assume more responsibility for supporting their personnel and those who surround them. For example, MLR employees help each other through times of financial need, parenting, death, illness, and many other life challenges (Maxwell 1998; Maxwell 2008).

The need for establishing spiritual well-being within organizations is not a new idea. O. A. Ohmann, in his classic 1955 *Harvard Business Review* article "Skyhooks," argued that people have lost faith in society's basic values and that a spiritual rebirth was needed in industrial leadership. He argued that never in human history have people had so much yet enjoyed so little real life satisfaction. Ohmann proposed that the god of production and profits had feet of clay and that a religion based on materialism, science, and humanism is inadequate. He explained that man, especially at work, is searching for new "skyhooks"—for an abiding faith around which life's experiences can be integrated and given meaning (Ohmann 1955). In exploring these issues, Ohmann asked fundamental questions: "Production for what?" "Do we use people for production or production for people?" and "How can production be justified if it destroys both personality and human values both in the process of its manufacture and by its end use?"

In answering these questions, Ohmann describes the successful executive as one who provides an invisible, fundamental structure of "skyhooks" into which the experiences of ever day leadership are absorbed and become the source of spiritual well-being. The skyhooks include,

- Providing a vision, without which the people perish.
- Philosophical and character values that help relate the over-all goals of the enterprise to eternal values.

- Setting the climate within which these values become working realities.

- Integrating the smaller, selfish goals of individuals into larger, more social and spiritual objectives of the group.

- Resolving conflicts by relating the immediate to long-range and more enduring values. (Ohmann 1955)

Ohmann makes a persuasive case for spiritual leadership and spiritual well-being. The two primary components of workplace spiritual well-being are the need for calling or being called (vocationally), which gives a sense of meaning and purpose, and the need for social connection, belonging, or membership. These two components of spiritual well-being are interconnected, universal, and common to the human experience.

Companies have begun to recognize that a focus on spiritual well-being through calling and membership is essential for overall employee well-being. Many people seek not only competence and mastery to realize their full potential through their work but also a sense that work has some social meaning or value. Professionals believe their chosen profession is a calling and is valuable—even essential—to society, and they are proud to be a member of it. Membership encompasses a sense of belonging and community; the cultural and social structures we are immersed in and through which we seek connections with others. As we devote ourselves to social groups; membership extends the meaning of our personality by joining us in a network of social connections that go as far as the group has influence and power, and backward and forward in relation to its history.

The previous chapter detailed the qualities of spiritual leadership and the values of altruistic love. In this chapter we heed Ohmann's original call for more "skyhooks" and offer further insights into spiritual leadership and the qualities of spiritual well-being. Finally, we again draw on the example of Maxwell, Locke, and Ritter LLP to illustrate how organizations can focus on enhancing employee spiritual well-being and, in doing so, maximize the Triple Bottom Line.

SPIRITUAL WELL-BEING.

Well-being can be defined as the state of being happy, healthy, or prosperous. Throughout human history there have been attempts to develop an understanding of well-being or "the good life" in terms of particular human characteristics and qualities that are desirable and worthy of emulation. Aristotle asserted that the only rational, ultimate goal of goals is happiness. Other philosophers and religious leaders have suggested that diverse characteristics—such as love, wisdom, and nonattachment—are the cardinal elements of a fulfilled existence. Some have argued for a focus on the emotional, mental, and physical pleasures and pains of daily living, and have claimed that the presence of pleasure and the absence of pain are the defining characteristics of a good life.

Demographic variables such as age, income, gender, and education do not account for significant differences in well-being. The way people perceive the world and their spiritual condition seem to be much more important to life satisfaction than objective circumstances. Regardless of the definition, there is agreement that well-being is a requirement for human existence—that human beings always and of necessity live on the basis of an understanding of what is a better, more desirable, or worthier way of being in the world.

Today it is generally accepted that individuals with abundant joy, peace, and serenity have the key ingredients of a good life. Joy is exultant satisfaction as a source of gladness or delight and is an emotion of keen or lively pleasure arising from present or expected satisfaction. Peace is a state of mind in which one is free from mental disturbance, strife, or agitation. Serenity is a deep inner sense that all is well. Taken together, joy, peace, and serenity go beyond our systems of emotional or rational intelligence. Rather, well-being is a state of intuitive or spiritual knowing that produces in us an inner experience of calmness, clarity, and awareness.

For a number of reasons, there is a growing interest in employee well-being and developing a healthy workplace. The *Sunday Times* newspaper list of Top 100 Companies to Work For has a category of "Best for Well-

Being," with companies such as Edward Jones, W. L. Gore and Associated, Marathon Oil, and NB Real Estate hailed as leaders in this respect. Companies are increasingly hiring well-being consultants, establishing well-being policies, opening well-being centers, and appointing well-being officers.

Corporate Heart is a consulting firm that works with organizations to increase organizational wellness, so that people and work processes synchronize to produce healthy, high-performance cultures. They define well-being as fostering the physical, mental, emotional, and spiritual status of each person—that is, a healthy body, an alert mind, emotional balance, and an inner essential presence of joy, peace, and serenity.

Corporate Heart conducts interventions and initiatives aimed at reducing stress and improving work-life balance—corporate chaplains, free career counseling, year-round day-care centers, work-at-home options, tuition reimbursement for professional development, discussion groups to address company and personal issues, free gym memberships, and mediation or quiet rooms. These interventions and initiatives are believed to enhance the value of human capital and the ability of people to deliver results, which in turn affects long-term organizational success through the holistic strategy of creating well communities at work.

The well-being interventions and initiatives that Corporate Heart and other organizations are implementing are attempts to answer Ohmann's call for "skyhooks" as a source of spiritual well-being at work. Ultimately the answer to these questions may lie with religious and spiritual traditions. These have argued for eons that spirituality lies at the heart of well-being. However, it is only within the last thirty years that mainstream scientific research in workplace spirituality, character ethics, and psychology have begun to recognize the power of spirituality in maintaining well-being. Research in the field of medicine also supports positive relationships between spirituality and physical and psychological health. Spiritual well-being is positively related to better coping with long-term and terminal illness, and to physical well-being, a sense of hope, self-esteem, social support, and better marital adjustment and intimacy. It is negatively related to anxiety, depression, feelings of loneliness, and risky

TABLE 5.1

Comparison of Scholarly Fields Emphasizing Spiritual Well-being

Spiritual Leadership	Religion	Workplace Spirituality	Character Ethics & Education	Positive Psychology
Hope / Faith **Vision** **Altruistic Love** • Integrity / Honesty • Trust / Loyalty • Humility • Courage • Patience / Meekness / Endurance • Kindness / Empathy / Compassion / Forgiveness / Acceptance / Gratitude • Excellence • Fun	• Vision of Service/ Letting Go of Self • Honesty • Veracity/ Truthfulness • Charity • Humility • Forgiveness • Compassion • Thankfulness / Gratitude	• Honesty • Forgiveness • Hope • Gratitude • Humility • Compassion Integrity	**Trustworthiness** • Honesty • Integrity • Loyalty **Respect** • Civility • Courtesy • Decency • Dignity • Autonomy • Tolerance • Acceptance **Responsibility** • Accountability • Excellence • Diligence **Perseverance** • Continuous • Improvement **Fairness Caring Citizenship**	• Optimism • Hope • Humility • Compassion • Forgiveness • Gratitude • Love • Altruism • Empathy • Toughness • Meaningfulness • Humor

SOURCE: Adapted and modified from Fry, L., "Toward a Theory of Ethical and Spiritual Well-being and Corporate Social Responsibility Through Spiritual Leadership," in *Positive Psychology in Business Ethics and Corporate Responsibility*, ed. R. Giacalone, C. Jurkiewicz, and C. Dunn, Greenwich, CT: Information Age Publishing, 2005: 47–83.

behaviors (for example, alcohol and substance abuse, unsafe sex, and driving under influence).

Finally, there is an emerging consensus that the dimensions of vision, hope/faith, and altruistic love in organizational spiritual leadership are necessary for spiritual well-being and, ultimately, positive human health and psychological well-being. This consensus is illustrated in Table 5.1, which compares the qualities of spiritual leadership outlined in the previous chapters to the views expressed by religion, proponents of workplace spirituality, positive psychology, and character ethics concerning spiritual well-being. While each of these fields has a different focus, they maintain a similar underlying premise: the importance of indentifying, increasing, and nurturing the positive virtues/values in strengthening human well-being.

Spiritual Well-Being in Religion and Workplace Spirituality

In terms of workplace spirituality, the entries in Table 5.1 represent dimensions of the spiritual well-being discussed in the earlier chapters. The table entries for workplace spirituality are also the focus of chapters in Giacalone and Jurkiewicz's pioneering *Handbook of Workplace Spirituality and Organizational Performance* (Giacalone and Jurkiewicz 2003).

Huston Smith, in his monumental work *The World's Religions*, observes that all religions espouse the values of humility, charity, veracity, and vision. Spiritual well-being is found in the pursuit of a vision of service to others through: humility, which is having the capacity to regard oneself as one, but not more than one; charity or altruistic love; and veracity, which goes beyond basic truth-telling to having the capacity to see things exactly as they are, freed from subjective distortions (Smith 1991).

Expanding on Smith's core values, Kriger and Hansen propose, in their article "A Value-based Paradigm for Creating Truly Healthy Organizations," a set of universal values—honesty, truthfulness, trust, humility, forgiveness, compassion, thankfulness, being of service, and stillness. They argue that these values are necessary for both economic and spiritual principles to thrive and grow in modern organizations (Kriger and Hanson 1999).

Spiritual Well-Being in Character Education

The Greek philosopher Aristotle defined good character as the life of right conduct both in relation to others and in relation to oneself (Lickona 1991). Since the beginning of mankind's quest for knowledge, we have recognized that there is a set of capital virtues and vices. To live well, one must live up to these virtues while overcoming the vices. Moral theology has traditionally identified prudence, justice, temperance, and fortitude as the "cardinal virtues". The values underlying them lead to morally good attitudes and behaviors or practices.

The ability to distinguish between acts that are morally good or evil is critical to the formation of character. It enables individuals to adopt the values and attitudes that lead to moral behavior and, ultimately, to well-being and "the good life." However, knowledge of ethical values and moral principles is futile unless the individual makes the effort to habitually incorporate them into his or her attitudes and behavior. Thus character constitutes an inner-directed and habitual strength of mind and will. This effort to create, teach, and model this core group of values is at the heart of character education.

Character education advocates a common ethical and spiritual ground, even though there are often intense conflicts in our society over moral issues such as abortion, homosexuality, euthanasia, and capital punishment. However, despite this conflict, we can identify basic and universal shared values. As Thomas Lickona argues in *Education for Character*: "There are rationally grounded, nonrelative, objectively worthwhile moral values: respect for life, liberty, the inherent value of every individual person, and the consequent responsibility to care for each other and carry out our basic obligations. These objectively worthwhile values demand that we treat as morally wrong any action by any individual, group, or state that violates these basic moral values" (Lickona 1991).

In character education, the "Six Pillars of Character" serve as a set of universal core ethical values that transcend race, creed, politics, gender, and wealth as a means to honor the dignity and autonomy of each person and cautions against self-righteousness in areas of legitimate controversy.

Trustworthiness. Don't deceive, cheat, or steal. Build a good reputation. Be reliable.

Respect. Be tolerant of differences and considerate of others' feelings.

Responsibility. Do what you are supposed to do. Be accountable. Persevere.

Fairness. Take turns. Share. Play by the rules. Don't take advantage of others.

Caring. Forgive others. Help people in need. Express gratitude. Be kind.

Citizenship. Obey the laws. Respect authority. Stay informed. Cooperate. (Lickona 1991)

These core values translate into principles that guide and motivate ethical conduct that promotes spiritual well-being. For example, honesty, a value of trustworthiness, gives rise to attitudes, behaviors, and principles in the form of specific do's and don'ts, including telling the truth, not deceiving, being candid, and not cheating.

People are not born with character; it must be developed. Building character is a process of instruction, training, and mentoring to instill within a person positive ethical values and principles. In situations in which we are confronted with conflicting values (for example, the desire for wealth and prestige versus honesty and kindness toward others), we resort to our core value system, which consists of the values we consistently rank higher than others. These values are the source of the attitudes and, ultimately, the behaviors we choose in any given situation. From this perspective, spiritual well-being is found through the day-to-day process of basing one's attitudes and behavior on these core values.

Spiritual Well-Being in Positive Psychology

Positive psychology attempts to refocus psychology away from a preoccupation with repairing the worst things in life and toward building positive qualities. Although there is an extensive literature about how people survive and endure under conditions of adversity, little is known about what makes life worth living, how people prevent life from being barren and meaningless, and how to achieve positive human health and psychological well-being. The purpose of positive psychology is to scientifically uncover a vision of "the good life" that is empirically sound while being understandable and attractive. It is not just concerned with illness, health, or fixing what is broken; it is about nurturing what is best in work, education, insight, love, growth, and play.

Positive psychology helps people identify and nurture their strongest qualities, what they own or are best at, and supports them in finding niches in which they best live out these positive qualities. Positive psychologists recognize that their best work lies in identifying, amplifying, and nurturing strengths rather than repairing client weaknesses, and developing contexts and cultures that reinforce and foster these strengths.

The most complete model of psychological well-being to date incorporates diverse features of what it means to be well (Ryff & Singer, 2001).

Self-Acceptance. One possesses a positive attitude toward the self; acknowledges and accepts multiple aspects of the self, including good and bad qualities; feels positive about his or her past life.

Positive Relations with Others. One has warm, satisfying, trusting relationships with others; is concerned about the welfare of others; is capable of strong empathy, affection, and intimacy; understands the give-and-take of human relationships.

Autonomy. One is self-determined and independent; is able to resist social pressures to think and act in certain ways; regulates behavior from within; evaluates oneself by personal standards.

Environmental Mastery. One has a sense of mastery and competence in managing the environment; controls a complex array of external activities; makes effective use of surrounding opportunities; is able to choose or create contexts suitable to personal needs and values.

Purpose in Life. One has goals in life and a sense of directedness; feels there is meaning to present and past life; holds beliefs that give life purpose; has aims and objectives for living.

Personal Growth. One has a feeling of continued development; sees self as growing and expanding; is open to new experiences; has a sense of realizing his or her potential; sees improvement in self and behavior over time; is changing in ways that reflect increasing self-knowledge and effectiveness.

Thus, one would experience greater positive human health and psychological well-being to the extent that one has a high regard for oneself and one's past life, good-quality relationship with others, a sense that life is purposeful and meaningful, the capacity to effectively manage one's surrounding world, the ability to follow inner convictions, and a sense of continuing growth and self-realization. Moreover, individuals who score high on these six dimensions not only experience greater psychological and spiritual well-being but also have fewer problems related to physical health in terms of allostatic load (cardiovascular disease, cognitive impairment, declines in physical functioning, and mortality).

SPIRITUAL WELL-BEING AND THE ORGANIZATIONAL SPIRITUAL LEADERSHIP MODEL

The deepest questions in life are spiritual in nature. They are questions concerning inner life and spiritual well-being through calling and membership—about the search for ultimate purposes, enduring truths, and how we relate in community with our fellow human beings: Why am I here? What am I meant for? What is worth my passion and life? How can I be for myself and also for others? Whom and what do I serve? These questions speak to the universal instinct toward connection with others and the discovery of our purpose and place in the larger web of life. In *The Healing Spirit*, Paul Fleischman seeks to address these questions. In doing so, he identifies calling and membership as two universal human needs essential for spiritual well-being regardless of gender, race, demographic group, or culture (Fleischman 1994).

According to a Zen Buddhist saying, work and pleasure should be so aligned that it is impossible to distinguish one from the other. People are happiest when they are engaged in interesting, intrinsically motivating activities, especially if it is in a supportive social setting in pursuit of common goals that are important and meaningful. In the organizational Spiritual Leadership Model, leaders and followers experience spiritual well-being through calling and membership. By committing to a hope/faith in vision of service to key stakeholders, workers develop a sense of calling through which they feel a sense of purpose and that their life has meaning and makes a difference. By receiving altruistic love through the care and concern for themselves and others, employees experience membership and feel a sense of belonging and community in which they feel understood and appreciated.

Calling—Finding Purpose and Meaning

Finding purpose and meaning in life is certainly not a new concept; individuals have been in search of their calling since the beginning of time. The essence of calling is captured in this statement from Sir Wilfred

Thomason Grenfell: "Real joy comes not from ease or riches or from the praise of men, but from doing something worthwhile" ("Wilfred Grenfell Quotes" n.d.). To be called is to have a deep inner conviction that one has a personal destiny or future goal that guides one's life. A calling provides a foundation for both meaningful human activity and utilizing one's individual and unique abilities.

Search for Calling

All of the world's major religious and spiritual traditions speak to the universal yearning for a calling, for a vocation that fulfills the world as it moves forward in one's own life, for a role that interlocks with the roles of others. Calling emerges through experiences in which one learns that true happiness cannot be found through external gifts or the trappings of success. Ask people what caused them to search for their calling and many cite a personal crisis, such as a death of someone close to them, a divorce, job loss, heart attack, alcoholism, or bankruptcy. Through calling one taps into the human ability to rise above these circumstances and care about something or someone beyond oneself.

Victor Frankl, founder of logotherapy (meaning theory), survived four different concentration camps during World War II, including Birkenau and Auschwitz. While in the camps, he endured almost unimaginable suffering. Early in his career he was a physician and neurologist and studied under two of the greatest minds of his time, Freud and Adler. While in the camps he used this experience as a way to field-test and validate his emerging theory of meaning. This extreme example of field research confirmed his theory that people with a clear sense of purpose and meaning through serving others were able to overcome the extreme suffering of the camps and retain their humanity and dignity (Frankl 1985).

Paul Fleischman, in his chapter on calling in *The Healing Spirit*, describes the inner life struggle that Carl Jung, the founder of analytical psychology, went through in the discovery of his calling to "dedicate himself to the service of psyche" (Fleischman 1994). By 1910, at the age of thirty-five, Jung was a close colleague of Sigmund Freud and already a world-renowned psychiatrist. But after several years of growing tension, Jung broke with Freud. In doing so he lost a beloved and awesome mentor and a close friend. Later in life he described his reaction to this event as intense, volcanic, idiosyncratic, and monumentally creative, and as leading to years of eerie self-absorption. During this period he was driven to new depths of self-knowledge, a new sense of isolation, autonomy, originality, and uniqueness. Ultimately his spiritual journey through the figures, fantasies, and characteristics of his dreams, visions, and unconscious led to his groundbreaking work on psychological archetypes and the collective unconscious.

When he looked backed upon it all and considered what happened to him during this period, he recognized that a message had come to him with overwhelming force. He experienced the "dark night of the soul" and ceased to belong to himself alone. From then on his life belonged to what he termed "the generality" in service to others through his beloved profession of psychiatry. He described this as hitting upon a stream of lava, and the heat of its fires reshaped his life. In this Jung saw a transformed self, from a successful and eminent professional and appointed heir to Freud, to a "called personality." He was no longer a scientist choosing a topic but instead felt himself chosen (Fleischman 1994).

Jung's work on himself and his patients convinced him that life has a purpose beyond material goals—one based in spiritual well-being. He believed the process of discovering one's calling has two stages. There is first an inner voice, a call to vocation that has the power of a law or God. This is followed by a free choice to obey the call. He believed that through calling one discovers and fulfills one's deep innate potential, much as the acorn contains the potential to become the oak or the caterpillar to become the butterfly. Based on his study of both Eastern and Western religions, Jung perceived that this journey of transformation through calling is at the mystical heart of all religions. He thought the spiritual experience of discovering one's calling and, therefore, one's purpose, that which gives life meaning, is essential to our well-being. It is a journey to meet the self and at the same time to meet the Divine.

August (Auggie) Turak provides another example, through his award-winning essay *Brother John,* of finding purpose and meaning in the simplest of circumstances. In the essay, based on a true story, the author describes an event during a contemplative retreat at a Trappist monastery that turns both magical and terrible when a simple monk, Brother John, offers to share an umbrella on a cold and rainy Christmas Eve. This simple act of loving-kindness proves almost more than Turak can bear and becomes the catalyst for a gut-wrenching reevaluation of his life's purpose and meaning ("The Power of Purpose Awards" n.d.).

He recounts going to eight services during the various monastic hours of Christmas Eve. Then after midnight mass there was a gathering in the refectory for the monks and visitors to break the long periods of silence and have some cookies, cakes, and cider while visiting with each other. Turak tells of being so tired after the day of working and services that he was about to fall asleep on his feet, so he decided to head for his cell several hundred yards away. He said,

> Halfway to the refectory door I heard the resurgent rain banging on the roof reminding me that I had forgotten to bring an umbrella. Opening the door I was cursing and resigning myself to a miserable hike and a wet monastic guest habit for morning services, when something startled me and left me squinting into the night. As my eyes adjusted, I made out a dim figure standing under an umbrella. . . . It was Brother John in a thin monastic habit, his slouched sixty-year-old body ignoring the cold.
>
> "Brother John, what are you doing?"
>
> "I'm here to walk the people who forgot their umbrellas back to their rooms," he replied softly.

They walked through the rain to his room and then as he said good night he noticed Brother John, with his flashlight, making his way back to the refectory to fetch the next pilgrim who had forgotten his umbrella. Turak recounts being disturbed by the spirit of this man who represented everything he longed to be but feared to be because he felt he could not be so gracious and hospitable without feeling deprived or resentful. But Brother John was also terrible because he was a living, breathing witness to Turak's own inadequacies. He had only to picture Brother John under his umbrella to feel as if "life is not worth living the way I live it." He was terrified that if he ever did decide to follow the example of Brother John, he would either fail completely or at best be faced with a life of unremitting effort without Brother John's obvious compensations. His greatest fear was that he would dedicate his life to others, to self-transcendence, without ever finding that inner spark of eternity that so obviously made Brother John's life the easiest and most natural life he had ever known.

Turak concludes in the end that it is fear that holds us back, and we avoid this fear through rationalization. We are afraid that if we ever did commit to emulating the Brother Johns of the world we would merely end up pulled apart between the poles of how we are living and how we ought to live, being unable to look away. We are afraid that if we ever did venture out we would find ourselves with the worst of both worlds. On one hand, we would learn too much about life to return to our comfortable illusions; on the other, we would learn too much about ourselves to hope for success.

It is through calling that one finds this miraculous transformation and the source of one's commitment to an authentically purposeful life that provides meaning and turns work into an effortless privilege. Ultimately, we must take a chance on faith, give in, make the commitment, and be willing to pay the price. We must commit to facing doubts, limitations, and self-contradictions head on while fighting distraction, futility, rationalization, and fatigue at every step. It may be hard to imagine how standing outside in the rain for others can be magically transformed from drudgery to a calling—an effortless privilege. However, according to Turak, to experience and reap this magic of transformation we must put aside doubts and act decisively.

Meaning and Purpose at Work

People are increasingly thinking about the words *meaning* and *purpose* as they apply to the workplace. Craig Neal, founder of the Heartland Institute—an organization that fosters social and spiritual transformation—believes that people want to find purpose in their lives at work because what we do all day makes a difference to ourselves, our communities, and our world. And when this call is answered, the undoable gets done and the impossible is possible ("Welcome to Heartland" n.d.).

One does not have to work to find life meaningful. However, many people spend most of their waking hours at work or in work-related activities. The search for calling in organizations has become especially relevant with the advent of the 24/7, global, Internet age. Today many people never really are away from their work and they want a sense of purpose rather than a sort of spiritual dying Monday through Friday.

As work becomes the centerpiece of life, individuals wrap the meaning of their life into the workplace. Therefore, if one's job hampers the achievement of their full potential, it becomes difficult for them to have a sense of purpose. Then work can be a source of frustration, boredom, and feelings of meaninglessness. In a recent survey, one in four workers indicated their job plays a vital part in defining who they are, while an equivalent number of managing directors believe they derive more meaning from work than from their home life.

Victor Frankl, in *The Doctor and the Soul*, explains that people can find meaning and purpose through work that allows them to use their creativity and unique abilities for the benefit of others; to both give to the world and learn from it. He found that people who report their lives are meaningful experience fulfillment and significance. Subsequent research has confirmed that meaning in life helps people make sense of senseless events and irrational behavior. It also positively influences psychological well-being and work wellness. By contrast, a lack of meaning has been shown to lead to psychopathologies such as anxiety, uncontrollable stress, burnout, suicidal thoughts, neuroticism, alcoholism, and substance abuse. Researchers have found that individuals who experience work as their calling are able to pursue work as an opportunity to enhance their sense of purpose, meaning, and wholeness in connection with others (Frankl 1986).

Pursuing a calling is much more than the choice of an occupation to satisfy economic needs for security, or of a particular profession that confers occupational status. Indeed, a calling can be found in any line of work, from neurosurgeon to sanitation worker, or in the simple act of walking someone to their cabin who has forgotten their umbrella. Through calling, work is integrated and organized into one's sense of self and the role one is destined to play in the fulfillment of a radiant world order.

Membership—Finding Community, Connection, and Belonging

Through calling, a person finds their role in life. Through membership this role is actualized through a social network and located in place and time. Membership is the universal need we all have to move beyond the isolation of one's individuality and have a sense of belonging. It manifests the desire to be understood and appreciated and to identify with others and to be identified by them. The role of interpersonal connection in pursuit of "the good life" cannot be understated.

More than two decades of research has provided evidence that developing good-quality relationships with others is central to optimal living. Healthy interpersonal and social functioning correlates with positive human health and psychological and spiritual well-being, whereas disconnection leads to despair and despondency. A sense of community plays a crucial role in increasing resilience, happiness, and well-being. Membership also provides the context for our communications in terms of whom we talk to and the language we use; to a great extent, it even determines what thoughts we think. In this sense our physical and psychological lives are ecological in that our values, thoughts, possessions, health, and even the food we eat and the air we breathe are interconnected lattices of webs reaching from person to person. As we weave these webs we define the reality of our lived-in universe. These realities are not spun alone. They overlap in multilayered depths in the sea of the intersecting human worlds of work, family, and community.

A sense of membership is primarily a result of giving and receiving altruistic love. As a component of spiritual well-being it is more than the act of joining a social organization or compliant attendance at a social function. Membership enables compassionate identification with others in community and fellowship that heals, or helps to heal, isolated individuals to whom it is extended. It becomes the source of personal ethics and leads to codes of conduct based on the universality of pain and suffering. The need for membership becomes central to those who, like Gandhi, sought the divine in every man. It eventually expands beyond humanity toward a sense of membership in the community of all living things.

Membership as a Place in History

Membership, therefore, is not abstract; it is the concrete, actual touch of other people and their ordering into time and history. There is no better example of this than Victor Frankl, who could not have found his calling to develop and practice logotherapy (meaning theory) without also experiencing a deep sense of membership. Readers of Frankl's classic *Man's Search for Meaning: Experiences in the Concentration Camp* will remember Otto as the fellow prisoner to whom he recited his final testament before being sent to a "rest camp" for the sick prisoners of Auschwitz.

"No one knew whether this was a ruse to obtain the last bit of work for the sick . . . or whether it would go to the gas ovens or to a genuine rest camp," Frankl wrote. The chief doctor offered that evening to take his name from the list. "I told him this was not my way; that I had learned to let fate take its course." Returning to the hut, he said, "I found a good friend waiting for me."

> Tears came to his eyes and I tried to comfort him. Then there was something else to do—make my will. "Listen, Otto, if I don't get back home to my wife, and if you should see her again, tell her that I talked of her daily, hourly. You remember. Secondly, I have loved her more than anyone. Thirdly, the short time I have been married to her outweighs everything, even all we have been through here." . . .
>
> What did happen? Otto, where are you now? Are you alive? What has happened to you since our last hour together?
>
> "Ah, yes, Otto," Frankl recalled in an interview commemorating his ninetieth birthday in 1995. "No, I heard nothing. One must assume he did not make it out." (Frank 1985)

As with Frankl, we do not choose the place and era of our birth. We live subject to the tidal wave of history. Whom and what we weave out of and into our lives are the result of both choice and fate. These interactions are not some self-selected, treasured feelings and daydreams; they essentially comprise our soul, as described in Chapter 3—the locus of ourselves, the place where we experience ourselves, the locus in reality where we experience the self. Its rhythm limits, guides, and channels what we may be.

Vicktor Frankl, as a holocaust survivor, could convey through his stories the way the world is subjective, local, and idiosyncratic. Yet his calling and ultimately the meaning and purpose of his life was deeply imbedded and determined through his membership in the holocaust community and the historical context from which it emerged.

Stories and myths from the world's spiritual and religious traditions place the individual in meaningful relationship within their current community as well as with those who created and sustained it over time. Inspired events in these traditions are the unforgettable lightning bolts that separate and organize time into history and provide continuity for community and membership. For Jews, it includes eating unleavened bread during the flight from Egypt. For Christians, the crucifixion of Jesus. For Muslims, the turning point when the angel Gabriel gave Mohammed the order to replace the old laws of the Bible with their final version, the Koran. For Buddhists, the distance in years from the time of the great Buddha. For Hindus, time and history in a recurring cycle of vast, infinite repetition and duration. For Mormons, the moment when the angel Moroni appeared to Joseph Smith and told him about the golden plates on which the Book of Mormon were inscribed.

Stories have also been dramatically harnessed by Alcoholics Anonymous (AA), in which a readily available and endlessly reconfirming sense of membership, coupled with its Twelve Step program, has been a key to the successful treatment of alcoholism in millions of cases. For AA, it was the pivotal day when Bill Wilson found Dr. Bob and they realized that only through a spiritual program practiced in fellowship could they and others recover from a hopeless state of mind and body. AA provides almost continuous social support in the form of daily meetings and the use of sponsors that together function like parents and family. It also provides a spiritual rationale to turn this social support into a form of membership. The principles of AA concerning finding a higher power, cleaning house, and helping others are found in their "Big Book." They read in part, "We made a decision to turn our will and our life over to God as we understand Him . . . made a list of all persons we had harmed and became willing to make amends to them all. . . . We try to carry this message to other alcoholics and practice these principles in all our affairs" (Alcoholics Anonymous 2003).

In each tradition, these and subsequent events give the future a focus, pointed toward days of judgment, spiritual awakenings, second comings, and Armageddon. They also punctuate time through holiday rituals and seasonal rhythms.

Destructive Membership

The need for membership can also deteriorate into a destructive force of paranoid in-groups. James Jones's Jonestown was one such group where the boundaries between membership and outsiders were rigid and absolute. The same could be said for Nazi Germany and Stalin's communist Russia. This "us or them" attitude toward outsiders demands an increase in inner-group cohesion. However, the sacrifice of autonomy and thoughtfulness to which the individual submits when he becomes part of the divinely sanctioned in-group is compensated for by the sense of membership that accompanies the envisioned immortality and the conquest of personal death and of human history that the communal herd incites. Religions can share some destructive aspects with other human groups and can exhibit destructive forces all their own. Witness the ongoing struggle in the Middle East that began with the Great Crusades more than a thousand years ago. Intertwined with these destructive forces are soothing, divisive sentiments: that one group has a special dispensation, that everyone else is outside the inner sanctum; unfortunately, hostility with a suggestion of violence is the expected outcome.

Thus membership can function to divide humankind into socially incestuous, exclusive group hatred or it can develop into a loving, pan-human embrace that reaches out to all other forms of life. A key element of the spiritual journey is to see ourselves in the heart of all beings, and to see all beings in our heart. All religious and spiritual traditions proclaim that it is God's will that man exploit nature for his proper ends but that all things in God's universe must be respected and loved. Saint Francis attempted to depose man from his monarchy over creation and set up a democracy of all God's creatures. In a similar vein, both Buddhism and

Hinduism stress the ancient view of Ahimsa or nonharmfulness to all; we are all part of Nature and, since Nature is divine, we are in Nature and Nature is in us. The challenge is to use the hunger for membership to grow outward, beyond embattled, self-justifying, paranoid, warring, incestuous, suicidal, murderous violence into identification with a larger group of interdependent stakeholders to embrace all living things that sustain us and our planet.

Membership at Work

Work provides an opportunity for employees to gain a sense of belonging to a larger, caring community. In membership one feels engaged in the body of the productive human community and has a sense of continuity. It can help people feel they are important, that they have value, and that they belong. Many of the spiritual needs met in earlier days by religious affiliation, extended families, and village communities are currently being met in the workplace. At its heart, membership connects us at work so that we experience deep communion with others as part of something larger than ourselves. An excellent example is Southwest Airlines, where the organizational culture includes a strong sense that employees are part of a big family. Employees take care of each other as well as customers, and employee families are also part of the extended Southwest Airlines family.

Membership at work requires an organizational culture based on the values of altruistic love so there is sense of mutual caring, support, and being connected to each other as part of a larger community based on mutual acceptance and trust. Through membership, employees feel a deep connection with their leaders and fellow workers. Social connections also enable shared change and organizational learning. Appropriate training, job enrichment, and policies of empowerment increase workforce competence and employees' ability to both achieve and participate as contributing members of the organizational community.

Creating, nurturing, and sustaining a sense of membership is also a key group-maintenance function. The maintenance process focuses on getting the group's psychosocial needs met as well as satisfying personal relationships. People want to be with good people who share similar values in an environment where these values are co-created. They need frequent interactions or personal contacts with others and need to perceive that there are relationships or interpersonal bonds marked by stability, care, and concern that will continue into the foreseeable future. Membership, as part of the maintenance process, includes issues of inclusion and participation, levels of influence, dealing with problem members, dysfunctional behavior, and dominance and risk-taking norms. Membership at work and the part we play in it helps us feel important, helps us feel we have value and belong. It builds a sense of trust in exploring and accessing synergistic possibilities with co-workers and creates a safe environment in which risk-taking and creativity can be exercised.

SPIRITUAL WELL-BEING: MAXWELL, LOCKE, AND RITTER

As discussed in the previous chapter, Maxwell, Locke and Ritter LLP (MLR) is a highly profitable company that has embraced a vision of service to their clients, their employees, and the greater Austin community based on the values of altruistic love. When wellness teams were implemented at MLR in early 2007, they further demonstrated the company's commitment to employee spiritual well-being; they showed that the firm was also going to provide support through its actions as a way for employees and the firm to grow and develop spiritually.

Coupling a wellness program with profit sharing and open-book management opened up a whole new avenue for ideas and solutions to reinforce MLR's vision and values while fostering spiritual well-being. Profit sharing coupled with open-book transparency enables employees to openly scrutinize spending decisions. Discussing both failures and successes facilitates interaction within and across teams on key issues. Teams begin to function as "think tanks" for innovative and creative solutions and strategies, which enables MLR to live its core values and treat everyone with honesty, dignity, and respect. Ultimately, this openness leads MLR's people to do unto others as they would have others do unto them.

Most important, profit sharing coupled with open-book transparency instills trust within the organization and supports the teamwork that has led MLR to become the world-class organization it is today.

This transparency also cultivates membership, community, and compassion. Earl Maxwell's definition of community is "a place where three or more people periodically gather who share common values." MLR believes businesses should assume more responsibility for supporting their personnel and those who surround them, as many people have no significant support systems. MLR's personnel help each other through many life challenges. They babysit for each other's children, help each other move furniture, lend money and vehicles to one another, sell cars and homes to one another, etc.

Building community or membership in organizational spiritual leadership also requires a family-friendly workplace that supports flexible work schedules. MLR firmly subscribes to the belief that "no success at work is worth failure at home" (Gorman, 2007). An Employers Support Parenting "ESP" brag bulletin board, located in a common area, functions like a home refrigerator where children's school accomplishments are prominently displayed. In addition to allowing parents to bring their children to work on days when there are childcare issues, MLR has implemented a policy that allows employees to participate in the education of their children by providing paid time off to attend school events as well as time to deal with issues surrounding aging parents, grandparents, and/or grandchildren. And four career tracks, with varying levels of commitment, including part-time, are available for workers who have heavy family obligations. MLR is also using technology to allow employees to work from home more and not have to be at the office at nights and on weekends. The result has been lower absenteeism, higher morale, and greater productivity. Annual turnover has averaged less than 10 percent, considerably less than the industry average.

In fall 2005 and fall 2007, Maxwell, MLR's managing partner, decided to administer IISL's Organizational Spiritual Leadership survey to measure the level of spiritual well-being within the organization (more about this measure in Chapter 7, "Implementing Organizational Spiritual

Leadership"). As expected, results from both surveys revealed high levels of spiritual leadership (vision, hope/faith, and altruistic love), inner life, spiritual well-being (calling and membership), organizational commitment, and productivity. The major comments/concerns were related to how to maintain MLR's vision and values in the face of explosive company growth.

In late 2007 Maxwell left MLR to lead Austin's St. David's Community Health Foundation as CEO. The foundation invests more than $60 million each year in care for the underserved and uninsured through hospital care in six St. David's hospitals and primary care in local safety-net clinics. The Foundation serves more than 25,000 area schoolchildren with mobile dental clinics, and collaborates with other central Texas agencies through grants, programs, and sponsorships to serve children, the elderly, the ill, and the homeless.

Steve Knebel, one of the first hires at MLR in the early 1990s, took over the reins as leading partner when Maxwell left. As one of the pioneers who has been on the MLR spiritual journey from the beginning, Knebel has maintained MLR's commitment to organizational spiritual leadership. MLR again administered the organizational spiritual leadership survey in the fall of 2009 and 2011. Results from this survey mirrored those from 2005 and 2007 and provided evidence that MLR exemplifies an organization that emphasizes spiritual leadership and spiritual well-being to maximize the Triple Bottom Line.

CONCLUSION

Spiritual well-being flows from spiritual leadership and is a result of satisfying the universal human needs for calling and membership. Calling is a sense that one's life has meaning, purpose, and makes a difference. Membership is a sense of belonging and community and that one feels understood and appreciated. The quest for spiritual well-being through meaning and membership is universal within the human condition and a basic human drive independent of specific demographics such as sex, age, and educational level. It may change its appearance through one's life, but it never disappears.

Spiritual well-being is not obtained by striving for it directly. Spiritual well-being cannot be engineered or manufactured. It is not produced when a company focuses on its monetary goals, but instead occurs through spiritual leadership that first establishes a healthy workplace culture grounded in altruistic values and hope/faith in a vision of service to key stakeholders. When members of an organization have a sense of belonging and a commitment to a common purpose, the organization is more successful in meeting or exceeding key stakeholder expectations and achieving sustainable financial performance—the Triple Bottom Line.

Maxwell, Locke, and Ritter LLP has a culture of excellence that encourages people to hit performance numbers that are very black and white, in a workplace where people celebrate, have fun, and relax to a much greater extent than is the industry norm. It also has a culture based in compassion, forgiveness, and acceptance that not only produces high levels of employee spiritual well-being; it also gives people permission to leave and offers them blessings and assistance in finding a better place to prosper.

Practical Tools

For those interested in maximizing the Triple Bottom Line, the major tools introduced in this chapter include the following:

Spiritual Well-Being provides a focus for satisfying employees' fundamental needs for calling and membership, which are essential for maximizing the Triple Bottom Line.

Calling provides workers with a sense of meaning and purpose: that they make a difference in the lives of others.

Membership provides workers with a sense of community and belonging: that they are understood and appreciated.

Chapter Six

Developing the Qualities of
Personal Spiritual Leadership

As we discussed in Chapter 3, having a conversion experience and becoming open to change are only the first steps in a lifelong process that is the spiritual journey. On our own, it is not easy to learn to rest in meditation, become mindfully aware, allow our dark side to come to full consciousness and let it go, give ourselves to a higher power for resolution, and figure out how we can love and serve others. However, the world's religious and spiritual traditions all work to provide a process or program for helping us along our spiritual journey. Many of these programs are through a fellowship or community that includes individuals who serve as sponsors or spiritual guides.

Self-help programs can guide us in finding out about our temperament, personality type, or conflict style. However, as the journey of the Fool taught us, the main thing we need to know about ourselves is that we are unable to do any spiritual work by muscling through life. By developing mindfulness through an inner-life practice, we start to develop and live the qualities of hope/faith, vision, and altruistic love of personal spiritual leadership. As we continue the spiritual journey we gain an increasing recognition of our weaknesses and the need to rely on some higher power. The more we realize that "our lives are unmanageable"—usually as a result of hitting bottom or having a conversion experience—the more the spiritual journey becomes an adventure in allowing a force beyond ourselves to move and accompany us in daily life.

Personal leadership is necessary, but not sufficient, for personal spiritual leadership. Personal leadership is the self-confident ability to crystallize your thinking and establish an exact direction for your life. It requires committing yourself to moving in that direction and then to take determined action to acquire, accomplish, or become whatever you identify as the ultimate goal for your life. To exercise strong personal leadership, you must:

- Recognize and believe in your untapped potential.
- Develop a strong self-image.
- Be self-motivated through a personal vision, fueled by both the desire and the belief that it will be realized.
- Define success in terms of the progressive realization of worthwhile, predetermined personal goals.

Exercising personal leadership also demands conscious assumption of control over your own destiny through the establishment of a personal mission based on goals that give depth and meaning to every action. Doing what you know is right and productive for you, regardless of obstacles or the opinions of others, is the essence of personal leadership.

However, personal leadership as a process is soulless. It comes alive and manifests only through a vision and a set of personal values. Therefore, both Joseph Stalin (who was responsible for the murder of 20 million of his countrymen in Russia) and Mahatma Gandhi (who was responsible for bringing political freedom to millions in India) had strong and effective personal leadership. However, Stalin's personal leadership was based on satisfying his own selfish needs; Gandhi's was based on love and service to his people, regardless of the sacrifices he might have to make, including his own death.

Most leaders recognize that there is a spiritual element to life. Personal spiritual leadership recognizes and incorporates the spiritual element into personal leadership. Personal spiritual leadership requires not only the exercise of strong personal leadership but also an inner-life practice that is the source of hope/faith in a transcendent vision and personal values based on altruistic love. By committing to a vision of service to our key stakeholders, we discover a calling to make a difference in other peoples' lives, and therefore life has meaning and purpose. In living the values of altruistic love through care and concern for and the appreciation of both oneself and others, we experience membership and the sense of being understood and appreciated. The combined experiences of calling and membership are the essence of spiritual well-being, which is the source of the individual outcomes of personal spiritual leadership—personal commitment and productivity, positive human health, psychological well-being, and life satisfaction.

As we discussed in Chapters 2 and 4, the Spiritual Leadership Model can be applied to both personal spiritual leadership and organizational spiritual leadership. Personal spiritual leadership is about leading and leader development of individual-based knowledge, skills and abilities associated with a formal leadership role, with an emphasis on the influence leaders have on their followers. Personal spiritual leadership then provides the foundation for organizational spiritual leadership. The primary emphasis of organizational spiritual leadership is on creating the context for employee inner-life development and workplace spirituality to foster hope/faith in a vision of service to key stakeholders through an organizational culture based on the values of altruistic love. Organizational spiritual leadership then positively impacts both leader and follower, spiritual well-being through calling and membership and, ultimately, employee well-being, sustainability, and financial performance—the Triple Bottom Line.

How do we develop and maintain the qualities of personal spiritual leadership necessary for organizational leadership and, ultimately, the Triple Bottom Line? To answer this question we will draw on the story of Patrick M. and how he used a Twelve-Step spiritual program of action coupled with a personal mission statement to develop and reinforce his inner life and the qualities of personal spiritual leadership, and to increase his spiritual well-being through calling and membership. In doing so he not only revitalized his personal life but also provided the necessary foundation for effective organizational spiritual leadership.

PATRICK M.'S TWELVE-STEPS TO PERSONAL SPIRITUAL LEADERSHIP

Patrick M. is a forty-two-year-old computer engineer living in Texas. He has been divorced for four years and is the father of a nine-year-old boy and a fourteen-year-old girl. Patrick grew up in a dysfunctional family, receives counseling from a licensed psychologist, and has been a member of Co-Dependents Anonymous (CoDA) for two years. He regularly attends CoDA meetings, reads its literature on a daily basis, has a sponsor who is helping him through the Twelve-Step CoDA program of recovery, and is active in service work in his home group.

Patrick's "birthing" into codependence began early in life. His father was a dedicated businessman who worked twelve to eighteen hours a day. Patrick felt pride in his father but had to work hard to receive attention from him. Since the behavior of his siblings was much more demanding and lively then his, the best way to get his mother's approval was by being quiet and invisible. The denial patterns in his family were so strong that nothing was ever acknowledged as a crisis or a difficulty. Anything that was painful or didn't fit the acceptable family image was ignored, discounted, or rationalized away. There was no process for dealing with conflict or grieving, just a great deal of energy and attention given to outward appearances and observances, all conveyed with the utmost of "southern" charm and graciousness. Thus there was an abundance of activity and physical presence, but little inner emotional substance available to him.

After college graduation Patrick thought he had it all; newly married, he was starting a career, had bought a new home, and in many ways, had acquired a new identity. Looking back he realized that he desperately wanted to be happy and believed that wanting it would make it so. As the years passed he focused more and more on his work and found himself becoming more and more like his father. He changed careers a couple of times, worked long hours, and spent less and less time at home. Five years ago, Patrick's wife left, informing him that she wanted a divorce because she was in love with another man. It was then that he realized that his workaholic and enabling behavior had destroyed his marriage.

As a result of his divorce and work-related difficulties Patrick hit bottom. To protect himself he became a people pleaser, even though he lost much of his own identity in the process. Often he would mistake any personal criticism as a threat. He realized he was unable to set strong boundaries in his relationships at work, with women, or with his children, who were beginning to show signs of dysfunctional behavior. These experiences and symptoms of codependence established him as a "co-victim," and recognizing this led him first to therapy and then to CoDA. There he found that he had several characteristics in common with other people who had been brought up in dysfunctional households. He also realized that, unless he made some life changes, he would continue to experience problems based on his own emotional programs of happiness and cultural conditioning.

THE TWELVE-STEPS RECOVERY PROCESS

More than seventy years ago, the Twelve-Step recovery process was pioneered by Bill Wilson and Dr. Bob Smith, who founded Alcoholics Anonymous (AA)(Alcoholics Anonymous 2003). Today there are more than 200 Twelve-Step recovery types of organizations (focusing on alcohol, drugs, relationships, work, gambling, shopping, food, etc.) with worldwide memberships numbering in the millions. The Twelve-Step process is a spiritual program that offers one way to surface and deal with the debris from the unconscious, become mindful, and enter the Level III Way of Knowing and Being. The twelve steps also provide a springboard for experiencing the ways of knowing and being in Levels II and I and the Three-Fold Path of Spiritual Transformation (all are discussed in detail in Chapter 3).

Twelve-Step programs assume a three-dimensional view of human existence: physical, mental (which includes the emotional), and spiritual. The physical dimension is manifested through obsessive-compulsive behavior and the inability to stop the behavior even after suffering extreme negative personal consequences. The mental dimension is often rooted in an obsession with altering the state of consciousness to escape unwanted thoughts or emotions. The spiritual dimension focuses on self-centeredness or selfishness, often manifested through excessive pride and an inflated self-concept. Conversely it can be demonstrated through self-negation, experienced as a sense of self that is dependent on external stimuli (for example, an addictive substance or the attention of significant others). As part of this spiritual dimension, all Twelve-Step programs have underlying spiritual principles or values that act as cornerstones to the steps.

Thomas Keating in, *The Human Condition,* argues that everyone is called to recover from something, even if it's only childhood. Unless we embark upon the spiritual journey, we are practically helpless to do much about escaping from our emotional programs for happiness and from our cultural conditioning, which leads to frequent, if not habitual, frustration (Keating 1999). As the pain of this frustration increases, the psyche then represses these traumatic experiences into the unconscious, which warehouses the negative energy in the body. This is why the religious and spiritual traditions suggest disciplines or programs to reduce the amount of energy we put into these emotional and cultural programs that seek external rewards and approval, often at the price of our own morals and integrity. Twelve-Step programs refer to this as emotional sobriety, which goes beyond the source of the addiction to address the deep emotional problems that are the source of addiction in the first place.

Modification of the Twelve Steps can guide us in developing personal spiritual leadership. At the heart of each step is a spiritual value that is a component or quality necessary for personal spiritual leadership. Please note that, although the term *God* is used in the steps, it does not necessarily refer to a supreme being or deity but instead is used to represent any higher power of your choice as you understand that higher power.

Step 1: We admitted that we were powerless over our self-centeredness, emotional programs for happiness, and cultural conditioning—that our lives had become unmanageable.

While Twelve-Step programs have evolved and become more inclusive in their scope, all focus on the spiritual domain with the aim of helping people overcome the spiritual root of their disorders. Here we offer a modification of AA's Step 1, which states "we admitted we were powerlessness over alcohol," to "We admitted that we were powerless over our self-centeredness, emotional programs for happiness, and cultural conditioning—that our lives had become unmanageable" for use in developing our personal spiritual leadership. But in this admission, who says our life is unmanageable? The answer is that it is something deep within us based on our personal experience of disarray through our relationships, business, or family. This first step emphasizes the fact that all human beings are subject to the universal human condition.

Spiritual Value: Honesty

To work Step 1, we must honestly accept the fact that we are powerless to control people, places, and things through acts of self-will. This admission provides an opening to the purgative way on the Three-fold Path of Spiritual Transformation and the Level III Way of Knowing and Being. This opening leads to what Ernest Kurtz and Katherine Ketcham, in *The Spirituality of Imperfection*, call the paradox of surrender, in which we are able to experience release or freedom only by letting go of what we are trying to control (Kurtz and Ketcham 1992). Surrender begins with accepting that we are not in control of the matter at hand (for example, children, spouse, job, illness). In fact, we are really not in absolute control of much of anything other than our attitudes and how we respond to our circumstances.

To be powerless means that you are helpless and can't change or fix something through your own willpower. Powerlessness is the result of frequent defeat; it can lead to despair, and that prompts people to avoid or numb the pain when it becomes too much to bear. As we continue the desperate attempt to find happiness through our emotional programs, a vicious addictive cycle begins that affects our whole life. The repressed negative energies and the resultant pain call for some kind of relief. We then resort to the past attitudes and behaviors that brought temporary relief or forgetfulness from the pain.

The vast majority of people who are not involved in an obvious addiction have no idea that much of their behavior is compulsive because they can usually fulfill the basic obligations of life. But some people, because of their emotional background, are always aggressive, withdraw, or tend to be angry and hostile. They don't realize that much of their behavior and ways of relating are unconscious, compulsive, the result of over-identification with cultural norms or a response to the instinctual needs that drive their emotional programs for happiness. Many never understand that the idea that their basic motivations and moral intentions are self-centered and selfish.

Patrick M.'s conversion experience came through his divorce, subsequent failed relationships, an inability to control his children, and his perceived injustices at work. His pain and frustration based on his inability to deal with these difficult problems on his own became so great that he sought the help of a psychologist who, after hearing his story and learning about his childhood experiences, recommended the CoDA recovery program. Patrick began attending CoDA meetings and started reading their literature, including the Twelve-Steps and related traditions and concepts. In doing so, he recognized his powerlessness and the unmanageability of his life and decided to get a sponsor to be his spiritual guide through the Twelve-Steps.

Patrick began to be honest with himself about living a life that was powerless and unmanageable. His sponsor had worked the steps and could show his compassion as well as the wisdom that came from dealing with similar circumstances. In addition, he kept reminding Patrick to face the truth of his feelings without identifying with them, acting them out, or blaming them on other people. He told him that if he attended meetings and worked at his program with the same energy for growth and health he formerly put into security issues, social approval, and controlling people, places, and things, he would begin to experience the fruits of the program—joy, peace, and serenity independent of his circumstances. He had taken the first step on the spiritual journey, with its beginnings in the purgative way, which begins when people who are living in Levels V and IV awaken to an awareness of a spiritual reality and seek the way of knowing and being in Level III.

Step 2: We came to believe that a Power greater than ourselves could restore us to sanity.

Spiritual Value: Hope

Hope gives us the ability to look beyond the circumstances of the present day. Through hope individuals can feel secure that change is possible. The second step is necessary to achieve ongoing recovery from the human condition because the first step has left a vacuum in our life. Our old programs for happiness are no longer working, and there is a need to believe in something that can help us overcome this sense of powerlessness, uselessness, and helplessness. The purpose of the second step is to find a power greater than ourselves that will fill this vacuum. This step releases us from the insanity of continuing the same failed behaviors and responses and expecting different results.

Recovery programs emphasize that embarking on the spiritual journey and seeking a higher power relieve us of being the center of the universe and allow us to transfer our problems to a power outside of and greater than ourselves. As we discussed in Chapter 3 as we explored Horton's continuum of God as a higher power, this higher power can take many forms, including some aspect of nature, a theistic God, or a group or humanistic social system. The only suggestion is that our higher power be loving, caring, and greater than ourselves.

Patrick initially used his CoDA group as a higher power and source of strength, especially after he discovered that he was not "terminally unique." His sponsor suggested that he also adopt a simple breathing meditative practice to help put "space between his thoughts" and quiet the incessant chatter that kept him ruminating about the past and worried and fearful about the future. It would also serve to give him the sense that a higher power transcends anything he can think about from the limited perspectives he has experienced so far in life. Patrick developed a ten-minute daily meditative practice to help him be present from moment to moment, to develop mindful awareness, and to move beyond his thoughts and feelings to become aware of his deeper motivations and to relate to the mystery of the nature of this higher power. He came to believe that CoDA offered hope that a higher power existed that could help him on his spiritual journey. This hope and the beginning of an inner-life practice marked the second step on Patrick's spiritual journey of developing the qualities of personal spiritual leadership.

Step 3: Made a decision to turn our will and our lives over to God *as we understood Him.*

Spiritual Value: Faith

Faith is a firm belief in something hoped for but yet unproved by evidence to be true. True faith in something or someone is demonstrated through action or work. Step 3 replaces the need to find happiness in the external world with faith in a higher power. Through this higher power we let go of ourselves as the center of the universe. Step 3 deepens the commitment to recovery from the human condition and the spiritual journey. We put honesty, open-mindedness, and willingness at the forefront of our lives because others in our spiritual community have said it is necessary and will work. This is an act of faith that opens the door for the rest of the Twelve Steps. At its heart is the belief that, in turning to a higher power for guidance, even if in the beginning it's our support group, whatever happens is the best possible situation for spiritual growth and that our current circumstances are just as they are supposed to be at this present moment, even if it is not what we wanted or expected.

Patrick initially balked at this step. He had been raised with the idea of a punishing God who was mainly interested in commandments with a bunch of do's and don'ts and who was looking for any excuse to plunge him into the depths of hell. The idea that a higher power is a source of happiness that can reduce the grief and constant emotional upheavals of daily life was foreign and strange. Others in his group had similar disbeliefs in the beginning. For them this higher power was not to be found through an institution or a political program. It was a state of consciousness.

Patrick began to have faith that with the help of those in his group and his sponsor, the Twelve-Step recovery process would work for him. He began to feel a sense of new power, peace of mind, and a faith that he could face life successfully. He realized he'd been playing God in trying to run his universe and that it didn't work. He decided that starting now this higher power would be his recovery group. He would have faith that this higher power would provide a path for happiness if he worked his program of spiritual recovery. As he became more accepting of this higher power, he began to lose his fear of today, tomorrow, and the here-after. Patrick's hope had become faith, a key element of personal spiritual leadership.

Step 4: Made a searching and fearless moral inventory of ourselves.

Spiritual Value: Courage

Courage, a central value of altruistic love, is what gives us the ability to confront fear, pain, and uncertainty. It allows us to make bold decisions despite opposition, shame, or discouragement. In undertaking the spiritual journey, we are starting a new way of life in an effort to be rid of the burdens and traps that controlled and prevented our spiritual growth. As part of this journey we must establish a searching and fearless moral inventory; we must sort through the confusion and contradiction our life has brought. In business, if a regular inventory is not taken the business usually goes broke. A major objective of an inventory is to disclose damaged or unsalable goods and to get rid of them promptly and without regret. This is exactly what we do with a moral inventory—we take stock honestly.

To conduct the inventory we sit down with paper and pen and ask our higher power for help in revealing the character defects that are causing us pain and suffering. Then we pray for the courage to be fearless and thorough; we pray that this inventory may help put our lives in order. Regardless of how we structure the inventory, its purpose is to reveal to our-

TABLE 6.1

Checklist of Character Defects and Assets

Character Defect	Opposite Asset	Character Defect	Opposite Asset
aggressive, belligerent	good-natured, gentle	jealous	trusting, generous, admiring
angry	forgiving, calm, generous		
apprehensive, afraid	calm, courageous	lazy, indolent	industrious, conscientious
argumentative, quarrelsome	agreeable	loud	tasteful, quiet
		lustful	healthy sexuality
arrogant, insolent	unassuming, humble	manipulative	candid, honest, noncontrolling
avoidant	faces problems and acts	overly emotional	emotionally stable
blocking	honest, intuitive	perfectionist	realistic goals
boastful	modest, humble	possessive	generous
careless	careful, painstaking, concerned	resentful, bitter, hateful	forgiving
controlling	lets go, esp. of other's lives	rude, discourteous	polite, courteous caring of others
defensive	open to criticism	self-centered	self-fulfilling
depressed, morose	hopeful, optimistic, cheerful	self-destructive, self-defeating	
envying	empathetic, generous, admiring	shy	outgoing
		slothful (lazy)	industrious, taking action
exaggerating	honest, realistic		
gluttonous, excessive	moderate	spiteful, malicious	forgiving
gossiping	closed-mouthed, kind, praising	stubborn	open-minded, willing
hypersensitive	tolerant, doesn't personalize	suspicious	trusting
		tense	calm, serene
impulsive, reckless	consistent, considered actions	ungrateful	thankful, grateful
		vain	modest, humble
indecisive, timid	firm, decisive	vindictive	forgiving
insecure, anxious	self-confident, secure	withdrawn	outgoing

SOURCE: "Fourth Step Inventory," n.d., http://www.royy.com/step4.pdf (accessed August 30, 2009).

selves as we really are. Table 6.1 gives a summary checklist of character defects, and Table 6.2 is a sample inventory worksheet for resentments that Patrick used.

Inventory Worksheet

The first step on the inventory worksheet is to identify all the resentments that are "renting space in our head" and causing us anguish and misery. We detail the cause of these resentments in Column 2. In Column 3 we

TABLE 6.2

Inventory Worksheet

Instructions for Completion

Complete each column top to bottom before proceeding to the next column. For example, list all names first, all causes second, etc. List real resentments, not imaginary or theoretical resentment. Is the resentment a problem for you? Does it cause you pain?

Column 1   *In dealing with resentments, we set them on paper. We listed people, institutions, or principles with whom we were angry.*

Column 2   *We asked ourselves why we were angry.*

Column 3   *On our grudge list, we set opposite each name our injuries. Was it our self-esteem, our security, our ambitions, our personal, or sex relations that had been interfered with?*

Column 4   *Referring to our list again: Putting out of our minds the wrongs others had done, we resolutely looked for our own mistakes. Where had we been selfish, dishonest, self-seeking, and frightened?*

Column 5   *This column is optional. List specific other defects to show your participation in the resentments.*

Reading from left to right, we now see the resentment (column 1), the cause (column 2), the part of self that had been affected (column 3), and the exact nature of the defect within us that allowed the resentment to surface and block us off from God's will (columns 4 and 5).

Tip: try and list resentments in groups—for example, family, school, relationships, work, etc.

REVIEW OF RESENTMENTS "SELF"

#	COLUMN 1 I'm RESENTFUL at:	COLUMN 2 The Cause	COLUMN 3 Affects My					COLUMN 4 My Own Mistakes				COLUMN 5 Specific Defects
			Self-esteem	Security	Ambitions	Personal Relationships	Sex Relations	Selfish	Dishonest	Self-seeking	Frightened	
	My Boss / Supervisor	He didn't give me the promotion I deserve to lead engineer.	X	X	X	X		X		X	X	

SOURCE: "Fourth Step Inventory," n.d., http://www.royy.com/step4.pdf (accessed August 30, 2009).

note whether our self-esteem, security, ambition, personal relationships, and/or sexual relations are affected by the resentment. Finally, we look at our own mistakes or what we did to contribute to each situation that led to the resentment. Usually this will be due to a character defect that is based in selfishness, dishonesty, self-seeking, or fear, although we have the option to list more specific character defects from the list in Table 6.1.

When Patrick worked on his moral inventory, he was resentful and angry at his boss because he had not received a promotion to lead engineer; instead the promotion went to a coworker. This led to sullen behavior on Patrick's part; he experienced a lack of motivation to come to work, which affected his job performance and relationships at work. His suffering caused him to think about quitting; he hoped he could find an enjoyable place to work where his abilities and professionalism would be better appreciated. His resentment stemmed from his bosses' lack of appreciation for the long hours and extra work he put in. Experiencing this resentment affected his self-esteem and sense of job security; it thwarted his ambitions and led to a significant deterioration in his relationship with the promoted coworker.

However, upon reflection he realized that the coworker had much more experience and had developed several new software programs that had led to significant increases in his project's performance. He saw that his resentment stemmed from his act of being prideful and having an overblown sense of his own accomplishments, along with being selfish, envious, sullen, and dishonest with himself about the true reality of the situation.

It took courage for Patrick to look within himself and be honest and truthful. It is important to realize that there is no bad news in our inventory; through a "searching and fearless moral inventory" we see that we are not bad, but human. In developing this type of courage—a central value of altruistic love—we are able to see our responsibility in any situation. This then opens the door to begin loving and serving others through personal spiritual leadership.

Step 5: Admitted to God, to ourselves, and to another human being the exact nature of our wrongs.

Spiritual Value: Integrity

It is through integrity that individuals look for alignment in values, attitudes, and behavior in personal and organizational spiritual leadership.
Integrity is the inner sense of "wholeness"; it requires honesty with ourselves and others in order to promote internal and external consistency
with reality. In recovery programs there is a saying that "you are as sick
as your secrets." The revelation of our faults and the discovery of the inner
motivation behind them is an essential part of the spiritual journey. This
is the power of Step 5; its ability to shatter our secrets. Unless we discuss
our character defects with another person, we will not acquire enough
humility, fearlessness, and honesty for effective personal spiritual leadership. If we expect to live happily in this world, it is essential that we be entirely honest with somebody; this can be a sponsor, spiritual guide, religious
clergy, or a close friend. When we reveal to another person our character
defects and the temptations behind them, we gain insights into their power
over us; it is by externalizing them that we see them.

According to Thomas Keating, in *Divine Therapy and Addiction: Centering Prayer and the Twelve-Steps,* sharing our secrets with a spiritual guide
or sponsor is all that is required to heal many temptations. Hiding a tempta-
tion due to pride, shame, or some other motive only makes it worse. As
soon as we hear ourselves telling the truth we're in a whole new world because, in exposing our temptations to the objective judgment of another
person who loves and cares about us, we can see them for what they are.
Then we can work with our sponsor or spiritual guide to come up with a
plan for how to better deal with the temptations. We begin to experience an
enormous inner freedom in being able to deal with the tempting thoughts
that travel through our heads and realize that it's not the thoughts that are
the problem but what we do with them.

Patrick's sponsor helped him explore his resentment toward his boss
and the character defects behind it. He asked such questions as: Where
do you think your attitude about this situation comes from? What is really behind your response to this situation? Is there a pattern of activity
here based on some frustration of your basic needs for security, power,
or approval and/or your cultural conditioning? Through these questions

Patrick was able to honestly strip away the dishonesty, isolation, fear, grandiosity, and self-will that were the root cause of these character defects.

Even though he was afraid to share his inventory, Patrick became able to trust the process and let go of the outcome. For the first time in a long time he could look the world in the eye as his fears receded. Steps 1 through 5 had been a guide for Patrick through the Purgative Way and an introduction to the way of Knowing and Being in Level III. He had begun his spiritual journey in earnest and laid a solid foundation. He awakened to a spiritual reality and began to discover the source of his addictions and attachments. He realized that following a spiritual path brought an added dimension to life. Most important, he began to experience a higher power that is a source of personal spiritual leadership as well as the priceless gift of peace of mind.

Step 6: Were entirely ready to have God remove all these defects of character.

Spiritual Value: Willingness

When we see and accept how our character defects affect our lives, we can let go of them and get on with a new life. If we want to live happy, joyous, and free, we must develop the state of willingness to let go of the character defects we identified in Step 4 and shared with another person in Step 5. It is through Step 6 that we consent to having our higher power remove these mental roadblocks, which manifest as character defects that are the sources of our suffering.

In working Step 6, Patrick renewed his readiness to wait with confidence and faith, knowing that his higher power was quietly at work in his life. His sponsor told him it was important that he not place unrealistic expectations on himself, since we are all human and wander off course. He tried to help him to be honest and willing to face his faults as they emerged and to listen to the reality that his unconscious was trying to express. He also warned Patrick that he might become doubtful that the higher power would see fit to relieve him of the burden of his most crippling defects.

Even though he might not be entirely ready, he was headed in the right direction.

Step 6 is where many people experience a "first dark night of the soul." Although Step 6 is about willingness, it is hard to have patience after we bring to the surface a character defect that has caused us suffering. It is only human nature that we want this burden relieved immediately. At this point we may feel that our progress toward recovery is stymied and that the abundant gifts we've received from our higher power are beginning to dry up. We're confused and begin to blame ourselves and wonder what am I doing wrong? The tendency here is to redouble our efforts, often only to experience more dryness and frustration. However, this is the inherent nature of the spiritual journey and a necessary step for developing the qualities of personal spiritual leadership.

Step 7: Humbly asked God to remove our shortcomings.

Spiritual Value: Humility

Humility is a result of getting honest with ourselves, which began with Step 1 and is essential for personal spiritual leadership. It is being content to be as poor and weak as we are and accept the truth of our lives, instead of wishing things hadn't happened as they did. This is the heart of true humility—to accept and honestly try to be ourselves. No one is perfectly good or bad. We are all people who are human, who have assets and liabilities. At the heart of humility is an understanding of the truth of who we are, coupled with a sincere desire to become what we can be. Humility is the capacity to accept whatever happens peacefully and then from that place have the clarity to accept the situation as it is or act to do something to improve or correct it. The main objective for the seventh step is to get out of our false self and strive to achieve the will of our higher power, which at its most basic is to love and serve others.

In humility we take satisfaction in the acknowledgment that we are powerless and dependent upon our higher power. We even become grateful for our character defects because we realize that our higher power is using them for our benefit. Without them we would have never been willing to begin and persevere through the spiritual journey. Through humility comes the realization that any suffering we experience is not some curse from a punishing higher power but just simply what happens to us as part of the healing and spiritual transformation process. Any failures we experience create the humiliation necessary for the true humility that is required for us to overcome our character defects. These very failures enable us to grow in humility so we are finally willing to have them removed by our higher power. This means that we still have to deal with the consequences of our actions, but now we know that we have a loving higher power to help us as we confront our character defects on our spiritual journey.

Patrick discovered that sharing with a spiritual guide and others in a spiritual community helps him avoid becoming morbidly serious about himself and his spiritual journey. Accepting the defects of others also helped him to become humble and paved the way for his own defects to be relieved. He found that if the shortcomings were real and he humbly embraced the chance to be rid of them, he would be more likely to experience peace of mind and a sense of well-being.

Like the journey of the fool, the journey through the Twelve-Steps is ongoing. As we use our higher power to chip away at our character defects, we attain balance because the good qualities we possess can at last shine. We work Step 7 because we want to have more to give—to our higher power, to ourselves, to others, and to life, all of which are manifestations of personal spiritual leadership.

Step 8: Made a list of all persons we had harmed and became willing to make amends to them all.

Spiritual Value: Altruistic Love

Step 8 gives us the ability to emphasize all the values of altruistic love that promote a sense of being connected to others in a way that provides feelings of completeness and joy. Moreover, it allows the values of altruistic love to become an integral part of day-to-day living. Altruistic love through care and concern for both ourselves and others is the first test of our newfound humility in that we are finally ready to mend damaged relationships.

The act of making a list of people we have harmed and then being willing to make amends to them begins the process of reconnecting with other people—a requirement to experience membership in personal spiritual leadership. In making the list we must openly and honestly examine our faults, admitting that we hurt others. This is not an easy step to take for it demands a new kind of honesty about our relations with others. Resentment, blame, grudges, and anger are not healing; taking responsibility for our actions is.

The eighth step is central to personal spiritual leadership because it starts the healing process of forgiveness and offers a big change from a life dominated by anger, resentment, worry, and fear. By the time we reach this step, we have become ready to first seek to understand rather than be understood. We recognize our own need to be forgiven and tend to become more forgiving. In doing so, we forgive others first for any harm they have done us and then, possibly, we are forgiven. We forgive ourselves before we make our amends in Step 9 because if we don't do that, the amends may be tainted by our resentments. As we discussed in Chapter 4, coming to forgive another in this manner is truly a freeing experience; it is the path to health, peace, and spiritual well-being through personal spiritual leadership.

Patrick's sponsor reminded him that the objective in Step 8 was only to make a list of harms; he should try not to think about making any actual amends at this time. He explained that Step 8 is an exercise in self-knowledge, gained by listing those he had harmed, many of whom he identified when writing his inventory lists in Step 4. As he prepared his harms list, Patrick began to realize that most, if not all of his relational problems were exaggerated demands that everyone should respect his needs for power and prestige, however unreasonable and unlimited and therefore unattainable. This had led him to think something was wrong with the other people, especially his ex- wife and people at work, since they did not provide what he had come to expect as a matter of right.

Step 9: Made direct amends to such people wherever possible except when to do so would injure them or others.

Spiritual Value: Forgiveness

Ultimately, Step 9 is about forgiveness, which is a must for personal spiritual leadership, as we make amends to the people on the harms list we developed in Step 8. This includes forgiveness of ourselves and our forgiveness of others' perceived transgressions against us. It may or may not include others forgiving our transgressions.

Typically we start with the amends that are the easiest to make and then move on to those that are more difficult or that we are less willing to make at this time. In doing so, we must be willing and ready to take the full consequences of our past acts and to take responsibility for the well-being of others. This means going to someone and admitting we were wrong—an act that's hard on the ego but good for our self-esteem. The most important thing is to take action and be ready to accept the reactions of those we have harmed with humility and patience.

A real amend is the right one for the relationship and involves much more than a simple, "I'm sorry." The key, whether the opportunity for an amend arises spontaneously or whether we plan a letter or a visit, is that it be simple and from the heart. In some cases we simply do our part to mend old conflicts by going to the person and humbly asking for an understanding of past wrongs and what we can do to set things right. Sometimes this will be a joyous occasion, especially when those harmed prove willing to let go of the bitterness; sometimes not. It is a successful amend, though, even if we are met with bitterness and humiliating responses from the person to whom it is offered. The main point is that when we make amends, we are doing it for ourselves, to lessen feelings of guilt and remorse and to feel relieved about the past. If an amend is not accepted we've done the best we could; we leave the results to our higher power and move on to the next person on the list. The main thing is that we go forward with a careful sense of timing and, with the help of our sponsor, exercise good moral judgment, prudence, and courage.

For Step 9, Patrick started making the amends that were possible and that he was willing to do immediately. Some involved people like his brother, who he believed at the time had sided with his wife in the divorce and had since passed away. After the divorce he never spoke to him again, even though his brother made repeated attempts at reconciliation. All Patrick could do now to make amends was to live life so that he would not hurt those closest to him through unforgiveness.

The most difficult amend to make was to his ex-wife. In retribution for her leaving him he had gone to court, made false acuasations, gotten custody of the children, and done everything he could to keep her out of the children's lives. Only now was he able to see his responsibility in the failure of his marriage—particularly how his anger and inability to forgive her had affected his children and contributed to the problems with them he was now dealing with. He went to her, acknowledged his part in their breakup, and asked her what he could do to make amends. She replied that she still wanted to be a part of the children's lives and suggested they go together to counseling and try to make that work. He agreed, thereby demonstrating strong personal spiritual leadership in that he was willing to ask for forgiveness and love and to serve those he had harmed.

Step 10: Continued to take personal inventory and when we were wrong promptly admitted it.

Spiritual Value: Perseverance

Perseverance is an aspect of personal spiritual leadership that acts as a form of assurance, providing us with an inner witness that encourages us to steadily continue on our chosen path despite daily difficulties and setbacks. In taking Steps 1 through 9 we worked to free ourselves from the wreckage of our past. Step 10 frees us from the wreckage of the present. The tenth step enhances our capacity to be detached from our unconscious motivations, those that interfere with our intentions and keep dragging us away from the present moment with thoughts about the past or future. This step is a maintenance step that challenges us to draw on our inner life to be mindful, live in the present moment, and stay true to ourselves. In continuing to take a personal inventory, we develop a habit of looking at ourselves, our actions, and our relationships on a daily basis. The basic practice is to notice when we are being self-centered or selfish and then immediately drop it.

As we continue to take inventory of our values, attitudes, and behavior, we find ourselves growing in self-acceptance and self-love, thereby further reinforcing our personal spiritual leadership. In conducting this daily inventory we review our feelings and what part we might have played in any problems that occurred. We survey what we have done, trying not to rationalize our actions. Regardless of how we do it, the key is to stop and take the time to allow ourselves the privilege of thinking about our actions, reactions, and motives. Did we cause someone harm? Do we need to admit we were wrong? Do we need to make an amend? The main thing is to handle these issues on a daily basis because, when left unaddressed, these things have a way of festering, which can lead us back to Steps 4 through 9. Taking a daily personal inventory affirms that spiritual growth is a process and that our needs, good points, and character defects are all important. We are a whole person who is lovable just as we are.

As Patrick practiced Step 10, he began to use three types of inventories. One is the spot-check inventory, which he could take at any time of the day. Upon discovering something or a situation that needs to be addressed, he adjusts his course with some little act, such as dropping a pen and going to one knee while saying "Help"—essentially asking to be guided to the right thoughts and actions from his higher power and to be saved from anger, worry, self-pity, or foolish decisions. The second is the occasional written inventory he takes, perhaps with his sponsor, to help him stay centered. The third type involves a personal retreat, allowing for a day or more of spiritual renewal.

Patrick found that, as a result of practicing Step 10, he started to be able to use his emotions as a barometer to monitor his thinking. Strangely, he now found delight in becoming aware and noticing the signals of his character defects, such as being angry, resentful, worried, or afraid.

Through perseverance in the use of these daily inventories he became able to recognize character defects as they emerged and take correction before they got the better of him. In doing so he was able to better practice personal spiritual leadership on a daily basis.

Step 11: Sought through prayer and meditation to improve our conscious contact with God *as we understood Him*, praying only for knowledge of His will for us and the power to carry that out.

Spiritual Value: Spiritual Awareness

The quality of being mindful in the present moment is spiritual awareness and essential for personal spiritual leadership. In Step 11, we seek to develop our inner life to the point where we see that our greatest need is for knowledge of our higher power's will for us in how we may better love and serve others and have the strength to carry out that love and service. Through our inner-life practice, the fruits of the spiritual journey are realized as the unconscious presence or the higher power becomes conscious. Through prayer we seek conscious contact with our higher power. Through meditation we achieve this contact. Step 11 helps us maintain it. When we remove our selfish motives and ask for guidance to love and serve others, we have a restored confidence and courage and a sense of peace and serenity. We find the means and the ways to perform tasks way beyond our capacities. We also acquire an awareness and empathy with other people that was not possible before working this step.

Step 11 helps us get our own selfish motives out of the way. It brings a deeper level of love into all other aspects of daily life as our actions begin to reflect the tenderness and goodness of our higher power. We become willing to let people and things be as they are without having to pass judgment on them. The urgency to be in control begins to fade, and there is the beginning of accepting the impulse to love and be of service to others through concern and care for their needs.

Patrick decided he wanted to expand and reinforce his spiritual program through a religious practice based on the Christian tradition. A friend in his home group invited him to attend a Christian nondenominational service at a church based on Father Thomas Keating's work on centering prayer and Contemplative Outreach, the organization he founded. He learned that centering prayer is a mindful practice for cultivating mindful awareness and improving his ability to listen and be with his higher power, whom he chooses to call God.

Patrick found the power of centering prayer restorative, healing, and a source for personal spiritual leadership. It helped him achieve conscious contact with a God that was one not of fear, but of trust and love. Going to this God helped him face his issues and make amends. He used it to start the day right, end it peacefully, and salvage it when it was falling apart. In making himself vulnerable, he found the courage to face the dark side of his personality. By deliberately attempting to "put space between his thoughts" for twenty minutes twice a day he began to understand the habitual thought patterns and emotions of his life. He began to awaken to not only his faults and weaknesses but also his basic goodness. This allowed him, with the help of his sponsor, psychologist, and close friends, both in and out of the program, to begin to gradually surface and process the undigested emotional material and attachments of a lifetime by allowing it to come to consciousness. This awareness gave Patrick the strength he needed to be free from the thought patterns that previously reinforced his emotional programs for happiness and cultural conditioning.

Step 12: Having had a spiritual awakening as a result of these steps, we tried to carry this message and practice personal spiritual leadership in all our affairs.

The message of the twelfth step is that, through experiencing a loving higher power, we learn to love ourselves and then, in turn, to love and serve others. In doing so, we experience the fruits of the spirit—joy, peace, and serenity independent of our circumstances.

Spiritual Value: Service and Gratitude

Service is the act of helping and contributing to the welfare of others. A vision of service to others is an essential ingredient of personal spiritual leadership. Step 12 is the affirmation that we have experienced a spiritual awakening. The essence of this spiritual awakening is the presence of a higher power in our lives and the beginning of recovery from the tyranny of our emotional programs for happiness and cultural conditioning. Through this awakening and helping others, we have embarked on the spiritual journey. We have begun to experience and satisfy our needs for spiritual well-being through calling and membership and come to this new life through twelve simple, but not easy, steps we can never outgrow. Each person experiences this awakening differently; we find our voice both singly and through fellowship in a spiritual community. Somewhere there is someone who needs to hear our voice and feel attracted to the hope and joy in our hearts and to see the peace in our eyes.

But it is a spiritual axiom that we can keep what was given to us only by sharing this gift of life with others who still suffer and are reaching out for help. Therefore this message is meaningless unless we live it. It is spread through attraction, not promotion, and can only be carried to someone who is asking for help. Our life actions give the spiritual journey meaning and ultimately attract others to inquire about the religious or spiritual underpinnings of such a way of life.

For Patrick, carrying the message requires that he attend meetings and is available to serve his spiritual community. He makes it known that he is available to sponsor others who suffer. Being a sponsor helps him to continue to practice the spiritual principles of his program. He also needs to communicate regularly with a spiritual guide to help him "stay on the beam" and maintain his spiritual program as he continues on his own spiritual journey. Honesty, humility, open-mindedness, and willingness help him treat others fairly. He discovers his decisions have become tempered with tolerance, and he has learned to respect himself. He tries to practice personal spiritual leadership in all his other affairs, especially at work. This includes taking time for community service in a variety of organizations.

REINFORCING PERSONAL SPIRITUAL LEADERSHIP ON A DAILY BASIS

When we work Steps 10, 11, and 12 and continue to clear away our emotional debris, we reinforce, on a daily basis, the qualities of personal spiritual leadership we outlined in Chapter 4. We also begin to experience the reality of Levels II and I—of love and service and the Nondual Way of Being. The first part of the spiritual journey asks, "Where are you?" This question concerns where you are in your spiritual journey. Have you completed a cycle and are now embarked on a new journey of inner discovery? Or are you stuck and find yourself trapped (hopefully not for long) by attachment or over-identification with security, power, a relationship, or what you do for a living? As long as we are identified with some role or persona, we are not free through our personal spiritual leadership to truly love and serve others in Level II or manifest the pure spirit or being of Level I. Therefore, a major part of the spiritual journey is a process of dropping whatever role you identify with. This role is not you. Your body is not you. Your thoughts are not you. Your emotions are not you. If you are not those things, who are you? That is the big question in the second half of the spiritual journey as you move through the Illuminative Way on the Three-fold Path of Spiritual Transformation.

As with the journey of the Fool in Chapter 3, Patrick's spiritual journey was also not so foolish after all. By being honest, open-minded, and willing, he embarked on the spiritual journey in search of his true self. Paradoxically, in the search for self, he discovered he could only find it by shedding it and embracing the all-knowing and encompassing pure spirit from which he came. He now has begun to move through the Unitive Way in the Three-fold Path of Spiritual Transformation. He is more fully aware of his place in the world and has started letting go or surrendering the illusion of absolute autonomy. His ego and life are becoming revitalized to a higher purpose and calling. He has begun to learn the lessons of life and the world and to balance his body, mind, emotions, and spirit and to love and appreciate the new life he has been given. He now has a strong foundation for the practice of both personal and organizational spiritual leadership.

As we take this journey, it becomes important to understand where we are and where we are going. This is best revealed in the development of a personal mission statement, our map to help guide us on our journey.

THE PERSONAL MISSION STATEMENT

As we draw more and more strength from our inner-life practice, our spiritual program, and our higher power, we accept our own weaknesses and lack of virtue, as well as life's unmanageability. We experience an inner resurrection that is manifested through the qualities of personal spiritual leadership. However, this manifestation cannot take place without a vision or destination and a compass (a set of values and moral principles). Mindful awareness as a result of our inner-life practice gives us the hope/faith to write our own script. We rescript ourselves so the paradigms from which our attitudes and behavior flow are in harmony with our vision, purpose, and mission in life and congruent with our deepest values.

The most effective way to begin this rescripting process is through a personal mission statement, which provides both a foundation and guidance for developing the qualities of personal spiritual leadership. A personal mission statement is not something you write overnight. It requires gestation and takes deep introspection, careful analysis, and thoughtful expression. It may take several weeks or even months and many rewrites before you feel it is a complete and concise expression of your innermost vision and the values that give depth and meaning to the long- and short-range goals that provide direction for your life. A personal mission statement is a living document that should be reviewed regularly and be revised as the years bring additional insights or changing circumstances. It becomes our personal constitution, the expression of our personal vision and values—the criterion by which we measure everything in life.

Taken together, a spiritual program and personal mission statement provide a deep sense of peace and security from knowing that our vision and values are timeless and circumstance free and that they do not change. Our vision and values transcend people and circumstances and encourage us to validate them through the practice of personal and organizational spiritual leadership.

Creating and Using a Personal Mission Statement

Envision yourself at a funeral. You park your car, get out, and walk inside the building. You notice the flowers and the soft organ music, see the faces of friends and family, and feel both the shared joy of having known the deceased and the sorrow of loss that emanates from the hearts of the people there. But to your horror, as you walk down to the front of the room and look inside the casket, you come face to face with yourself. This is your funeral and all these people have come to honor you, to express feelings of love and appreciation for your life. According to the program, there are four speakers. The first represents your family and all your relatives, who have come from all over the country to attend. The second speaker is one of your lifelong friends, who will give those attending a sense of what kind of person you were. The third speaker is from your work or profession; she will speak of you as a coworker and will relate your accomplishments. The fourth person is from your church, spiritual community, or a community organization in which you have been involved in service.

Now think deeply about what you would like each of these speakers to say about you and your life. How would they say you fulfilled your major roles in life—husband or wife, mother or father, daughter or son, sibling, friend, and coworker? What would they say about your character and achievements? Look carefully at those there to pay their last respects to you. What difference would you like to have made in their lives?

The process inherent in creating a personal mission statement is as important as the product. Writing or reviewing a personal mission statement is a process of change because it forces you to think through your priorities deeply and carefully and to align your values, attitudes, and behavior. As you begin to live your life according to your personal vision and values, others begin to sense that you are not being driven by the externalities of your situation—that you have a sense of vision, purpose, and mission of love and service grounded in altruistic values that provide intrinsic motivation and excitement for your life and what you are trying to do.

Visualization and Affirmation

Visualization is the force that turns dreams into reality; it is exercised by successful high achievers in every profession. It is an act of mentally picturing ideas, events, circumstances, and concrete objects that gives more accurate knowledge than any other sense. The practice of visualization is supported by the fact that we customarily think in terms of pictures rather than words. When you can picture a vivid picture of yourself in possession of your goals, you stimulate and spark the desire, creativity, and intrinsic motivation that are necessary for planning and the other efforts necessary for successfully accomplishing them.

When based on your core values, visualization and affirmation can transform your thinking, your attitudes, and finally your behavior. Through the powers of your imagination, you can visualize your own funeral, as we did earlier. If you are married, another effective exercise is to visualize a distant anniversary (say your twenty-fifth or fiftieth). Have your spouse visualize it with you. Visualize your retirement and detail the achievements you would want to have accomplished. What about after retirement? How will you exercise personal spiritual leadership and continue to live your vision and values and satisfy your needs for calling and membership? As you do so, expand your mind and visualize your life in rich detail. Envision that you find out you will die within five years. What would your spouse say at your funeral and afterward at the gathering of family, friends, coworkers, and others from the community? Do this for your other key stakeholders as well. Are there differences in these visualizations? If so, explore the reasons why and whether this should be so.

A useful technique for focusing your creative power of visualization is the practice of affirmation. Affirmation—often also called self-motivation, self-commands, auto-suggestion, or self-talk—are positive declarations of something you believe to be true or something you expect to become true and desire to live by. They should be your own creation and be based on your goals; they should describe the person you want to be, and what you want to do and have in terms of your key stakeholders.

By repeating and visualizing your affirmations in action, you build the needed internal commitment, confidence, and determination to overcome obstacles, accomplish your goals, and improve your personal commitment and productivity. Affirmations are particularly useful for building con structive attitudes. For example, if you want to be a better communicator, remind yourself daily, "I communicate my ideas clearly and persuasively. I listen attentively when others speak." Another example might be, "I enjoy knowing people I work with as individuals. I listen when they talk and understand both their words and their feelings. I respect them and their right to be themselves."

The egoic mind is like a computer. It controls thinking, emotions, and actions based on the information it is given to work with. In other words, the old adage for computers "Garbage in, garbage out" is also true for your mind. If you feed it negative ideas, it can only respond negatively. But when you give it positive affirmations through constructive, confident directives, it responds with positive motivation for committed, positive action. The following guidelines can help as we write powerful affirmations:

- *Effective affirmations use the first person pronoun, "I."* Affirmations are useful only when they are internalized; the use of "I" serves to forge a personal commitment to live according to what you affirm.

- *Affirmations are most effective when written in the present tense.* Many people have trouble with this aspect; they find it difficult, for example, to state, "I am calm and peaceful in all situations," when that is not presently the case. If however, you use the future tense to say you will be calm, your mind is likely to use this as an excuse to procrastinate in taking the actions necessary to make it so. The goal essentially remains forever in the future. Through visualizing the affirmation in the present tense you can experience in the present moment how it feels to possess your goal.

- *State affirmations as positives.* Negative affirmations are much more difficult to picture mentally. For example if you say, "I do not procrastinate starting important activities," it is difficult to picture "not procrastinate." If you say instead, "I enjoy getting started on important projects and making steady progress," you can picture yourself getting started on important work and enjoying the sense of accomplishment that results from productive actions. (Meyer 1994)

Once you have written some affirmations, keep them where you can see them (for example, on the bathroom mirror, the sun visor of your car, or the refrigerator). Repeat them frequently so they reinforce your desired attitudes and behaviors. Then visualize your affirmations in rich detail. You can think, feel, and see yourself working on that important project and successfully completing it. Or you can see yourself handling that difficult personal situation with all the love, power, and self-motivation you have captured in your affirmation. You can also use a personal mission statement as a source for affirmations for your spiritual journey. And if you do this day after day your behavior will change. You will no longer be acting out scripts based on your failed emotional programs for happiness and cultural conditioning. You will be living out your personal spiritual leadership based on hope/faith, a transcendent vision of service to others based in the values of altruistic love.

When we seriously make the effort to identify what matters most to us in our lives—who we want to be and how that looks in terms of what we do and have—we become reverent and more open to the spiritual journey. We start to think in larger terms and become willing to do more than satisfy our own egocentric desires. We begin to realize that meaning in life comes from making a difference in the lives of others and that in doing so we receive love, understanding, and appreciation in return.

Identifying Stakeholders, Issues, and Goals

An effective personal mission statement requires vision, purpose, mission, and value statements. It also identifies our key stakeholders and their expectations, issues related to unmet expectations, and a set of integrated goals and strategies to resolve these issues. Figure 6.1 is an example of worksheets that can be used as an aid in this process.

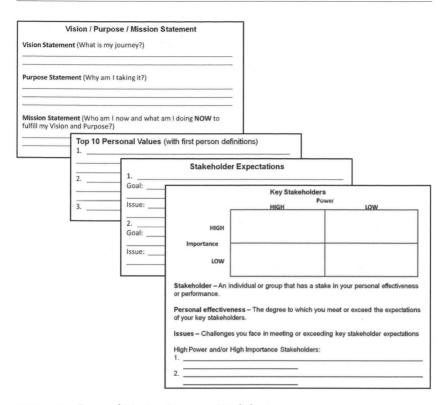

FIGURE 6.1 Personal Mission Statement Worksheet
Source: International Institute for Spiritual Leadership

The vision (what is my journey), purpose (why this journey is important), and mission (what I'm doing now to fulfill my purpose and vision) work together to identify key personal stakeholders. A vision/purpose/ mission vividly portrays a journey that, when undertaken, will give hope/ faith to pursue the vision. It also forms the basis for our ethical system and the personal values based in altruistic love underlying it. These values serve as a primary means of communicating, reinforcing, and rewarding appropriate behavior. In personal spiritual leadership, we set the stage for personal change by striving to be authentic, and we model these values through our everyday attitudes and behavior, drawing on both our spiritual program and our personal mission statement for guidance.

The stakeholder effectiveness analysis utilizes a stakeholder approach in viewing individuals as being imbedded in levels (individual, group, organizational, societal) with various internal and external constituencies (boss, coworkers, customers/clients, spouses, family members, government agencies, etc.), all of whom have a legitimate strategic and moral stake in our personal commitment and performance. The focus should be on those stakeholders that have high power and/or high importance. Each of these stakeholders may have different values and interests as well as different relationships with other individuals, groups, and organizations. For example, your boss may have power over you in terms of position and authority but not be that important to your personal mission. Conversely, your friends may be an important part of your social life but may not be have the power to influence you like your spouse or higher power.

In addition to our vision/purpose/mission and values, key stakeholder expectations and issues associated with not meeting these expectations are identified. It is usually best to select only the top one or two issues to focus on for personal change. All change is difficult, and to focus on more than one or two areas can make the task of change seem overwhelming and may dissipate our energy for change. Avoid this possibility by setting goals to address the issues. The steps in goal setting are not complex, but they do require that we be patient and keep an open mind until the overall pattern of activity begins to unfold. Effective goals should be clear, specific, and challenging; they should focus on results rather than activity. In particular goals should:

Begin with an action verb, preceded by "to" (to sell, to build, to increase, to learn, to improve, to decrease).

Identify a key result area that is the performance target (attitude, attendance, community service).

State a performance indicator or measurement standard (percentages, monetary units, average time/task).

Provide a time frame by which the result will be produced (Friday noon, each week, by the IRS deadline).

Examples might be "To exercise for fifteen minutes three times a week first thing in the morning after I have my coffee" or "to decrease time lost by equipment failure to no more than ten minutes per day during the next quarter."

It is imperative that goals be written. Written goals create psychological commitment and ensure that we identify the achievements that are most meaningful. They force us to clarify and crystallize our thinking. They marshal the forces of our untapped potential, create and make use of a positive self-image, and act as a fuel for self-motivation based on desire held in expectation with the hope/faith the goal will be realized. Other significant benefits of written goals include:

- *They save time.* There are continually demands on your time. Written goals keep you on course to minimize and focus your attention on what is most important to do next.
- *They help measure progress.* Motivation is highest when there are goals for measuring progress and monitoring accomplishments.
- *They produce motivation.* Each time you review your goals you renew your sense of purpose, strengthen dedication to their achievement, and become more excited about working toward them.
- *They reduce conflict.* Conflicts between your values, priorities, and use of time become obvious when goals are written, thereby eliminating damaging frustration.
- *They form a basis for action.* Properly written goals provide the action steps for moving from the daydream stage to the reality of solid accomplishments, actual success, and increased commitment and productivity.
- *They stimulate visualization.* You can see future results more easily and clearly with your goals written out. You then have more hope/faith in the possibility of success and are more motivated to reach your goals.

The main purpose of the goal-setting process in personal mission statements is to guide us on our personal journey from dream to fulfillment. Just remember that we are where and what we are today because of life's events, which have unfolded over time, and the choices we made in response to those events. So making changes in our attitudes or habits or in developing new values that will lead to spiritual growth and increase our personal effectiveness will also take time. Goals unify our efforts and give meaning and purpose to all we do. They work to stimulate effort and commitment while helping to identify where we want to be and determine where we are. They give us important information on how to get where we want to be and let us know when we have arrived. Ultimately, goals guide daily activities so that we are proactive and making things happen through personal spiritual leadership each day by providing structure and an organized path for our personal mission.

Patrick M.'s Personal Mission Statement

Patrick found it was important to give direction and guidance for his journey of personal spiritual leadership by developing his own personal mission statement. His vision/purpose/mission statement reveals him to be a man who is a professional engineer, working on a graduate degree, who is family-oriented and dedicated to helping and enriching the lives of others.

Vision: (My life's journey). I love life and the relationships that I have with my family. I am constantly looking to help others. I am an individual who loves to voluntarily help and serve those who are less fortunate. I am creative and caring.

Purpose (Why I am taking this journey). To enjoy my family. To provide opportunities for individuals who seek my help. To use my many skills to enrich the lives of others.

Mission (Who I am and what I'm doing now to fulfill my vision and purpose): I am a professional engineer; I am a good leader and follower in my company's efforts to exceed the expectations of our customers. I attend graduate school to further my education to help me accomplish my personal goals and be a better employee. I volunteer for community service activities to help others and be a positive role model for my children.

Values: These values reflect how I seek to relate to God, family, students, friends, boss, co-workers, and community. (Patrick's values reflect the values of altruistic love and the need to draw upon the strength of a higher power he chooses to call God.)

- *God.* Relationship with God: "If the Lord takes you to it, He'll get you through it." My personal relationship with God is my number-one priority.

- *Compassion.* I understand we are all human and make mistakes. I give empathy and understanding in all situations.

- *Responsible.* I am a person others can depend on during everyday situations and in times of crisis.

- *Honest.* I am truthful with others and myself.

- *Determined.* I am a person who reaches for the stars, and nothing can stop me until I have reached them.

- *Golden Rule.* I treat others as I would like to be treated.

- *Excellence.* I give 100 percent in everything I do.

In his personal mission statement, Patrick identifies below seven key stakeholders and their expectations of him. The expectations he gives for each stakeholder provide a definition for the effectiveness of his personal spiritual leadership. In other words, he will be personally effective to the extent he meets or exceeds the expectations of (in order of importance) his God, children, friends, boss, coworkers, community service agencies, and fellow graduate students.

Stakeholder Effectiveness

God: *To Act Out of Belief and Love.* To worship and keep him in my heart. To love and serve others that he puts in my path.

Children: *To Provide Love, Support, and Motivation.* To provide for and love them unconditionally and to meet their needs.

Friends: *To Be Caring and Supportive:* To be there for them and accept and love them unconditionally.

Boss: *To Be Hardworking and Capable.* To be a good decision maker, support my boss and his or her decisions, and do my job to the best of my ability.

Coworkers: *To Be Responsible and Honest.* To be a motivated team player, to support team members and their ideas, and to provide guidance when asked.

Community Service Agencies: *To Be Supportive and Dedicated.* To be a reliable and committed individual who's willing to do what it takes to help those in need.

Students: *To Provide Leadership and to Be a Role-Model.* To pull my weight on group projects, to be dependable and to take the lead when necessary.

Upon reflection, Patrick identified two issues. The first was in response to a conflict between his family and his community stakeholders. In writing his personal mission statement he realized he was not meeting the expectations of his family, primarily due to his increased time commitments to graduate school while trying to maintain a significant level of community involvement. As a response he set two concrete and specific goals. He would reduce his community involvement to one committee until he graduated. Plus he would set aside Wednesday evenings and Sunday afternoons for family time and activities.

The other issue was his continuing resentment against his boss. He resolved to do a fourth step in writing on this resentment and to share this with his sponsor. This will reveal his part in the resentment and what actions he should take, which may include making an amend if he has harmed his boss in any way, perhaps by not giving his best efforts.

CONCLUSION

Personal spiritual leadership requires a spiritual program to develop mindfulness and guide us on our spiritual journey. As we illustrated through Patrick M.'s story, one such program is the Twelve-Step recovery process. Although it is just one of many spiritual and religious traditions that can be used for this purpose, the Twelve-Step process is a widely accepted approach that can be universally applied by anyone seeking to develop the qualities of personal spiritual leadership. It entails recognizing that at least one area of your life is unmanageable (Step 1); discovering a loving higher power (Steps 2 and 3); clearing away the debris of the past (Steps 4 through 9); beginning to practice your spiritual program on a daily basis (Step 10); adopting an inner-life practice to become more mindfully aware or conscious (Step 11); and, having had a spiritual awakening as a result of these steps, practicing personal spiritual leadership in all your affairs (Step 12).

Twelve-Step recovery programs offer the following promises to those who work the steps on a daily basis:

> We are going to know a new freedom and a new happiness. We will not regret the past nor wish to shut the door on it. We will comprehend the word serenity and we will know peace. No matter how far down the scale we have gone, we will see how our experience can benefit others. That feeling of uselessness and self-pity will disappear. We will lose interest in selfish things and gain interest in our fellows. Self-seeking will slip away. Our whole attitude and outlook upon life will change. Fear of people and of economic insecurity will leave us. We will intuitively know how to handle situations which used to baffle us. (Alcoholics Anonymous 2003, 83–84)

A personal mission statement provides focus, guidance, and direction for the exercise of personal spiritual leadership. An effective personal mission statement requires that we identify the vision, purpose, mission, and values we draw upon to love and serve our key stakeholders. Then we identify issues related to unmet expectations of these stakeholders. Finally, we develop goals and strategies to address these issues.

Because people cannot lead others unless they can lead themselves, personal spiritual leadership is necessary for anyone seeking to lead a group or organization. Thus, personal spiritual leadership combined with a personal mission statement is necessary for organizational spiritual leadership and ultimately maximizing the Triple Bottom Line. How to do this is the subject of the next chapter, on implementing organizational spiritual leadership.

Practical Tools

For those interested in maximize the Triple Bottom Line, the major tools introduced in this chapter include the following:

Personal leadership involves the self-confident ability to crystallize your thinking, establish an exact direction for your life, commit yourself to moving in that direction, and then take determined action to acquire, accomplish, or become whatever you need to attain your ultimate goal in life.

Personal spiritual leadership requires the exercise of strong personal leadership, plus an inner life practice that is the source of hope/faith in a vision of service to your key stakeholders through altruistic love.

A spiritual or religious program of action provides a process for developing and reinforcing the qualities of personal spiritual leadership.

A personal mission statement serves as a personal constitution that gives personal spiritual leadership focus, guidance, and direction.

Chapter Seven

Implementing Organizational Spiritual Leadership

Although retired Procter & Gamble (P&G) CEO A. G. Lafley might not think of himself as a spiritual leader, he exhibited many of the characteristics of both personal and organizational spiritual leadership in the company's successful turnaround between 2000 and 2010. Lafley transformed P&G from an unfocused collection of famous brands into an aggressive, innovative machine driven by ideas from consumers rather than eggheads in research and development. Through huge acquisitions, including a $57 billion deal for Gillette, he gave P&G global reach that goes beyond that of most governments (Kimes, 2009).

During the 1990s P&G had struggled to introduce new brands, which were considered by many to be the sustaining force and lifeblood of the legendary consumer products company. Durk Jager, the previous CEO, had lasted just seventeen months and was removed by his board in 2000 after failing to reverse P&G's decline and lackluster performance. At the time, half of P&G's top fifteen brands were losing market share, and employee morale was at an all-time low. The dynamics of the industry were changing as power shifted from manufacturers to massive retailers like Wal-Mart. P&G was in danger of becoming another Eastman Kodak or Xerox, once great companies that had lost their way (P&G, n.d.).

Lafley's biggest challenge was to transform what had become an insular organizational culture. P&G employees view themselves as a family. They often start out there and grow up together. Promotion from within is the norm, and few outsiders are hired. Cincinnati, P&G's corporate home, is a small town where employees live near each other and go to the same churches, health clubs, and restaurants. They view themselves as company men and women and are proud of it. P&G had long been famous for its resistance to new ideas, even though its last big breakthrough had been in 1983 when it had a huge hit with Always (feminine protection pads). P&G's research and development operations stubbornly held to the notion that worthy ideas and inventions could come only from within P&G.

Lafley moved quickly to establish a vision for transformational change that reflected an outwardly focused, flexible company with the characteristics of a learning organization. The central tenet of his vision was that P&G should do only what it does best and nothing more. He spent a significant amount of his time patiently communicating his vision and how he wanted P&G to change through slogans like "The consumer is boss" and "Our key assets at P&G are our people and our brands." The company focused on "the first moment of truth" when the consumer first sees the product on the shelf and the "second moment of truth" concerning the consumer's experience at home with the product.

Lafley cut costs by focusing on what was selling and pouring resources into those brands while cutting the rest. He eliminated 9,600 jobs and closed down several new-product-development projects that were consuming resources with no clear probability of success. He pulled new products from the market that had not met their market projections and sold off product lines he did not see as strategic fits, including Jif and Crisco (Reingold, 2009). At the same time he signaled the need to reach outside the company for ideas by asserting that half of P&G's new products should come from external sources. P&G also began entering alliances with other companies to develop new products, including competitors like Clorox, with which it codeveloped the highly successful Glad Press and Seal ("Procter & Gamble (P&G) Dividend Stock Analysis" 2009).

To motivate managers to improve their performance, Lafley revealed everyone's financial results at a meeting each quarter. He established rewards for business units that share their ideas with others to break down the barriers within P&G and get employees from different divisions to talk, which they had not traditionally done. As a symbolic gesture to drive home the importance of removing barriers between units, Lafley embarked on a highly visible redesign of the fabled eleventh-floor executive suites at the P&G head office. He moved all five division heads to the same floors as their staff. Then he and other top executives were assigned cubicles on half the floor. The other half was transformed into a center for employee learning where executives teach and get involved in employee development. A willingness to train others is another key to advancement. The idea is that if your direct reports aren't ready for promotion, then neither are you. This forms the foundation for a rigorous training program called "Build from Within," which tracks the performance of every manager, making sure they are ready for the next slot (Reingold, 2009).

In addition to demonstrating many of the characteristics of organizational spiritual leadership, A. G. Lafley also displayed many of the qualities of personal spiritual leadership. He listened more than he talked and is living proof that the messenger is just as important as the message, patiently communicating how he wanted P&G to change. Through a process he calls "peeling the onion" he developed a reputation as a boss who stepped back to give his empowered staff plenty of responsibility while helping shape decisions by asking a series of keen questions. The table in the conference room where he and twelve other top P&G executives met every Monday used to be rectangular and executives were told where to sit. He brought in a round table so executives could sit where they liked. An outsider might have had trouble distinguishing the CEO: he occasionally joined in the conversations, but most of the time the executives talked as much to each other. Robert McDonald, who took over the reins from Lafley as CEO in 2010, says "People wanted to follow him. I frankly love him like my brother."

Like other top companies, P&G stumbled in the massive market meltdown of 2009. However, the legacy of Lafley's leadership continues to be impressive and propel P&G as a Triple Bottom Line leader. While Lafley focused P&G to seek external opportunities, he embraced and reinforced P&G's family culture and turned it into a source of competitive advantage. P&G also embraced sustainability in terms of product safety, environmental and social responsibility, and caring for the communities in which they operate. Robert McDonald is determined to expand this legacy worldwide through his new vision: "To touch and improve more people's lives, in more parts of the world, more completely."

P&G's financial performance was also outstanding under Lafley's leadership. In 2005 nineteen of P&Gs top-selling brands gained market share. In 2000 P&G earned $5.53 billion on sales of $40 billion. In 2005 it earned $10.4 billion on sales of $57 billion. And in 2008 it earned $12.1 billion on sales of $83.5 billion. As of January 2010, over the last eleven years P&G has managed to deliver a greater than 10 percent average increase in earnings per share and dividends to shareholders.

Organizational leaders, like Lafley, face major challenges in the twenty-first century. They must understand and cope with a rapidly changing, global, Internet-driven environment, while successfully developing and implementing transformational organizational change. Such transformation seeks to create massive changes in an organization's orientation to its environment, vision, goals, strategies, structures, processes, and organizational culture. Its purpose is to affect large-scale, paradigm-shifting change. An organizational transformation results in new models and methods for organizing and performing work. The overall goal is to simultaneously improve organizational effectiveness and individual well-being.

This often means radical change to a learning organization. A learning organization incorporates a broad range of techniques and strategies that are characterized by flatter, less hierarchical, and more flexible, networked, diverse, global structures, and work arrangements. Central to the learning organizational paradigm is developing, leading, motivating, organizing, and retaining people to be committed to the organization's vision, goals, culture, and values. It involves qualitatively different ways of perceiving, thinking, and behaving. Learning organizations continuously transform themselves. People in learning organizations continually expand their capacity to create the results they truly desire; new and expansive patterns of thinking are nurtured; collective aspiration is set free; and people continually learn together to produce quality products and services that exceed stakeholder expectations.

Regardless of whether A. G. Lafley considers himself to be a spiritual leader, his leadership in P&G's turnaround illustrates a successful organizational transformation to a learning organizational paradigm based on a vision of service to key stakeholders and cultural values centered on care and concern for employees—the essence of organizational spiritual leadership. In this chapter we provide a roadmap for implementing organizational spiritual leadership and highlight specific organizational transformation and development interventions. First, we discuss organizational spiritual leadership as a source for organizational and team transformation. Then we detail specific organizational development interventions necessary to implement and sustain organizational spiritual leadership. Finally, we describe a field experiment using two public elementary schools to illustrate the use of the Organizational Spiritual Leadership Survey and a vision/stakeholder effectiveness analysis, which are necessary for implementing organizational spiritual leadership.

ORGANIZATIONAL TRANSFORMATION THROUGH SPIRITUAL LEADERSHIP

Although a paycheck is still necessary for employee survival, today's high performance workers also seek leadership that provides: (1) interesting work that permits them to learn, develop, and have a sense of competence and mastery, (2) meaningful work that provides a sense of purpose, (3) membership through a sense of connection and positive social relations with their coworkers, and (4) the ability to live an integrated life, so that one's work does not conflict with who they are as human beings. Satisfying these employee needs is central to organizational spiritual leadership.

Organizational spiritual leadership addresses three vital questions: (1) How will individuals know what to do? (2) How will they be trained and developed? and (3) What will motivate them to do it? The foundation for addressing these questions is built around three principles. First, employee involvement and commitment based on intrinsic motivation is the most effective source of control. Involvement and commitment create intrinsic controls because employees have a sense of ownership and they focus energy and creativity on the improvement of processes and the attainment of organizational objectives. When involved and committed to their work it is possible for all employees to add significant value to the organization.

Second, a learning organization based on spiritual leadership utilizes team-based work designs. This team-based approach to organizing should be centered on issues relating to products and customers rather than the traditional functions of the organization.

Finally, it is necessary to implement organizational spiritual leadership as a driver of a business model that impacts the organization's effectiveness by setting direction, defining the agenda, adjusting strategy to address the changing business environment, and serving as a role model for leaders throughout the organization.

To implement organizational spiritual leadership, strategic leaders must recognize the need for:

- Selectively recruiting new personnel who identify with the company's vision and values;
- An organizational design based on self-managed teams and decentralized decision making;
- Comparatively high compensation that is contingent upon organizational performance;
- Extensive training;
- Transparency of financial and performance information; and
- Reduced positional status distinctions and barriers.

The development and implementation of these key components requires a new mind-set and a learning organizational paradigm, one that recognizes the importance of organizational spiritual leadership, sustainability, and maximizing the Triple Bottom Line.

Organizational activities, systems, and processes based on organizational spiritual leadership train, develop, and reinforce top leadership teams that are more effective at surfacing and debating information. This leads to superior situation assessments, more accurate problem definition, and the generation of a richer set of alternative solutions. And, ultimately, higher-quality strategic decisions lead to higher performance. Leaders serve as role models for the rest of the organization to develop a culture that is comfortable with identifying failures and using them as opportunities for learning. Most important, to identify emerging failures, leaders interact with frontline employees to get a feel for how their decisions are being implemented and to learn about any unintended side effects. These observations are then brought back to the top leadership team for further review and action.

Sometimes top leaders, usually in the face of decline, are able to overcome their own cultural biases and perceive the need to change the organization's culture because its values are dysfunctional for survival and growth in a changing environment. More often, though, leaders who brought their company to stagnation or the brink of failure cannot lead their company through it. They must be replaced by leaders who unfreeze the present system by highlighting the threat to the organization if change doesn't occur while at the same time instilling in its people the belief that change is possible.

Organizational spiritual leadership also requires top leadership teams to create vision and value congruence across organizational levels as well as develop effective relationships between the organization and environmental stakeholders. To facilitate this congruence, several key ongoing practices are critical for the implementation of organizational spiritual leadership.

Administer the Organizational Spiritual Leadership Survey. Conduct a periodic assessment of organizational spiritual leadership using the spiritual leadership survey methodology that has been developed and extensively tested for over twelve years by the International Institute for Spiritual Leadership. This survey is used to establish a baseline for the variables in the spiritual leadership model. The survey, usually administered in intervals of twelve to twenty-four months, also identifies key issues for organizational transformation and/or development intervention.

Conduct a vision/stakeholder analysis. Using the results of this assessment, the top leadership team should conduct a vision/stakeholder analysis to establish and reinforce the values, attitudes, and behaviors of organizational spiritual leadership, identify key stakeholder issues, and provide a basis for an organization-wide dialogue concerning the appropriate goals and strategies to address these issues.

Conduct organizational development interventions and skills training. Organizations wishing to implement organizational spiritual leadership must develop strategies for intervention and training to implement and sustain these goals and strategies. At a minimum, these include implementing elements of team empowerment—collaborative, consensus-based decision making; managing conflict; managing and overcoming resistance to change; and dealing with anger, resentment, and fear through forgiveness acceptance, and gratitude.

Align changes with key organization design variables. Organizational development and transformation through spiritual leadership requires congruence or fit among the organization's reward systems, structure, information and production technology, and recruiting and selection processes.

The Organizational Spiritual Leadership Survey:
Establishing a Baseline

The first step is to gather information through surveys and interviews to establish a baseline for possible organization transformation or development intervention. The organizational Spiritual Leadership Survey has been given to thousands of employees and conducted in numerous organizations ranging in size from a few employees to more than 1,200, including schools, military units, cities, police, and for-profit companies. These studies have confirmed the Spiritual Leadership Model and its reliability and validity. While the questions are randomly distributed on the survey, they cover the basic components or variables of spiritual leadership: inner life, vision, hope/faith, altruistic love, meaning/calling, membership, employee life satisfaction, organizational commitment, and productivity, plus any other outcomes that might be of interest to the organization (for example, unit quality, customer satisfaction, or sales growth). The variable definitions and items for the organizational Spiritual Leadership Survey are:

Vision, which describes the organization's journey and why we are taking it; vision defines who we are and what we do.

I understand and am committed to my organization's vision.

My organization has a vision statement that brings out the best in me.

My organization's vision inspires my best performance.

My organization's vision is clear and compelling to me.

Hope/Faith, the assurance of things hoped for, the conviction that the organization's vision, purpose, and mission will be fulfilled.

I have faith in my organization and I am willing to "do whatever it takes" to ensure that it accomplishes its mission.

I demonstrate my faith in my organization and its mission by doing everything I can to help us succeed.

I persevere and exert extra effort to help my organization succeed because I have faith in what it stands for.

I set challenging goals for my work because I have faith in my organization and want us to succeed.

Altruistic Love, a sense of wholeness, harmony, and well-being produced through care, concern, and appreciation for both self and others.

The leaders in my organization "walk the walk" as well as "talk the talk".

The leaders in my organization are honest and without false pride.

My organization is trustworthy and loyal to its employees.

The leaders in my organization have the courage to stand up for their people.

My organization is kind and considerate toward its workers and, when they are suffering, wants to do something about it.

Meaning/Calling, a sense that one's life has meaning and makes a difference.

The work I do makes a difference in people's lives.

The work I do is meaningful to me.

The work I do is very important to me.

My job activities are personally meaningful to me.

Membership, a sense that one is understood and appreciated.

I feel my organization appreciates me and my work.

I feel my organization demonstrates respect for me and my work.

I feel I am valued as a person in my job.

I feel highly regarded by my leaders.

Inner Life, the extent to which one has an inner life or spiritual practice

I feel hopeful about life.

I consider myself a spiritual person.

I care about the spiritual health of my coworkers.

I maintain an inner life or spiritual practice (for example, spending time in nature, prayer, meditation, reading inspirational literature, yoga, observing religious traditions, or writing in a journal).

My spiritual values influence the choices I make.

Organizational Commitment, the degree of loyalty or attachment to the organization.

I feel like "part of the family" in this organization.

I really feel as if my organization's problems are my own.

I would be very happy to spend the rest of my career with this organization.

I talk up this organization to my friends as a great place to work.

I feel a strong sense of belonging to my organization.

Productivity, efficiency in producing results, benefits, or profits.

In my department, everyone gives his or her best effort.

In my department, work quality is a high priority for all workers.

My work group is very productive.

My work group is very efficient in getting maximum output from the resources (money, people, equipment, etc.) we have available.

Satisfaction with Life, one's sense of subjective well-being or satisfaction with life as a whole.

The conditions of my life are excellent.

I am satisfied with my life.

In most ways my life is ideal.

If I could live my life over, I would change almost nothing.

So far I have gotten the important things I want in life.

Vision/Stakeholder Effectiveness Analysis

After the survey data are gathered and summarized, the next step is to conduct a vision/stakeholder effectiveness analysis with the organization's top leadership team to implement organizational spiritual leadership. This process focuses on identifying and addressing key stakeholder issues, discovering what works well, why it works well, and how success can be extended throughout the organization. There are three basic assumptions to this process. First, organizations are responsive to positive thought and positive knowledge. Second, both an image of the future and the process for creating that image produce the energy to drive change throughout the organization. Last is the belief in the power of visualization and positive affirmation; if people can envision what they want, there is a better chance of it happening. By using this approach, organizations can discover, understand, and learn from success, while creating new images for the future.

The vision/stakeholder effectiveness analysis utilizes a stakeholder approach in viewing social organizations as being imbedded in layers or levels (individual, group, organizational, societal) with various internal and external constituencies (employees, customers, suppliers, government agencies, and so forth), all of whom have a legitimate strategic and moral stake in the organization's performance. The organization should focus on stakeholders who have high power and/or high importance. Each of these stakeholders may have different values and interests as well as different relationships with other individuals, groups, and organizations. Government agencies may have power over the organization in terms of regulatory authority (for example, the Environmental Protection Agency) but not be central to the company's mission. Conversely, each individual customer at Walmart is important, but no individual customer has the power to significantly influence Walmart's operations.

An organizational vision/stakeholder effectiveness analysis worksheet is given in Figure 7.1 as a tool to aid in this process. The visioning process for an organization follows the elements discussed in Chapter 6 for vision development in personal spiritual leadership. The vision (what our journey is), purpose (why this journey is important), and mission (what we do as employees to fulfill our purpose) work together to identify key stakeholders. Taken together, the vision, purpose, and mission must vividly portray a journey that, when undertaken, will give employees a sense of calling, a sense of one's life having meaning and making a difference.

The vision, purpose, and mission then form the basis for the social construction of the organization's culture and the ethical system and values underlying it. Cultural values serve as a primary means of communicating, reinforcing, and rewarding appropriate organizational behavior. In spiritual leadership, these values are prescribed and form the foundation for a culture based on altruistic love that gives employees a sense of membership, of belonging and being understood and appreciated. To set the stage for initial change efforts, strategic leaders must be authentic and model these values through their everyday attitudes and behavior.

All members or representatives of the organization should ultimately be offered the opportunity to participate in the vision/stakeholder analysis process. The critical goal is for all employees to know, believe in, and be fully committed to hope/faith in a vision of service to key stakeholders through a culture based on altruistic love. As this process unfolds, key stakeholder expectations and issues associated with not

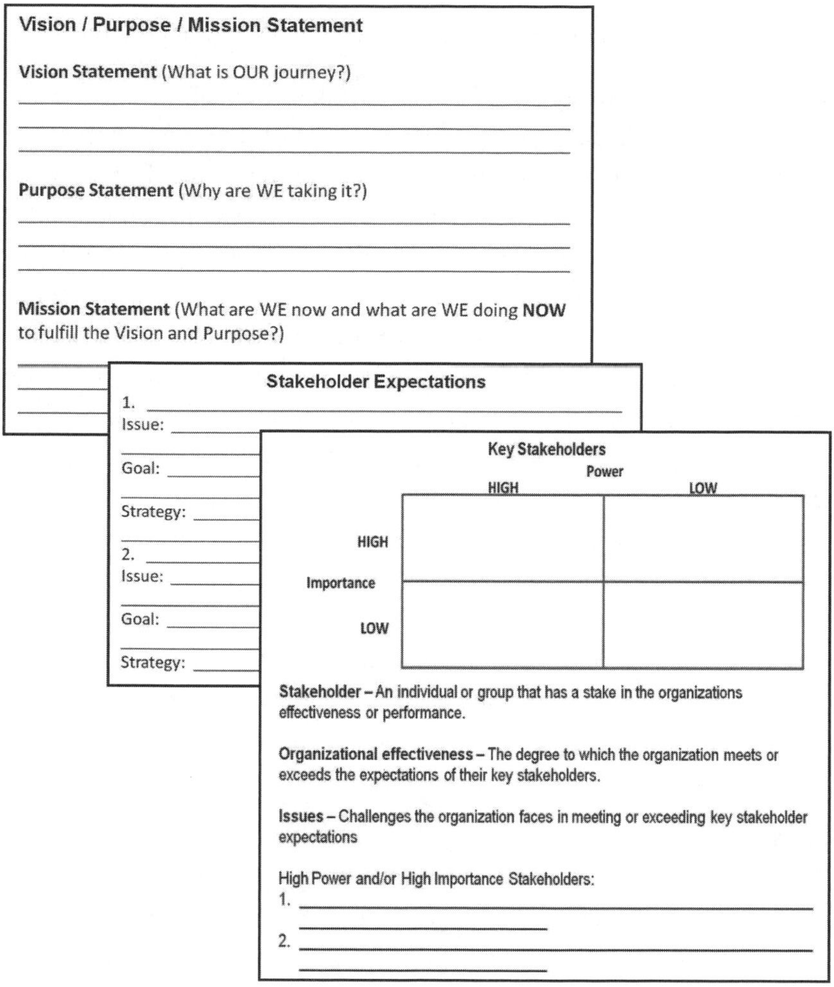

Vision / Purpose / Mission Statement

Vision Statement (What is OUR journey?)

_____

_____

_____

Purpose Statement (Why are WE taking it?)

_____

_____

_____

Mission Statement (What are WE now and what are WE doing **NOW** to fulfill the Vision and Purpose?)

_____

_____

Stakeholder Expectations

1. _____

Issue: _____

Key Stakeholders

Power

HIGH   LOW

Goal: _____

Strategy: _____

HIGH

2. _____

Issue: _____   Importance

Goal: _____   LOW

Strategy: _____

Stakeholder – An individual or group that has a stake in the organizations effectiveness or performance.

Organizational effectiveness – The degree to which the organization meets or exceeds the expectations of their key stakeholders.

Issues – Challenges the organization faces in meeting or exceeding key stakeholder expectations

High Power and/or High Importance Stakeholders:

1. _____

_____

2. _____

_____

FIGURE 7.1 Organizational Vision/Stakeholder Effectiveness Analysis Worksheet
Source: International Institute for Spiritual Leadership

meeting these expectations are identified. Then empowered teams are formed of members most affected by these key issues. If necessary to effectively address the issues, organization development intervention strategies are adopted to apply techniques and technologies for facilitating change.

Organizational Development Interventions

The issues that are identified in the vision/stakeholder effectiveness analysis process often require organizational development interventions for their resolution. In contrast to organizational transformation, which is about radical organizational change, organizational development is the planned development, improvement, and reinforcement of strategies, structures, and processes that lead to organizational effectiveness. Organizational development interventions based on organizational spiritual leadership should not be initiated until the organization has established a baseline for intervention through the Spiritual Leadership Survey and conducted a thorough vision/stakeholder effectiveness analysis that has identified key issues.

In this regard, it is essential to have a general understanding of the interventions that are essential for implementing organizational spiritual leadership—the elements necessary for team empowerment, for managing conflict, for collaborative, consensus-based decision making, for managing resistance to change, and for overcoming anger, resentment, worry, and fear through forgiveness, gratitude, and acceptance.

Elements of Team Empowerment

Empowerment is power sharing through the delegation of power and authority. It creates the cross-level connection between team and individual jobs, provides the basis for strong intrinsic motivation, and meets the higher-order needs of individuals. Empowered employees are more committed to the organization through trust, hope, and faith. In particular:

- Empowered teams receive information about organizational performance.
- Employees receive knowledge and skills to contribute to organizational goals.
- Employees have the power to make substantive decisions.
- Employees understand the meaning and impact of their jobs.
- Employees are rewarded based upon organizational performance.

Managing Organizational Conflict

Conflicts take many forms in organizations. There are the inevitable clashes between formal authority and power, differences over how resources should be allocated, how the work should be done, including jurisdictional disagreements among individuals and departments. These include subtler forms of conflict involving rivalries, jealousies, personality clashes, and struggles for power and favor. Organizational conflict, though, is not all bad. It can be positive and seen as a constructive learning experience that creates involvement and positive relationships that lead to improved communication and problem solving. Yet it can also be a destructive force that diverts energy from tasks and widens differences, creating irresponsible behavior and lower morale, with reduced commitment and productivity.

There are several sources or types of conflict:

- *Relationship conflicts:* strong negative emotions, misperceptions or stereotypes, poor communication, or repeated negative behaviors.
- *Data Conflicts:* lack of information needed to make wise decisions; misinterpretations; competing assessment procedures.
- *Interest conflicts:* competition over perceived incompatible needs; the belief that in order to satisfy one's needs, the needs of another must be sacrificed.
- *Structural conflicts:* caused by external forces such as geographic constraints, time, and organizational change.
- *Value conflicts:* perceived or actual incompatible value or belief systems.

The model of conflict is adapted from the work of Thomas Killmann (Kilmann & Killmann, 2004). It is used to assess an individual's or group's style in conflict situations when the concerns of the parties appear to be incompatible. In such situations, we can describe behavior along two basic dimensions: (1) assertiveness, the extent to which the individual or group attempts to satisfy their own concerns, and (2) cooperativeness, the extent to which the individual or group attempts to satisfy the other party's concerns. These two basic dimensions can be combined to define five specific methods or styles of dealing with conflict:

Accommodating Style (I Lose, You Win): putting aside your needs and desires and acquiescing to the other person's requests or demands. This style is appropriate when a high value is placed on the relationship with the other party or when the outcome is of low importance to the specific individual but is of high importance to the other party.

Avoid (I Lose, You Lose): sidestepping or withdrawing from the conflict situation. This style can be appropriate when emotions are high. However, when a conflict is prevented or postponed, it remains unresolved and neither party wins.

Compromise (We Both Win, We Both Lose): Resolving the conflict by seeking a fair and equitable split between the two positions. Each side concedes on some issues in order to win others. This style is often appropriate when two parties with equal power are strongly committed to mutually exclusive goals and there is a need to achieve temporary settlement of a complex issue, or when there is time pressure.

Compete (I Win, You Lose): Seeking to win the one's position at the expense of the other party losing theirs. This style is appropriate when only one party can achieve their desired outcome. It is best used when there is little time for collaboration or the outcome is extremely important and the relationship between the parties is of low importance.

Collaboration (I Win, You Win): cooperating to find an integrative solution that satisfies both party's concerns when they are too important to be compromised. This style is appropriate when there is a need to join with the other party to compete against the situation, issue, or problem instead of against each other. Each side must feel that the outcomes gained through collaboration are better than they could achieve on their own.

People learn their approach to dealing with conflict based on their early-childhood experiences with their family. Some children grow up in families and seldom hear their parents speak a cross word. Others grow up in families where it's world war at the dinner table most nights. Although it is most effective to be able to draw on all five styles depending on the situation, by adulthood most people learn to depend on one or two of the conflict styles if faced with conflict. And all five styles have disadvantages if relied upon too much or too little. For example, one who is overly completive will try to dominate others and tend to surround himself with "yes" people and have subordinates who are afraid to admit or point out mistakes. Conversely, people who will not compete or be forceful in asserting their interests often feel powerless in situations and have trouble taking a firm stand.

Those who are over-accommodating feel that their ideas and concerns are not getting the attention they deserve. Individuals who are low on accommodation have trouble building goodwill with others, are often regarded as unreasonable, and have trouble giving up and admitting they are wrong. Over-avoiders have trouble giving input on important issues and often feel they are overwhelmed with problems that never get resolved. People who do not avoid conflict when it's appropriate find themselves hurting others' feelings and stirring up hostilities and drama. Those who compromise too quickly give up on satisfying their concerns too rapidly and may be more intrigued with the gamesmanship inherent in bargaining and trading in compromise. People who are not willing to compromise find it hard to make concessions and may have trouble gracefully exiting from destructive arguments and power struggles. Over-collaborators want to make sure everyone is included and may spend too much time and energy trying to get everyone's input or discussing issues in depth that do not deserve it. Under-collaborators find it hard to explore or seek to understand differences that offer opportunities to learn and solve problems for joint gain.

Implementing this organizational development intervention first requires that team members or individuals assess and understand their conflict style and grasp the conditions or circumstances in which a certain style is appropriate. Team leaders then model an ongoing process whereby conflict situations are acknowledged and team members are encouraged to engage in dialogue about the conflict process and how to best resolve it.

Collaborative, Consensus-Based Decision Making

The fundamental building block of a learning organization is an empowered team that encourages constructive conflict as key to effective decision making. Conflict resolution can often be achieved through a collaborative process of problem solving and the willingness of the individuals to trust one another, openly explore issues and alternatives, and actively listen to one another. For important issues, the collaborative style should be used first to attempt to generate a consensus decision that people are committed to implement. This is because initially resorting to win-lose and lose-lose methods of managing conflict creates a clear "we-they" distinction between the parties rather than a "we versus the problem" orientation. In win-lose and lose-lose conflict, energies are directed to the other party in an atmosphere of victory and defeat, and each party sees the issue only from their own point of view rather than defining the problem in terms of mutual needs.

The process of collaborative, consensus-based decision making is depicted in Figure 7.2. The initial focus is on common ends or goals rather than differences, with emphasis on addressing the issue rather than defeating the other party. Consensus is not unanimity but rather a situation where each party is open-minded, honest in sharing facts and opinions, and willing to participate responsibly to satisfy both their and the other party's needs. By definition, once a consensus decision is reached, all parties support the decision and will actively work to implement it.

The first step in the collaborative process is to review the actual conditions that exist, related to the conflict itself, its context, and the history and current state of the parties' relationship. The key is to encourage trust and the honesty, open-mindedness, and willingness to share information that has been hoarded or distorted for the advantage of some group members. Another step in the process is to do a reality test of the parties' perceptions of themselves and the other party.

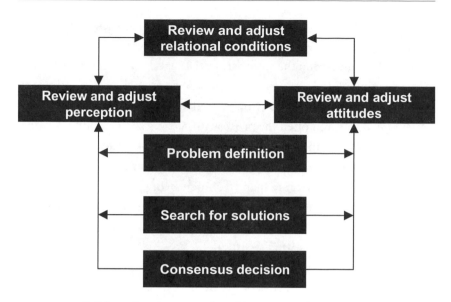

FIGURE 7.2 Collaborative, Consensus-based Decision Making Process
Source: International Institute for Spiritual Leadership

The attitudes and perceptions of the parties form a screen through which information about conditions or attributes of the parties is distorted. If the review and adjustment of relational conditions, perceptions and attitudes to foster a climate of trust is not successful, it may be better to use some other conflict style to make the decision.

For collaborative problem solving to take place, the ends or goals of the parties must be identified. They may have different goals, but each party must accept the stated goals of the other and not consider the problem solved until a solution is found that is acceptable to both parties. It is important to recognize that not all problems can be resolved through collaboration. Some issues, for example, involve fixed resources that must be divided between the parties. Then one party's gain is at a cost to the other party. In such situations the best solution is one that is considered fair by both parties. The key is to take collaboration as far as possible, then resort to the other conflict styles if consensus is not possible.

Parties that have issues are responsible for defining their needs. However, anyone may have a high-quality, highly acceptable alternative or solution. For this reason the emphasis in the search for solutions is to generate as many solutions as possible without first judging or evaluating any particular one. This key step is often neglected and leads to suboptimal decision making. Too often the process unfolds by sequentially offering a solution and evaluating it before considering other solutions. The alternatives should be evaluated only after an acceptable set of feasible solutions has been generated. There are many techniques for preventing this, including brainstorming, discussion groups, surveys, and the nominal group (decision making method for use among groups) and Delphi techniques (a structured communication technique).

Evaluation of all viable solutions and arrival at a consensus decision that is acceptable to all parties is the final step in the collaborative process. Consensus is based on the principle that every voice is worth hearing and every concern is justified. If a solution makes a few people, even one person, deeply unhappy, and there is a valid reason for that unhappiness, and if it is ignored, then acceptance and the implementation of the decision will suffer. There may be the need for a person, who can be a team member, to serve as a process facilitator. The facilitator observes the process of the meeting to keep the meeting focused and moving. Commonly people will drift off the subject under discussion and begin talking about something else. The facilitator reminds them what the subject is, and if necessary arranges for later discussion of new issues raised ("Introduction to Consensus Decision-Making" n.d.).

Managing and Overcoming Resistance to Change

The one constant in the twenty-first-century global, Internet age is change. Rapid social, economic, and technological external change calls for similar internal organizational changes to meet these external challenges. Jack Welch, the former long-time chairman and CEO of General Electric, was famous for his saying that the end was in sight for an organization when the rate of change outside exceeds the rate of change inside. One of the biggest problems facing today's organizations is the failure to adapt to rapid environmental change. Although there are many reasons for the failure to change and adapt, there is little doubt that effective leadership is necessary to keep change efforts moving forward. Leaders must serve as the main role model for change and provide the vision, values, and motivation to facilitate change in followers and help their organizations adapt to external threats and new opportunities.

The Stool of Change

We have found the idea of the "Stool of Change" as illustrated in Figure 7.3 to be useful to help organizations understand how change happens. The idea is that change will not take place unless all three legs of the stool are in place. The stool also recognizes that organizational change is both a top-down and a bottom-up process. First is the need for top management support. This requires a compelling vision that establishes a sense of urgency and is communicated widely throughout the organization. The vision helps to establish a perceived need to change in other leaders, followers, and stakeholders. There is also the requirement to find an idea and a set of strategies that fits the need.

For the change process to succeed there must be a shared commitment to empower employees and change teams throughout the organization to act on the vision for change. This means using the tools for managing conflict and collaborative, consensus-based decision making while giving employees the knowledge, resources, and discretion to make things happen as they generate short-term wins. Major changes take time. Leaders should plan initially for relatively easy performance improvements, enable them to happen, and hold celebrations to broadcast these achievements. A change effort loses momentum if there are no short-term accomplishments that employees can recognize and celebrate. Breaking the change effort into a series of identifiable steps allows for change agents to make adjustments as the change progresses, as well as bring along hesitant employees who become willing to show support once there appears to be a chance of success.

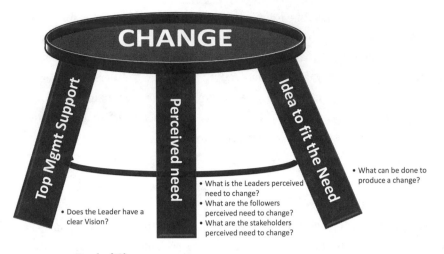

FIGURE 7.3 Stool of Change
Source: International Institute for Spiritual Leadership

Overcoming Resistance to Change

In addition, many good ideas are never implemented due to failure to anticipate or prepare for resistance to change because, no matter how good the idea, its implementation will conflict with some party's interest and jeopardize current alliances in the organization. These conflicts, threats, and potential losses require strategies to increase the probability of a successful change transition. Creating such strategies calls for widespread communication, participation, involvement, and training (as in the interventions we cover here) to help employees understand and cope with their role in the change process. Perhaps the best strategy for overcoming resistance is to make sure the change meets a real need; the process of overcoming resistance to change requires that the change be good for those who have to implement it.

Another effective weapon in the battle to overcome resistance to change is a volunteer idea champion who is deeply committed to the change. An idea champion helps keep up and sustain the sense of urgency, building on the credibility and momentum of the short-term wins to tackle bigger problems. The idea champion has the courage and perseverance to instill in people the energy and power to take on more difficult issues.

They see to the technical aspects of changing systems, structures, and policies, including hiring and promoting people who can best implement the vision and making sure employees have the time, resources, and authority they need to pursue the vision.

Aligning Organization Design Variables

The organization will then need to focus on aligning key organizational design variables to implement any changes. A model for organizational design that is adapted from Jay Galbraith's work is given in Figure 7.4 (Galbraith 2007). The basic idea behind organizational design is that there are several key variables—structure, task, information technology, people, and reward systems—that must fit or be in alignment for an organization to implement its vision, values, goals, and strategies. A change in any one of the design variables will call for adjustments in the others; they all must form an integrated whole or system. The values that comprise the organization's culture form the glue that holds the system together.

For example, the bureaucratic and learning organizational paradigms require different organizational designs for organizational effectiveness. Bureaucratic designs use highly centralized, formalized, and standardized structures to organize highly routine tasks with centralized, highly restricted information systems. The employees are tightly controlled, easily replaceable people who require minimum training and are primarily led by means of a command-and-control leadership style, often controlled through the production technology, and motivated through extrinsic rewards. Successful bureaucratic cultures tend to be performance-driven and customer-oriented but often at the expense of care and well-being of their employees. There are numerous profitable examples of these organizations, including food franchises (such as McDonalds) and retail outlets (such as Walmart).

In contrast, learning organizational designs are decentralized and much less formalized and standardized; tasks are performed by empowered teams using information systems that are accessible to anyone in the organization with a need to know. Employees are recruited and selected

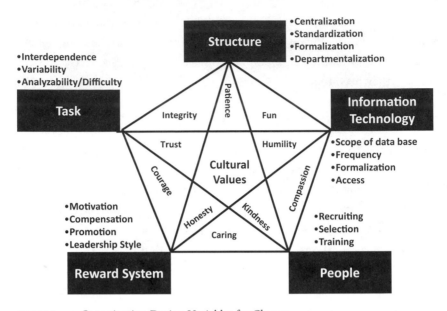

FIGURE 7.4 Organization Design Variables for Change
Source: International Institute for Spiritual Leadership

based on how well their values fit the organization's values; they are highly trained and work in an empowered team environment. Learning organizations based on organizational spiritual leadership include those discussed earlier (including Tomasso Corporation, Interstate Batteries, and Maxwell, Locke, and Ritter LLP) as well as some companies that have the characteristics of a learning organization but don't expressly embrace spiritual leadership (including Procter & Gamble).

Ultimately, change is fully accepted and implemented when it is steeped in the organization's culture and becomes "the way we do things around here." Until the new behaviors are rooted in social norms and shared values, the organization will digress as soon as the pressure for change is removed. This stage requires that leaders make a conscious attempt to communicate how the new approaches, behaviors, and attitudes have improved organizational performance. It also requires that the people and reward-system design variables are adjusted so that the next generation of leaders really reflects the new order. This is where many, if not most, organizational change efforts fail. If, for example, an organization must change its emphasis from engineering off-the-shelf products to providing and implementing customer's system solutions to survive, it must change from an engineering-driven to a marketing-driven culture. If, however, the reward and promotion systems still reward and promote successful engineers rather than successful marketers into leadership positions, the change won't stick.

Overcoming Anger, Resentment, Worry, and Fear Through Forgiveness, Acceptance, and Gratitude

One of the consequences of organizational and personal conflicts is the stimulation of the destructive emotions of anger, resentment, worry, and fear. All of us are aware that the workplace is not devoid of emotions and that people don't just check their feelings at the door. Organizational development interventions can target and alleviate these emotions by focusing on the spiritual values of forgiveness, acceptance, and gratitude.

Anger and Resentment

Anger is the emotional response to a real or perceived injustice. We feel angry when we do not receive what we think is fair or just, what "should have been." According to a Yale School of Management Study, *The Experience of Anger at Work: Lessons from the Chronically Angry*, anger at work is most commonly caused by the actions of supervisors or managers (Gibson & Barsade, 1999). Other major causes for workplace anger include other coworkers or employees, others not being productive on the job, and tight deadlines or a heavy workload. Employees also may have deep-seated feelings of hostility toward others because of their gender, ethnicity, sexual orientation, political beliefs, religion, or other factors. In addition, the threat of downsizing and layoffs, coupled with having to do more with less and knowing you could lose your job tomorrow, no matter how productive you are, creates an ongoing climate that facilitates anger (Gibson & Barsade, 1999).

Anger in general is a mixed blessing and, as with all emotions, can be healthy to the extent that it is expressed and channeled so that one is not ruled by it. However, people who bottle the anxiety, anger, fear, guilt, or pain that is generated by a major loss or conflict pay a huge price. Those who suppress or try not to feel their emotions start to somatize; they begin to get such physical symptoms as headaches, migraines, and high blood pressure. And the cost to both the organization and its employees can be great even when anger does not result in overt aggression. Anger can also lead to damaged interpersonal relationships and poor communication that can be very costly in terms of low organizational commitment and productivity and high employee absenteeism and turnover. Failing to deal with workplace hostilities can also have legal consequences for organizations that do not adequately insure their employees' health, safety, and welfare in dealing with excessive and potentially violent people. We seem to be confronted frequently with stories of workers "going postal" and taking aggressive and often violent actions due to some perceived wrong, particularly against superiors.

Resentment is a negative combination of thoughts, emotions, and actions resulting from unresolved anger. Ongoing resentment is emotionally debilitating and can produce touchiness or edginess, denial of anger or hatred, and provocation or anger arousal when thinking of the resented person or when the person is present. Resentment can also lead to severe long-term effects, such as the development of hostile, cynical, sarcastic attitudes, lack of personal and emotional growth, difficulty in self-disclosure, trouble trusting others, and loss of self-confidence.

Worry and Fear

Fear is an unpleasant, sometimes strong emotion caused by anticipation or awareness of being threatened in some way (not necessarily physically) and is often accompanied by a sense of anxious concern or anticipation of loss. Anger is born out of fear as a result of a sense of inadequacy and/ or anticipation of loss; often those who act out their insecurities in anger are the most fearful. Therefore, fear and anger work together; fear is the catalyst that fuels anger and anger is a primary sign of fear.

Worry is a form of persistent fear that adds anticipation, memory, imagination, and emotion to the feared event, circumstance, or situation. It manifests as a troubled state of mind that has no peace and experiences anxiety, uneasiness, and stress. For many people, fear and worry seem a normal way of life. People worry about their job security or about being attacked and criticized by coworkers and/or superiors. These fears fuel further worry about not getting that desired raise or promotion or failing because of having too many responsibilities. Many employees are afraid to present their ideas or opinion before a group for fear of being ridiculed even though they know someone else may present the same idea and get credit for it.

Worry and fear in the workplace hinder personal, team, and organizational effectiveness. Fears keep people from taking risks and doing their best in challenging and changing the status quo. Fear creates an atmosphere of powerlessness that diminishes employee confidence, commitment, enthusiasm, imagination, and motivation. Most damaging is that workplace fear can weaken or destroy trust and the open communication that goes with it. When people are afraid to speak up, important issues are suppressed and problems are not solved effectively. Leaders do not get accurate feedback when fear is high, which distorts the reality of a situation and denies the opportunity for effective conflict management and collaborative, consensus-based decision making.

The Spiritual Aspects of Anger, Resentment, Worry, and Fear

A person experiencing anger, resentment, worry, and/or fear has a troubled mind that is not at peace. Often an organization's vision, cultural values, and organization design creates a context that produces and reinforces these toxic emotions. Not only does this negatively affect employee well-being, it also wastes untold amounts of energy, effort, and money, which is detrimental to organizational effectiveness. It is therefore important for companies to have a vested interest in identifying conditions that precipitate these emotions and implement organizational development strategies and interventions to help alleviate them.

To cast out anger, resentment, fear, and worry one must first get past the ego, develop mindful awareness, escape the tyranny of the past and future, and become present. Ultimately, dealing with anger, resentment, worry, and fear is an individual matter. Only the person experiencing these emotions can make the decision to do the work necessary to over-come these toxic emotions and seek the peace of mind that is the source of joy and serenity. If this is true, then the question becomes "What can an organization and its leaders do to establish, facilitate, and reinforce a workforce that is conscious and present from moment to moment?" The answer is that an organization can, through its recruitment, selection, training, and organizational development processes, create a context that raises the level of employee awareness of these issues. This makes it more likely people will become honest, open-minded, and willing enough to take what is, in effect, the beginning of the spiritual journey to the Level III Way of Knowing and Being that we described in Chapter 3.

Although there is a large and growing industry comprised of consul-tants and firms whose aim is to help companies stop or prevent workplace hostility and anger, few of these recognize or attempt to address the spiri-tual issues that underlie these emotions. Nor do they also address the fears and worries that are often the source of anger. The end result with these approaches is that—no matter how sophisticated the technique or how supportive the organization or group—the undetected anger, resent-ment, worry, and fear remain under the surface, masquerading behind a dozen different masks. Ultimately, those emotions toxify every relation-ship they touch to the detriment of the organization and the parties involved.

The Healing Effects of Forgiveness, Acceptance, and Gratitude
While forgiveness, acceptance, and gratitude were discussed in detail in Chapter 4, it is important to understand the role they also play in healing organizations.

Through forgiveness, we reframe our view of the offense so that the thoughts and feelings related to the transgression are transformed from negative to neutral or positive. This frees us from the bondage of anger and resentment. Only then can we become more productive, relate to co-workers in a positive manner, and become able to develop and implement the skills necessary for effective conflict management and collaborative, consensus-based problem solving. Through forgiveness we are also more proficient at generating creative alternative solutions to problems and implementing those solutions.

Acceptance embraces all things, good and bad, as they are in the moment without denying their full reality. It views everything as a gift, which allows us to draw strength from a higher power, be peaceful in the moment, and have a sense of what can be improved or changed and what can't.

Gratitude provides meaning in life by embracing life in the now or present as the ultimate gift. A grateful focus also helps us confront and find the strength to overcome worry and fear over future challenges. When we have truly accepted ourselves and our situation fully as it is in the present moment, we give thanks for all we've received, no matter what it might be.

Acceptance and gratitude stimulate moral behavior that is motivated out of concern for others, reinforce a culture that can improve worker well-being, lower toxic emotions in the workplace, and provide a starting point for the transformation necessary for forgiveness. Acceptance and gratitude also work to improve performance, commitment, and organizational citizenship behaviors.

Interventions for Forgiveness, Acceptance, and Gratitude

If the Spiritual Leadership Survey reveals that there are problems with employee anger, resentment, worry, and fear, the organization may need to emphasize interventions that target the cultural values of forgiveness, acceptance, and gratitude.

Chapter 3, on the spiritual journey with its levels of knowing and being and the organization's Three-fold Path of Spiritual Transformation, provides models and tools for training that both leaders and employees can draw upon to become free of anger, resentment, worry, and fear. In addition, most of the practices outlined in Chapter 1 can be useful. Interventions that focus on specific leadership and management activities that reinforce the values of altruistic love and, in particular, forgiveness, acceptance, and gratitude include:

- A room for inner silence.
- Testimonial meetings.
- Meetings between three people and a high-ranking manager.

- Meetings with laid-off or dismissed employees.
- Shared community meals where management serves the meal and eats after everyone else.
- A gesture where people are called on to contribute and share with others.
- The annual one-on-one personal conversation.
- A dinner for four and pre-hiring interviews.
- A moment of silence during meetings.
- A shared bonus.
- Spiritual support groups (for example, prayer groups or sacred text study groups).
- A personal days policy that includes paid days off for spiritual re-charging.
- Creating an employee advocacy group within the organization to sustain openness and provide a discussion forum for workplace spirituality issues.
- Access to a nondenominational, on-demand chaplain who offers support, in person or via phone, to employees during emotionally or spiritually trying times. ("Our Project: Reconciliation of Human Well-being with Productiviy and Profits," n.d.)

These are just few of the many interventions available to help overcome anger, resentment, worry, and fear through forgiveness, acceptance, and gratitude.

Necessary Conditions for Implementing Organizational Spiritual Leadership

Finally, in order for organizational spiritual leadership to be implemented, it is necessary to follow a few underlying principles.

Competitive Working Conditions

Any talk of spiritual leadership and workplace spirituality has little chance of being heard by the workers if their salaries barely allow for a decent family life while the owners and leaders live in abundance. Working conditions within the organization must be competitive with those in the market in which it is operating. It goes without saying that the company itself must be competitive and successful enough to be able to pay for the working conditions that have been aligned with those of the market. Competitive working conditions reinforce the vision and values of organizational spiritual leadership.

The Primacy of People and Human Well-being

An assumption of the Spiritual Leadership Model is that the organization exists to serve people and not to make people serve it. Therefore human beings are more than human capital or human resources. Organizational spiritual leadership recognizes that spirituality is important for both the individual and the organization. Reconciling spirituality and daily life is just as possible for an organization as it is for people; the same tensions are present in both. The primacy of people is essential to implementing workplace spirituality in the day-to-day activities of work. Implementing workplace spirituality through organizational spiritual leadership contributes to the importance given to humans, but the two must be present: the primacy of people along with competitive performance.

Freedom

Implementing organizational spiritual leadership must be carried out by respecting individual and collective freedom. Top leadership proposes spiritual activities, but the spiritual values in each person vary, and people must be free to participate or not. However, the leadership team must first create favorable conditions so that the employees are able to participate in the activities, and it must invite the employees to participate in them. One of these conditions requires that workers be paid during their participation in these activities because they are organizational development interventions.

Costs Versus Benefits

While data is still limited, Robert Ouimet of Cordon Bleu-Tomasso reports that the cost of the activities represent less than one half of 1 percent of sales if the time needed for managers to organize and operate them is counted. This cost is quite reasonable because when people feel their work

contributes to their development and they are treated with love and respect and feel understood and appreciated in a climate of discipline and
rigorous planning, it's not only teamwork and motivation that increase but
also creativity in terms of new ideas, products, and services. Economic
competitiveness also increases when people feel they are making a difference and their life has meaning in service to key stakeholders. It is above
all a question of balance because when people invest in their spiritual lives
they live more serenely with themselves and the people around them.

Recruiting

It is important to recruit people who will not only be at ease with the
spiritual orientation of the organization but who can also contribute to
its success. In addition to technical and professional competence, candi-
dates should aspire to serve others through the values of altruistic love.
Careful recruiting makes it possible to ensure a certain homogeneity of
values in the organization without being unfair to anyone, and thus
to respect everyone's freedom. Recruitment must aim at hiring people
who will be active in embracing organizational spiritual leadership and
who also will be highly effective and productive in their own daily work.
Jim Collins in *Good to Great* describes this process as first getting the
right people on the bus (and the wrong people off) and then worrying
about where to drive it. In doing so, top leaders place greater weight on
ethical thinking, integrity, the quality of a person's character, and their
fit with the vision and values of the organization rather than focusing on
a person's educational background, managerial competencies, expertise
or work experience (Collins J. , 2001).

Strong Top Leadership Team Personal
Spiritual Leadership.

Since an organization or business is a structured whole in which each person has a role, the top leadership team must show strong personal spiritual
leadership if they want to implement spiritual leadership throughout their
organization. In doing so, they must authentically live their spirituality
on a day-to-day basis, not only in word but also in deed. This is why the
top leadership team and progressively all levels of leadership must be in-

tensely interested in the importance of spirituality in their lives and in the day-to-day running of the workplace. They must increasingly implement the tools that make it possible to foster organizational spiritual leadership and workplace spirituality, all of which contribute to human development, corporate social responsibility, and financial performance—the Triple Bottom Line.

TRANSFORMING PUBLIC SCHOOLS THROUGH SPIRITUAL LEADERSHIP

Here we report a study based on research conducted to measure the effects of implementing organizational spiritual leadership. Although this is a study of a public, nonprofit organization, the methods and tools we used here can be applied to any organization, whether public, private, profit, or nonprofit.

The study was funded by the Texas A&M University's Regent Initiative to examine issues regarding teacher retention, identify ways to retain qualified teachers, and stem the growing tide of teacher turnover in public schools. The research was a response to the increasing criticism of deterioration and decay throughout the U.S. public education system. Especially alarming is the growing difficulty schools face in filling their annual quota of new recruits and the mass exodus of early and mid-career teachers. Recent statistics show that between 40 percent and 50 percent of newly certified teachers leave the profession within five years. In Texas there is no shortage of certified teachers; but there is a shortage of certified teachers *who are willing to teach*. A major reason for this is the intense stakeholder pressure to make sure students are taught in a way that ensures they will pass achievement exams like the State of Texas Assessment of Academic Readiness (STAAR) test.

The challenge in today's educational process is to develop an educational delivery system model that encompasses the fluid aspects of society that schools encounter while producing achievement results certified by the public sector. A major challenge for public education is to create an organizational paradigm in which the teacher's professional commitment is translated into organizational commitment and productivity. Public school leaders are challenged with reestablishing throughout the ranks the role of intrinsically motivated professional educators who are esteemed for educating our children.

Overwhelmingly, public schools rely on bureaucracy as a dominant paradigm, with its excessive reliance on standardized curriculums and externally imposed standardized testing to measure, sort, and rank schools and children. Increasing pressure for higher test scores is found at the local, state, and national levels. Opponents of this accountability system argue that mandated continuous improvement and required scores for campus accountability ratings drive the educational system without regard to the needs of students in the formulation of skills and resources critical to perpetuating a connected, caring, and loving society of people. More and more it appears that the field of education should adopt the learning organizational paradigm—a paradigm that, we argue, requires organizational spiritual leadership.

The purpose of the research was to determine if there is a relationship between the qualities of organizational spiritual leadership and teacher commitment and productivity. A one-year field experiment was conducted with two elementary schools using the organizational Spiritual Leadership Survey and a vision/stakeholder effectiveness analysis intervention performed in one school, with the other school acting as a control. Based on the Spiritual Leadership Survey, target issues for improvement were identified and organizational development strategies and interventions were implemented to apply techniques and technologies for change.

The two schools selected for the experiment were both elementary schools (pre- kindergarten to third grade). They were adjacent to one another geographically and were similar in terms of size and teacher, student, and parent demographics. Both schools took the organizational Spiritual Leadership Survey at the end of the 2001 and 2002 school years (in this study we did not measure inner life and life satisfaction). The survey has a five-point response scale with 1.0 representing "strongly disagree" and 5.0 representing "strongly agree." Averages on the seven organizational Spiritual Leadership Survey measures (vision, altruistic love, hope/faith, meaning/calling, membership, organizational commitment, and productivity) can range from 1.0 to 5.0.

Ideally an organization would want the responses on all of the variables to average over 4.0 ("agree" to "strongly agree"). Our extensive experience with this survey has shown that averages in the mid-3 range indicate areas that can be improved through organizational development interventions. Averages below 3.0 indicate an organization in crisis and in need of organizational transformation. Initial survey results revealed that both schools had averages over 4.0 for hope/faith, meaning/calling, and productivity. School one also had averages over 4.0 for vision and membership. The main organizational outcome variable of interest for this study was organizational commitment; past research suggests that increased organizational commitment strengthens motivation and reduces turnover. The averages for organizational commitment for schools one and two were 3.5 and 3.4, respectively. Overall both schools showed evidence of organizational spiritual leadership but with the need for improvement, especially in the area of altruistic love.

Next a vision/stakeholder effectiveness analysis was conducted with school one's site-based decision committee (SBDM). This is a top leadership team that all schools in the district were required to have to serve as advisers to the school principal and their key administrators. After training on the use of the organizational Spiritual Leadership Model, the Spiritual Leadership Survey, and the vision/stakeholder effectiveness analysis process, the eighteen SBDM participants completed the initial draft—a process that usually takes two to three two- to three-hour sessions. This analysis was then shared at the grade level, where it and the initial spiritual leadership survey results served as input for top-down/bottom-up dialogue that produced the final draft of school one's vision/stakeholder effectiveness analysis, as laid out below.

School One Vision/Stakeholder Effectiveness Analysis

Vision: To educate all children, without exception, to become successful citizens ready for the world. *Motto:* We light the Lamp Within.

Purpose: To provide healthy experiences that foster emotional, social, physical, and academic growth of the whole child.

Mission: School One's empowered team of skilled teachers and staff, with the meaningful involvement of parents and community partners, educates students in a safe, clean, caring, and fun environment that celebrates the noble effort.

Values: These values reflect how we seek to relate to students, parents, teachers, school staff, district, school Board, and community partners

- *Compassion.* Serving and accepting others to become successful citizens ready for the world.

- *Integrity.* Conducting ourselves in an ethical and respectful manner.

- *Excellence.* Meeting the needs and striving to exceed the expectations of those we serve through continuous innovation and improvement.

- *Courage.* The willingness to test/explore unproven or established solutions and face challenges.

- *Fun.* Instilling the joy of learning and celebrating creativity and accomplishments.

Stakeholder Effectiveness Criteria

Students (Low Power/High Importance). Learning as fun. Caring teachers and staff, good school supplies and equipment, fun after-school programs, and a clean and safe environment.

Parents (High Power/High Importance). Quality education, qualified and caring teachers, well-equipped learning environment, clean and safe environment. Feel welcome. Individual attention. *Issue:* Need more information from them (for example, attitude survey; comparison between computer-literate versus non-computer-literate parents).

Teachers (High Power/High Importance). Parental training and support, better disciplined parents and students, uninterrupted teaching time, time for interaction and collaboration, resources for changing curriculum , administrative support in setting priorities, adequate equipment and supplies, and a safe environment.

Issues: (1) What we're doing is not enough. (2) Lack of celebration and cross-grade collaboration. (3) Focus on negative, not positive. (4) Kindergarten—involve in scheduling aides. (5) Specialists—feel isolated (no e-mail). (6) 1st Grade—no time for interaction or team collaboration. (7) Better parent feedback on TAKS Report Categories not measurable. (8) Input on evaluation of Administration/Staff (360 feedback). (9) Need help with parent orientation, parenting skills, health and nutrition, counseling, and after-school tutoring.

School District (High Power/Low Importance). Acceptable TAAS Scores. Teach TEKS. Comply with OASIS System. Implement emotional Intelligence training and culture. *Issues:* (1) Handling ever-increasing requirements, especially TAAS test, as it adversely affects school culture and teacher and student well-being. (2) No assessment or placing in a lower priority of current programs before they are replaced

Staff (High Power/High Importance). Administration: Meet paperwork deadlines. Communicate student issues. Support: Be polite and civil. Respect and recognize their contributions.

Input from all areas of the school operations is evident in the school vision, purpose, and mission statements. For example, during the creation of the school mission statement the custodial staff requested that the word "clean" be inserted to accurately depict their contribution to the environment. They also chose to adopt a motto, "We light the lamp within." Mottos act as a lightning rod that signals to customers and clients what they should expect as well as to employees the product or service they should provide. The school also chose to include the word "empowered" in their mission statement, conscious of the commitment this required from the school's leaders.

For their cultural values, school leaders and employees decided to rank their stakeholders in order of importance and acknowledge that these values form the foundation for their relationship with them. The specific values (compassion, integrity, excellence, courage, fun) were chosen as best representing the values of altruistic love for their school.

School District Stakeholder

The vision/stakeholder effectiveness analysis brought to the surface a variety of issues for the parent, teacher, and school district stakeholders. The issues identified for the school district reinforce and support the idea that the school faces an onerous, overly bureaucratic district administration and that teachers are experiencing high levels of pressure to have their students pass the state-mandated achievement exams. The school teachers and staff felt that they were bombarded with requirements to continually impose new accountability programs from the ever-growing number of district superintendent administrators with little or no input and no relaxation of previous requirements or programs. In interviews, the teachers likened this to being a full glass of water that was under a running faucet. They also recognized that it was beyond their power to significantly address these issues.

Parent Stakeholder

The main issues within the school's power to address were better leadership and management of its parent stakeholder group. This emerged from dialogue with the teachers relative to their expectations, which included expectations for better parental training, support, and discipline. Much of this was due to the fact that the two schools in the study had high percentages of Title 1 students. Title 1 is a federally funded program that provides supplemental funds to school districts to assist eligible public and private schools with the highest student concentrations of poverty to meet school educational goals. The realization emerged that there were two distinctly different parent subgroups based on this distinction. The parents of the Title 1 students on average had an eighth-grade education and were mostly computer illiterate. The remaining parents, on average, had a high school education with some college and were computer literate.

Title 1 parents included a high percentage of parents that were either teenagers, in jail, on parole or probation, or had problems with drugs and alcohol. It was not uncommon for their children not to have a permanent address due to the itinerant nature of the parent's lifestyle. Often these parents would use their children's names to get credit for basic services, like utilities, because they had no credit. Most important, the nature of the interactions with these parents tended to be more defensive and combative when they came to school to deal with an issue relating to their child. This group of parents also tended to have the attitude that it was the school's job to educate their children; they had little sense of the need to be actively involved in their child's education.

Based on this dialogue, it became clear that the school needed more information and special initiatives to deal with the parent stakeholder group. Several initiatives were developed, including a parent survey, a grade-specific parent information book that included the school's vision, purpose, and mission; values; and both student and parent expectations. Rather than one general school orientation where attendance was optional, mandatory parent-student orientations by grade were required at the beginning of the school year. The school also changed the process by which parents gained access to the teachers to deal with an issue. No longer could they go directly to the classroom and confront the teacher. Instead parents were required to first go to the office and have their issue evaluated. Then it was determined who was the person to best deal with the parent.

Teacher (Employee) Stakeholder

Another issue targeted for intervention was the teachers' expectations for more time for interaction, collaboration, and celebration. At the time, teachers had a forty-five-minute conference period organized by grade, which kept them from coming together across grades or as a school community during regular school hours. This led to a sense of isolation and frustration because it was difficult to raise and address issues that had school-wide or cross-grade implications. There was also a lack of opportunity to come together and celebrate achievements and accomplishments. The constant bombardment of new programs and the ongoing intense pressure to perform on the student achievement tests left the teachers and staff with an ongoing sense of "What we're doing is not enough." The top leadership team decided to address this issue by scheduling school-sponsored "away days" two afternoons a month for all students. This time was used to address issues and/or come together to socialize and celebrate as a school community.

The planning for these interventions took place during the 2001 summer break, and the organizational development interventions were implemented at the beginning of the next school year. The final survey was administered in May 2002 to both schools. Summaries of our results are given in Figure 7.5, which was used as feedback to the survey respondents, the two school principals, and the school district superintendent. Inner life and life satisfaction organizational spiritual leadership variables were not measured in this study.

The bar graphs depict the dispersion for the seven spiritual leadership variables for the initial and final survey for each school. Survey responses that average between 1.00 and 2.99 represent "disagree"; "neither" is an average scale value between 3 and 3.99; and "agree" average scale values are between 4.00 and 5.00. Ideally organizations would want all their employees to have high average scale scores (above 4) and report high (above 60 percent) percentage levels of "agree" for all variables. Moderate or low levels of averages and percent agreement on the variables indicate areas for possible organizational development or transformation intervention. The labels under the bar graphs indicate the initial and final averages; an asterisk denotes that the averages are statistically significantly different.

In field experiments, control groups are used to further validate that an organizational development intervention or experiment is statistically significant. Unfortunately, conditions deteriorated dramatically at school two, thereby limiting its usefulness as a control for our field experiment study. However, these results do illustrate the discriminate validity of our Spiritual Leadership Survey—that it can indeed pick up or measure differences in organizational spiritual leadership. Initially vision and altruistic love were significantly lower at school two relative to school one. The final survey revealed that all seven variables were significantly lower for school two. For school two, averages on all but altruistic love dropped significantly from the initial to the final survey. Even for altruistic love the percentage of respondents agreeing that the organization showed care and

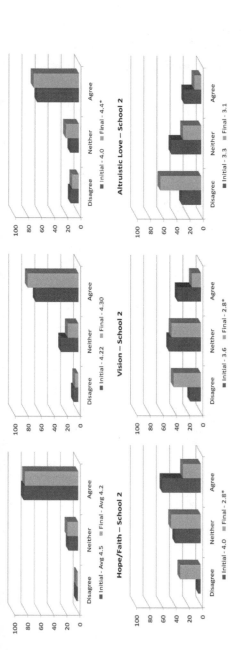

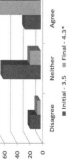

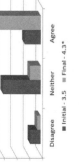

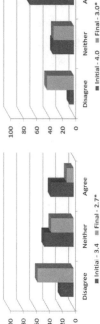

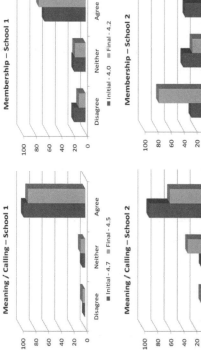

FIGURE 7.5 Field Experiment Results for Elementary School Study
Source: International Institute for Spiritual Leadership

concern for them dropped from 24 percent to 11 percent, while the percent of respondents disagreeing rose from 29 percent to 62 percent. For membership, the percentage agreement dropped to zero! In other words, no survey respondent agreed that they felt understood and appreciated at school two. Open-ended survey comments and personal interviews with people familiar with the situation at school two revealed that both leadership and personal issues between the administration and teachers had led to a very intimidating, hostile, and conflict-ridden environment during the period between the two surveys.

In contrast, the results of the second survey show school one to have high levels of organizational spiritual leadership and that the interventions significantly increased vision, altruistic love, and organizational commitment. There were no significant decreases in any of the variables. All variables had averages above 4.0, and agree responses ranged from 67 percent for productivity to 90 percent for calling. Vision increased significantly, from 4.0 to 4.4. Altruistic love significantly increased from a 3.9 to 4.5. Most important, the average for organizational commitment rose significantly rose, from 3.5 to 4.3. The agree percentage for commitment also dramatically increased, from 25 percent to 78 percent, while the "neither" and "disagree" groups dropped 42 percent and 11 percent, respectively. This finding is especially encouraging since past research has clearly shown that increased organizational commitment strengthens motivation and reduces turnover—a major and ongoing problem in our public schools and the major variable of interest to the Texas A&M's Regent's Initiative group, which funded the study.

Ongoing Effects of Organizational Spiritual Leadership at School One

Events after the study reinforce our finding of high organizational commitment at school one. Teacher turnover dropped to almost zero after accounting for retirements and teachers leaving due to the necessity of a family move. The school found it had a waiting list of teachers who wanted to join the faculty and staff. Most telling were reports from interview teams set up by the principal who helped make new hire decisions. These teams were comprised of individuals who would work closely with the new individuals. They reported that the criteria they used was whether the person held the cultural values of the school and enthusiastically embraced the school's vision. This reflects our view that using employees as a central part of the interview process is a key strategy and is necessary to implement and sustain organizational spiritual leadership.

In terms of accountability and performance, the sustaining impact of organizational spiritual leadership at school one is evidenced in the 2002–2003 and 2003–2004 Academic Excellence Indicator System report required by the Texas Education Code as the accountability system at that time for public education in Texas. In May 2003 the Texas Assessment of Academic Skills (TAKS) in force at that time for school one revealed a significant increase over the 2002 scores in that 100 percent of the Hispanic population at the school passed both the reading and the math portions of the test. The Hispanic population accounted for 15.4 percent of the student population. The White population, which constituted 30.6 percent of the population, had a pass rate of 100 percent also in the areas of reading and math. African American students comprised 48.2 percent of the school population and posted a pass rate of 95.3 percent on the math test. The pass rate for African American students in the area of reading was 90.2 percent. These areas indicate a very high level of content mastery. An area of needed growth for 2002–2003 was economically disadvantaged students, of whom 66.2 percent passed the reading and math tests.

In May 2004 the results for school one continued to be strong, even though the standards for passing the TAKS test increased. No major changes in ethnic distribution of the student population occurred during this period. In math, the pass rate for the Hispanic student group was 97 percent, the White student group 100 percent, and the African American student group 88 percent. Reading scores were 90 percent or above in all three ethnic groups. A very large increase was achieved in economically disadvantaged students, with 88 percent passing the math test and 99 percent passing the reading test. This accountability data suggests that the time and energy invested in the spiritual leadership process through articulation of the campus mission, values, and stakeholder expectations, coupled with the organizational development intervention strategy to address parent and teacher stakeholder issues was worth the effort in terms of sustainable improvement.

Especially important was the commitment of the campus principal in this implementation process. The principal at school one was deeply committed to the spiritual principles that underlie the vision and values of organizational spiritual leadership. She stated, "Everything we did as a campus was a result of the campus vision and values, which was a direct result of our work with the spiritual leadership model." And "The vision and values we developed through the spiritual leadership process have endured and are still the foundation we rely on to guide our day-to-day activities."

CONCLUSION

The spiritual leadership implementation process is initiated and reinforced by periodically administering the organizational Spiritual Leadership Survey, which is used to measure and establish a baseline for the Spiritual Leadership Model. The survey results provide input for a vision/stakeholder effectiveness analysis to achieve consensus on the organization's vision, purpose, and mission; cultural values; stakeholder expectations; and the key issues that are within the power and influence of the organization to resolve. These issues are addressed by empowered teams, in which employees are provided with the knowledge, training, resources, and power to make the consequential decisions necessary to address the issues.

The teams and employees who are tasked with developing and implementing any initiative to tackle an issue may need to utilize organizational development models. As part of a standard employee development program to implement organizational spiritual leadership, training should be incorporated for four key organizational development interventions including managing conflict; collaborative decision making; managing change; and overcoming anger, resentment, and fear through forgiveness, acceptance, and gratitude. The focus of the training should be on learning and applying the organizational development models and interventions as they apply to an issue that was identified through the vision/stakeholder effectiveness analysis.

The school study is an example of how organizational spiritual leadership can be implemented. It illustrates how to use the Spiritual Leadership Survey to generate data for the subsequent vision/stakeholder effectiveness analysis. It also shows how the survey can be used for a comparative study of organizational units to further assess the effectiveness of any organizational development interventions.

Practical Tools

For those interested in maximize the Triple Bottom Line, the major tools introduced in this chapter include the following:

The **organizational Spiritual Leadership Survey** measures the variables in the organizational Spiritual Leadership Model to provide a baseline for the vision/stakeholder effectiveness analysis organizational analysis and subsequent organizational development interventions.

Vision/stakeholder effectiveness analysis defines a process for establishing and reinforcing the values, attitudes, and behaviors of organizational spiritual leadership, identifying key stakeholder issues, and generating an organization-wide dialogue concerning the appropriate goals and strategies to address these issues.

Organizational development and transformation interventions provide models, training, and methods for implementing organizational spiritual leadership and addressing the key issues identified thorough the Spiritual Leadership Survey and vision/stakeholder effectiveness analysis.

The **organization design model** identifies the key variables that must fit together or be aligned for an organization to implement organizational spiritual leadership.

Chapter Eight

SPIRITUAL LEADERSHIP: THE DRIVER OF THE TRIPLE BOTTOM LINE

For both public and private organizations, the global, Internet age has ushered in a new era of instant communication, transparency, and accountability. Companies are increasingly being held responsible not only for their own activities but also for the impact of these activities on key stakeholders, including employees, suppliers, customers, and the communities where they are located. Companies are being called to account not only by shareholders and investors who have a financial stake but also by politicians, whistleblowers, the media, employees, community groups, prosecutors, class action lawyers, environmentalists, and human rights organizations.

Moreover, since September 11, 2001, when homeland security became a top priority, the operating environment for CEOs has also fundamentally changed. National governments are increasing financial regulation in order to monitor flows of money that could be used to finance terrorist activity. Corporate scandals such as Enron and WorldCom and the more recent failures of Bear Stearns, Lehman Brothers, and AIG and the collapse of the world's financial markets, in which so many highly touted financial institutions proved worthless, have led to even more scrutiny and government oversight.

As a result, companies are being forced to respond to the human and social consequences of their actions. One example is Walmart, which is now grappling with the high cost of its relentless low-wage, efficiency-driven culture. When Sam Walton founded Walmart in the 1960s, one of his core values—respect—was based on the assumption that if you trusted employees with important information and decisions, provided ample opportunities for advancement, and tied their compensation to performance, they would repay the company with dedication and hard work (Daniels, 2003; Holt, 2004). For years this formula worked. Over the last several years, however, the relationship between Walmart's management and its employees has been strained due to a succession of lawsuits claiming that Walmart pressures hourly workers to work overtime without pay, systematically discriminates against women, and knowingly hires undocumented immigrant workers as janitors to get by with paying them less than minimum wage. Walmart claims that there could not be a systematic policy to get hourly workers to work without pay or to discriminate against women because these decisions are made at the store level and that it vigorously opposes and sanctions such actions. Critics concede this point. However, they argue that, although Walmart may not have such policies, its hard-driving, cost-containment culture, which is strongly supported by top management, has created an environment that can encourage and reward such abuses.

McDonald's is another American icon that has been forced to deal with both employee and social responsibility issues—the McJobs and obesity controversies. McDonald's has to face the fact that the people who comprise its key recruiting pool are increasingly reluctant to work for a company that treats them like cogs in a machine. A striking example of this is the slang term "McJob"; closely associated with McDonald's, it was recently added to both *Merriam-Webster's Collegiate Dictionary* and the *Oxford English Dictionary* as a legitimate word connoting a low-paying, low-prestige, dead-end, mindless service job in which an employee's work is highly routine, regulated, and micromanaged (Aldridge, 2006; Noe, 2006). McDonald's has tried to shore up its image in recent years by improving wages, adding employee benefits, and pointing out that many of its key top executives, including its CEO Jim Skinner, began their careers working in the restaurant's kitchen. McDonald's has also come under fire and been forced to respond to an increasingly health-conscious society. It has been subject to a lawsuit filed on behalf of several obese teenagers who claim the fast-food company is responsible for making them fat. Although dismissed, the case created much negative publicity and criticism that the company did not adequately provide information on the health risks associated with fast food, and that children developed health problems such as diabetes, high blood pressure, and obesity from eating its products. This negative publicity and resultant concerns about marketing fast food to children are cited as reasons the Walt Disney Company dissolved its ten-year promotional partnership with McDonald's ("McDonald's Targeted in Obesity Lawsuit" 2002). Both companies subsequently issued denials that the controversy and concerns were a factor in the decision to terminate their long-standing relationship. At the same time, McDonald's has responded with a more health-conscious menu and an expensive campaign to promote it. It has also contributed money to scientific studies on the causes of childhood obesity and type-2 diabetes.

The best-run companies are responding to such stakeholder concerns before they become targets of groups that have an environmental or social, rather than financial, stake in the firm's performance. Companies are discovering that outside stakeholders can be loyal, creative, and helpful business partners that help generate enormous financial benefits. These organizations cultivate relationships with key stakeholders, get lots of business ideas from outside the company, and use joint ventures at the local, regional, and global levels to bring them to fruition. For example, Procter & Gamble (P&G) is known for its emphasis on human resource development and employee well-being. Now the company is figuring out how to develop and sell products to the desperately poor in ways that lift them out of poverty. It has joined the Safe Water Drinking Alliance, self-described as a public-private collaboration whose goal is to help households in some of the world's poorest countries obtain a regular supply of safe drinking water. P&G's involvement is centered on its new water-purification product, PuR, which is economical and easy for poor people in the developing world to use. A powder that costs about 10 U.S. cents, that it yields clean safe drinking water for 10 liters (Berner, 2003). PuR is a product with a potentially enormous market that, from the perspective of social responsibility, places it far ahead of competitors. P&G also actively supports the Alliance's educational programs, which teach poor rural families about the importance of hygienic practices, such as washing hands with soap, in halting the spread of infectious diseases. P&G obviously stands to benefit financially from an emerging billion-person developing world market for its soap products.

This chapter builds upon the previous one, with its emphasis on stakeholder analysis and organizational spiritual leadership. We also bring together advances in performance measurement, balanced scorecards, and the sustainability movement to offer a Spiritual Leadership Balanced Scorecard Business Model that maximizes the Triple Bottom Line. First, we discuss developments in sustainability, conscious capitalism, and the Triple Bottom Line. Next, we cover the latest developments in measuring strategic performance and the Triple Bottom Line. Then we introduce the Spiritual Leadership Balanced Scorecard Business Model. Finally, we offer an illustrative case study of the Centre for Excellence in Leadership (CEL) as a real-world example of an organization that developed a business model to maximize the Triple Bottom Line through spiritual leadership.

THE CALL FOR SUSTAINABILITY, CONSCIOUS CAPITALISM, AND THE TRIPLE BOTTOM LINE

The sustainability movement has emerged in response to the excesses of CEO and corporate greed. Sustainability respects the interdependence of the organization with other elements of society and acknowledges the needs and interests of other key stakeholders. Sustainability respects the diversity of human experience, including family life, intellectual growth, artistic expression, and moral and spiritual development.

The only way for organizations to succeed in today's interdependent world is to embrace sustainability. This means operating a business that earns a profit while recognizing and supporting the economic and noneconomic needs of a wide range of stakeholders on whom the organization depends.

For several decades, companies emerging out of the culture of the 1960s have been emphasizing a new breed of capitalism that emphasizes sustainability. It is a capitalism that recognizes the power of purpose, the principle of interdependence, and the need to serve stakeholders other than investors and management. It is capitalism that sees leaders who act as stewards and facilitators as a source of empowerment. And it is a capitalism that embraces the co-creative and synergistic nature of businesses as living and learning systems, and is directed toward fulfilling the potential of business and the marketplace to be a powerful force for positive change. This is a Conscious Capitalism, embodied by Conscious Capitalists.

Perhaps the most organized movement working to promote Conscious Capitalism, worldwide sustainability, and the triple bottom line is the Conscious Business Alliance (CBA). The CBA is a select group of companies, organizations, and individuals dedicated to transforming the way business is conceived, conducted, and perceived. A division of Conscious Capitalism, Inc., co-founded by John Mackey and Michael Strong, CBA is dedicated to "liberating the entrepreneurial spirit for good." For CBA, to live consciously means to "be awake, mindful, and open to perceiving the world around and within us, to understand our circumstances, and to decide how to respond to them in ways that honor our needs, values, and goals."

A Conscious Business is built on three core principles:

Deeper purpose: Recognizing that every business has a deeper purpose than merely profit maximization, a Conscious Business is clear about and focused on fulfilling its deeper purpose.

Stakeholder model: A Conscious Business focuses on delivering value to all of its stakeholders and works to align and harmonize the interests of customers, employees, suppliers, investors, the community, and the environment to the greatest extent possible.

Conscious leadership: In a Conscious Business, management embodies conscious leadership and fosters it throughout the organization. Conscious leaders serve as stewards of the company's deeper purpose and its stakeholders, focusing on fulfilling the company's purpose, delivering value to its stakeholders, and facilitating a harmony of interests, rather than on personal gain and self-aggrandizement. Conscious Leaders cultivate awareness throughout their business ecosystem, beginning with themselves and their team members, and moving into their relationships with each other and other stakeholders. (Mackey, 2007)

Companies that practice Conscious Capitalism embody the idea that profit and prosperity go hand in hand with social justice and environmental stewardship. They utilize creative business models that are transformational and inspirational and that can help solve the world's many social and environmental problems. They are dedicated to the Triple Bottom Line as their definition of success in order to provide positive value in the domain of people, planet, and profit.

In addition to providing investors financial results that range from adequate to superior, a Conscious Business seeks to operate with a systems view, recognizing and benefiting from stakeholder connectedness and interdependence. Some of the practices such companies have adopted include:

- The forming of wellness-affirming workplace cultures
- Improved employee benefit programs
- Use of fair trade materials for manufacture or sale
- Assistance to communities who supply raw materials
- Assistance to communities who manufacture materials
- Local community-outreach programs (Mackey, 2007)

Conscious Businesses also seek to minimize their impact on the environment and work to replenish it when they can, through practices that include:

- Robust recycling programs
- Building "green" or "zero-impact" workplace facilities
- Using solar or wind energy in the workplace
- Purchasing materials from organic or sustainable farmers
- Purchasing renewable and sustainable materials

- Working with environmentally conscious distributors
- Urging manufacturers and distributors to adopt better environmental practices
- Adopting sustainable product packaging (Mackey, 2007)

Many of these companies, their founders and leaders—Kip Tindell and the Container Store, John Mackey and Whole Foods Market, Chip Conley and Joie de Vivre Hotels, Sally Jewel and REI, to name a few—are purposefully coming together to share their experiences and support one another as they address the pressing issues they face with their companies. They are collectively working to catalyze a broader Conscious Capitalism Movement and spread the Conscious Capitalism theme to other businesses, the investment community, consumers, employees, and other stakeholders.

Conscious Businesses choose to use their resources to benefit social and environmental programs that are not directly related to the creation or distribution of their product or service. Frequently, they will donate employee paid time, money, or products toward nonprofit organizations. Sometimes a Conscious Business will create a foundation that works with one particular cause. Some Conscious Businesses become involved with social or political campaigns to protect the environment, animals, or people, and they often dedicate significant amounts of their profits to these causes. Furthermore, a Conscious Business will sometimes work closely with suppliers in either farming or manufacturing communities in a developing country to help develop the local economy and replenish it environmentally.

John Mackey co-founded Conscious Capitalism, Inc., to provide a home for the Conscious Capitalism Movement and to create community and content to deepen and broaden the movement. He chose the term *Conscious Capitalism* to capture the depth and complexity of the changes in the business operating model that are needed. The term heralds the fact that more people today are at higher levels of consciousness about themselves and the world around them than ever before. Mackey believes this is due in part to natural evolution, but also to the rapid aging of society, which has resulted in a higher proportion of people in mid-life and beyond who have become more conscious of spiritual issues and needs. Moreover, the Internet has accelerated and cemented this trend by enabling billions of people to become connected in real time and by placing increasing demands for transparency on companies.

Mackey argues that "great companies have great purposes." He has outlined four such high ideals for companies aspiring to become Conscious Capitalists:

The Good: Service to others, expressing love and care. Example companies include Southwest Airlines, The Container Store, and Nordstrom—all have made gold-standard customer service a major part of their missions.

The True: Discovery and the pursuit of truth. Examples include Google, Wikipedia, and Genentech, which strive to collect and make available vast arrays of knowledge.

The Beautiful: Excellence and the quest for perfection. An obvious example is Apple, which has built a reputation for beautifully designed technology.

The Heroic: Changing and improving the world. Examples include both Microsoft and its founders' Gates Foundation, which is currently working to eradicate malaria, as well as the Grameen Bank, which seeks to eliminate poverty by providing Third World entrepreneurs with tiny loans to start their own very small businesses. (Mackey, 2007)

By his own admission, Mackey has been on a quest for meaning and purpose since his teens. In college he found himself espousing the typical left-wing philosophy of the time that viewed both business and capitalism as exploiters of consumers, workers, society, and the environment. When he started his first health-food store, Safer Way, in his garage in Austin in 1978, he held the belief that profit, although a necessary evil, was certainly not a desirable goal for society. However, he quickly found himself on the dark side. Customers complained his prices were too high. Employees thought they were underpaid. He felt trapped by the government due to an endless barrage of fees, licenses, fines, and taxes. Worst of all, he found himself becoming a greedy, selfish capitalist ("Conscious Business" n.d.; "Conscious Capitalism" n.d.; Stacks 2009).

This realization led to an identity crisis that put him into an existential tailspin. Then Mackey discovered the writings of Milton Friedman and Ayn Rand, two gurus of modern free-market capitalism. He found himself embracing the ideas of voluntary cooperation and spontaneous order that, through free markets, lead to the continuous evolution and progress of humanity. This provided the foundation for his early thinking on Conscious Capitalism—that self-interest and altruism can coexist and thrive simultaneously without government intervention. Conscious Capitalism thus refutes the assumption that human beings must either be greedy or selfish, and think only of themselves or else they must be saints.

Four years later after his libertarian rebirth, when he was twenty-nine, Mackey had an even more powerful spiritual rebirth. He was doing a connective breathing exercise with his therapist when he had an overwhelming experience of being in the birth canal that was a spiritual awakening for him. For years he had been an atheist, but soon after his rebirth experience in therapy he discovered and became a devout practitioner of A Course in Miracles, a guide to enlightenment and inner piece channeled from Jesus through a Columbia psychology professor, Helen Schucman, in the 1970s. He credits his own wisdom to a "Higher Intelligence" that, to the degree individuals and organizations become more skilled at accessing it, will be the driving force behind the evolution of humanity to solve the seemingly intractable problems we face.

Whole Foods Market, the company Mackey started with one small store in Austin, Texas, in 1980, is itself a study in the compromises necessary to maximize the Triple Bottom Line. From the beginning Whole Food's philosophy has been a marriage between the "food of indulgence" and "food as health," summed up as their mission statement: "Whole foods—Whole people—Whole planet." Their mission is institutionalized through their cultural values:

- Selling the highest-quality natural and organic products available
- Satisfying and delighting our customers

- Supporting team member excellence and happiness
- Creating wealth through profits and growth
- Caring about our communities and our environment
- Creating ongoing win-win partnerships with our suppliers (Stacks, 2009)

In support of his commitment to sustainability, conscious capitalism, and the Triple Bottom Line, Mackey professes to be aloof about Whole Food's stock price and its impact on shareholders. "The only thing in the human body that grows just for growth's sake is cancer. I think sometimes businesses do that because they get drunk off bigger market share or more power and bigger perks and bigger egos, and I don't think all that scale growth is always healthy" (Stacks, 2009).

However, this attitude does not insulate his company from economic recession and the need to retrench. In 2009 his company experienced the first negative same-store sales decline ever. In response, Whole Foods slowed growth and opened fewer stores. But in order to preserve as many jobs as possible, the company instituted a hiring freeze and reduced their global staff by 5 percent, mainly by attrition. They also froze all employee and store team leader pay. In addition Whole Foods found itself saddled with debt due to the acquisition of Wild Oats at the peak of the market before the 2008 crash. This forced Mackey to raise $425 million in the private equity market.

In addition to investor disapproval of the downturn and increase in debt, Mackey is also being criticized by environmental stakeholders because Whole Food's astronomical growth—essentially doubling in size every four years through aggressive acquisitions of nineteen of its competitors has entailed social and environmental trade-offs. The company purchases most of its produce from agribusiness instead of local producers for its highly efficient 40,000-square-foot, nonunion stores. In 2008 Ceres, a green-investment watchdog, rated the chain's environmental record among the lowest of all corporations. Mackey finds itself in this conundrum because Whole Foods is facing the dilemma of trying to heal the planet without sacrificing profits, but in order to do so, he needs to continue to tax it with more, still bigger stores.

Another example of this stakeholder conflict is the criticism that he is abandoning Whole Foods' "healthy food" roots for the sake of the bottom line. He concedes that he is selling "a bunch of junk" like frozen turkey corn dogs and natural grilled cheese puffs because as Whole Foods has gotten larger, they've tapped a middle-class customer, and this is what they're voting for with their purchase dollars. So while he's feeding the cravings of his customer stakeholders and satisfying his shareholders, he seems to be doing so at the expense of the company's healthy foods mission. Mackey counters by saying that everywhere in their stores and on their Web site and in their promotions is the theme of healthy living through whole foods and that this message is what he hopes will get through to those who make less healthy food choices.

This is the major dilemma faced by Whole Foods and other organizations that aspire to maximize their Triple Bottom Line. How can you work to meet the expectations of your key stakeholders when Wall Street watches your every move and unloads shares when earnings are two cents below what was expected? Mackey acknowledges that conflict between the various stakeholders is inevitable from time to time simply because each stakeholder wants more. For example Whole Foods donates 5 percent of its profits to the community stakeholder, much to the chagrin of investors, who tend to believe that corporations should stick to what they do best, which is maximizing profits, and then let the individual shareholders themselves engage in philanthropy ("Whole Food's Market Values" n.d.).

Much of the challenge lies in managing stakeholder expectations. Stakeholders tend to see themselves as primarily pursuing their own interests separate from each other and the business. This type of attitude ignores the interdependence among stakeholders and the business and the fact that they often have a shared purpose and common values that provide the opportunity to create and evolve together. This is the challenge of leadership for Conscious Capitalists who aspire to maximize the Triple Bottom Line—to develop solutions that continually work for the common good. According to John Mackey, "The art of excellent leadership seeks the win-win-win-win-win in the context of competitive market processes that optimizes the value of the entire business system and for each of the stakeholder participants within that business system" ("Conscious Business" n.d.).

Moving companies to focus on purpose instead of profit underscores the importance of all the stakeholders the organization must satisfy. When all stakeholders' interest are considered and become the focus for strategy formulation and implementation, all will flourish, including shareholders and the bottom line. Ultimately, businesses that consciously focus on making a positive difference in the world not only make the world a better place; they also achieve higher profit and return on profit—a win/win for all.

Sustainability through Conscious Capitalism is therefore not simply a matter of good corporate citizenship or merely a matter of business ethics—of earning brownie points for cleaning up toxic waste or doing the right thing when confronted with a moral dilemma. No, sustainability is central to the financial success and longevity of all public and private organizations. While the practice of sustainability is still an emerging art, the measurement of sustainability is becoming a science, including specific goals and metrics by which any organization can measure its strategic performance and judge their progress on implementing the Triple Bottom Line.

DEVELOPMENTS IN MEASURING STRATEGIC PERFORMANCE AND THE TRIPLE BOTTOM LINE

A growing number of companies around the world are measuring and reporting their Triple Bottom Line. The Triple Bottom Line captures the essence of sustainability through Conscious Capitalism by measuring the impact of an organization on its key stakeholders. A positive Triple Bottom Line reflects an increase in the organization's value, including its human and societal capital, as well as its profitability and economic growth. It can serve as a balanced scorecard that captures in numbers and words the degree to which any organization is or is not creating value for its shareholders, employees, and for society.

As we mentioned in Chapter 1, the emphasis in the 1980s on total quality management prompted management to decentralize decision making and empower individuals and teams with the authority needed to make processes more efficient and effective. Since then empowerment, quality, and continuous improvement are increasingly viewed as necessary components of employee and organizational learning. These components are also necessary for creativity and innovation, which must come from those who are in touch with the voice of the customer and the voice of the process. It cannot come from people acting only on instructions from top managers who are immersed in a fog of information about financial results.

In the 1980s and early 1990s, two milestone developments in performance measurement were developed—the Baldrige National Quality Program and Kaplan and Norton's Balanced Scorecard model ("Baldrige National Quality Program" 1992–2005; Fuchsberg 1992). The Baldrige approach focuses on business results in the areas of (1) leadership (2) strategic planning, (3) customer and stakeholder focus, (4) measurement, analysis, and knowledge management, (5) human resource focus, (6) process management, and (7) business results. Organizations that adopt the Baldrige National Quality Program establish measures for these areas to ensure that strategies are balanced and there are no conflicts among important stakeholders, objectives, or short- and longer-term goals that might impair business results.

Then Kaplan and Norton, in their classic Harvard Business Review article "The Balanced Scorecard—Measures that Drive Performance," introduced the Balanced Scorecard, which is also intended to ensure that strategies are balanced (Kaplan and Norton 2004; Kaplan and Norton, *The Balanced Scorecard* 1996). As shown in Figure 8.1, they provide a framework for capturing metrics at the executive level based on the categories of (1) customer satisfaction, (2) financial performance, (3) internal processes, and (4) employee learning and growth. Nonfinancial measures provide the balance needed to supplement financial measures and align employees with strategy. Kaplan and Norton define strategy as "a set of hypotheses about cause and effect" and maintain that every measure

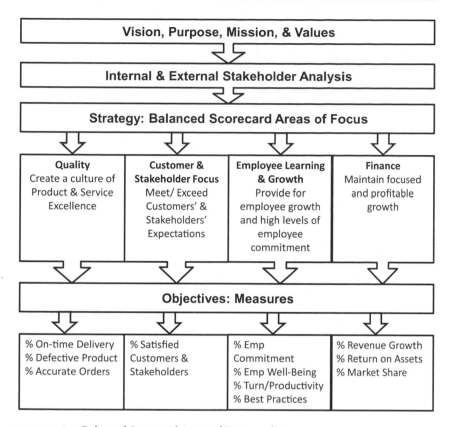

FIGURE 8.1 Balanced Scorecard Areas of Focus and Measures
Source: International Institute for Spiritual Leadership

should be identified in a chain of outcome measures and corresponding performance drivers of the outcome measures. Although specific measures will vary across organizations, there are generic, core outcome measures such as customer satisfaction, financial data and employee skills that are common across strategies and industries. The nonfinancial measurement perspectives—customers, internal business processes, and learning and growth—represent an investment in intangible assets that build the capabilities for a company's future growth that ultimately drive firm performance.

Balanced Scorecard

Quality	Goal	Jan	Feb	...	Dec
% On-time Delivery					
% Defective Product					
% Accurate Orders					
Stakeholder Focus					
% Satisfied Customers					
% Satisfied Stakeholders					
Learning & Growth					
% Employee Commitment					
% Turnover					
% Employee Well-Being					
% Productivity					
% Best Practices					
Finance					
% Revenue Growth					
% Return on Assets					
% Market Share					

FIGURE 8.2 Balanced Scorecard
Source: International Institute for Spiritual Leadership

Similar to the Vision/Stakeholder Effective Analysis we covered in Chapter 7, the Balanced Scorecard's strategic areas of focus are derived from the organization's vision, purpose, mission, and values in conjunction with an internal and external stakeholder analysis. The actual scorecard reports strategic performance indicators in those areas of focus that have been derived from the firm's strategic plan and for which quantifiable performance objectives have been established. An example of a Balanced Scorecard for sustainability and the Triple Bottom Line is shown in Figure 8.2. In the learning and growth area, five common and core outcome measurements are identified: employee well-being, organizational commitment, retention or turnover, employee productivity, and implementation of best practices. By examining monthly trend data and performance versus targets, performance gaps can be identified that, if closed, will provide the firm with a competitive advantage.

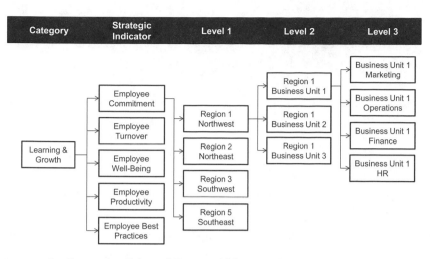

FIGURE 8.3 Integrating Balanced Scorecard Measures Across Functions, Business Units, and Regions
Source: International Institute for Spiritual Leadership

Figure 8.3 provides an example for developing a strategic performance measurement system to a firm's strategy and objectives vertically and horizontally across organizational functions and units. The figure starts with the core measures for learning and growth, and shows how the data can be segregated to measure each region, business unit, and function, thereby linking individual, department, and business unit efforts in a common and integrated direction.

Both the Baldrige and Balanced Scorecard approaches to performance measurement recognize the pivotal role that employees play in the achievement of quality and internal operational results and that the knowledge, skills, creativity, and motivation of employees is central to an organization's success. Valuing employees by committing to employee development, learning, and well-being leads to continuous improvement of key processes, higher-quality products and services, and customer satisfaction, all of which are necessary for performance excellence. According to Baldrige, organizational and personal learning will lead to a more flexible, responsive, and efficient organization, which will result in a sustainable distinctive competency and market advantage. Kaplan and Norton assert that the learning and growth perspective is *the* driver for achieving performance outcomes in the other categories (Kaplan and Norton, "Using the Balanced Scorecard . . ." 1996).

THE SPIRITUAL LEADERSHIP BALANCED SCORECARD BUSINESS MODEL

Proponents of Conscious Capitalism, sustainability, and strategic performance measurement all stress the need for a new business model. In emphasizing the Triple Bottom Line, leaders operating under this new model will give equal emphasis to other nonfinancial predictors of financial performance such as leadership, operating/internal measures, quality, customer satisfaction, employee well-being, and social responsibility.

Such an approach is offered by the Spiritual Leadership Balanced Scorecard Business Model, given in Figure 8.4, which utilizes organizational spiritual leadership as a driver to maximize the Triple Bottom Line. An example of a spiritual leadership balanced scorecard with measures for the four Balanced Scorecard Performance Categories is given in Figure 8.5. The strategic management process begins with the development of a vision, purpose, and mission, followed by an internal and external stakeholder analysis. This analysis forms the basis for development of the organization's strategic objectives and action plans. These objectives form the basis for the leading and lagging indicators that are selected for the Balanced Scorecard Performance Categories. Leading indicators and metrics are used to measure the performance of ongoing company operations. Generally, the more strategic the level of the scorecard in the organizational chart, the more results-oriented and lagging are the specific measures that are reported in the scorecard. These measures comprise the learning and growth, quality, customer and stakeholder satisfaction, and financial Balanced Scorecard Performance Categories. For example, the quality of a firm's products and services are outputs that are leading indicators of customer satisfaction, which in turn, is a leading indicator of financial performance. However, quality is also a lagging indicator

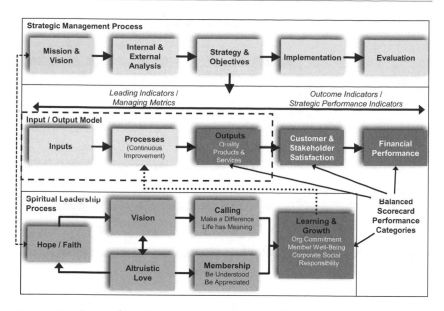

FIGURE 8.4 Spiritual Leadership Balanced Scorecard Business Model
Source: International Institute for Spiritual Leadership

of the efficiency and effectiveness of the organization's key production processes.

According to Kaplan and Norton, employee learning and growth is the central Balanced Scorecard Performance Category because it is a leading indicator that drives the other performance categories (Kaplan and Norton, "Using the Balanced Scorecard" 1996). As shown by the dotted line from the learning and growth category to processes, employees who have high levels of organizational commitment, have a sense of well-being, and are socially responsible will strive to increase productivity and continuously improve organizational processes to produce quality products and services that satisfy customers and other key stakeholders who, ultimately, determine the organization's financial performance. In turn, the learning and growth outcomes of organizational commitment, employee well-being, and social responsibility are lagging indicators that are outcomes driven by the organizational spiritual leadership process.

SPIRITUAL LEADERDSHIP BALANCED SCORECARD															
	1	2	3	4	5	6	7	8	9	10	11	12	13	YTD	Target
Learning & Growth															
% Agree Inner Life															
% Agree Vision															
% Agree Altruistic Love															
% Agree Hope/Faith															
% Agree Calling/Meaning															
% Agree Membership															
% Agree Life Satisfaction															
% Agree Commitment															
% Agree Productivity															
% Best Practices															
Quality															
% On Time Delivery															
% Defective Products															
% Accurate Orders															
Stakeholder Focus															
% Satisfied Customers															
% Environmental Protection Agency Satisfaction															
% Community Satisfaction															
% OSHA Satisfaction															
Finance															
% Revenue Growth															
% Return on Assets															
% Market Share															

FIGURE 8.5 Example Spiritual Leadership Balanced Scorecard
Source: International Institute for Spiritual Leadership

Strategic leaders are responsible for creating vision and value congruence across all organizational levels. As shown by the dotted line, the strategic management process influences the spiritual leadership process. The spiritual leadership process is initiated by challenging employees to persevere, be tenacious, "do what it takes," and pursue excellence in achieving challenging goals through hope/faith in a vision of service of others through altruistic love. Through vision, hope/faith, and altruistic love, employees begin to develop, refine, and practice their own personal spiritual leadership that embodies a vision for their own lives and gives them a sense of calling and that their life has meaning and purpose. By incorporating the values and attitudes of altruistic love in social interaction with others, workers also experience a sense of membership and feel understood and appreciated. Calling and membership then become the source for the learning and growth category outcomes. Then, the learning and growth of employees drives the other categories. In other words, personal and organizational spiritual leadership is necessary for conscious, stakeholder-focused sustainable organizations that maximize the Triple Bottom Line.

SPIRITUAL LEADERSHIP BALANCED SCORECARD BUSINESS MODEL: THE CENTRE FOR EXCELLENCE IN LEADERSHIP

The Centre for Excellence in Leadership (CEL) serves as a role model for maximizing the Triple Bottom Line through spiritual leadership. CEL is a stellar example of a public sector organization that embraced organizational spiritual leadership, employee well-being, and sustainability while maintaining high levels of financial performance. Their CEO, Lynne Sedgmore, has a strong inner life and spiritual practice and has been open about her commitment to workplace spirituality and spiritual leadership. Her leadership was pivotal to leading CEL through its spiritual journey, including several "dark nights of the soul," to a place of preeminence in the United Kingdom's Further Education (FE) sector (Centre for Excellence in Leadership 2004; Centre for Excellence in Leadership 2008a; Sedgmore, Winter 2000/2001).

CEL was established in October 2003 as a national agency funded by the United Kingdom's Secretary of State within the "Success for All" initiative. It was formed through a national bidding process commissioned by the then Department for Education and Skills (DFES), which is now the Department for Business and Innovation (BIS). CEL's charge was to foster and support leadership improvement, reform, and transformation throughout the UK FE sector. The Further Education system is the equivalent of the U.S. junior college system in place in most states. Funded by the UK government, in 2004 it comprised 600,000 staff, 7 million learners, 389 colleges, and nearly 2,000 workplace training organizations. The CEL business model was to be a new form of public organization that was relatively autonomous from government and, ultimately, had to be financially self-sufficient.

CEL was launched officially on October 8, 2003, by Margaret Hodge, the education minister, and Anita Roddick, CEO of the Body Shop and a pioneer in Conscious Capitalism and advocate of the Triple Bottom Line. Initially, CEL was a partnership comprised of the Learning and Skills Development Agency (LSDA), Lancaster University Business School (LUMS), and the Ashridge Business School. This partnership was considered ideal in that three prestigious organizations would be supporting and developing leadership in FE.

CEL's leadership team initially consisted of an interim CEO (from LSDA) and a senior team made up of personnel from the three partners. Startup funding was £14m over three years, with annual goals of 500 participants and a 75 percent average customer satisfaction rating. CEL's ultimate goal was to be financially self-sufficient by March 2006 (Centre for Excellence in Leadership 2004).

This was a complex time for CEL, as it was a new experiment and lacked a unifying vision and had no history of partnership or collaboration between the three autonomous and prestigious partner organizations. Although the partners had never worked together, between them they had considerable leadership expertise and resources. Because of this, the Centre was committed through its partners to carrying out innovative research into leadership and management in CEL's market and committed £3 million of its £14 million to this end.

A number of issues created a range of difficulties from the beginning. The interim CEO had never been in a CEO role before. Everyone was on assignment; no one was employed directly by CEL. The new CEL project was a potentially high risk, so staff remained committed to the perks and positions within their home/host organizations. It soon became clear that the interim CEO was struggling to pull the new senior team together mainly because the financial and reward systems were geared to encourage loyalty and commitment to the partners rather than to CEL. Most alarming was that all of the first-year funding was paid to the partners in development costs, with only 90 participants going through programs from October 2003 to April 2004.

Serious conflicts began to emerge between the partners on leadership pedagogy, nature of programs, the nature of research, and who should be the lead partner. Much of this was because the leadership team never developed a common CEL vision and therefore was torn between the partners; self-interests. Another complication was that the FE colleges felt resentful that two higher education organizations were brought in to "sort out" their leadership when there was a strong belief that the sector could do this for themselves. The FE colleges sensed that the CEL partners were committed not to FE but instead to their own corporate ends. As a result they did not believe that CEL could be effective. For example, partners frequently used their own organizational names when working with participants rather than the CEL name and brand. Program participants' feedback supported this in consistently reporting that they experienced three separate organizations, not one.

However, CEL had to be successful, at least politically, because it was a project that was visibly supported at the ministerial and secretary of state levels. Because the government's funding of £14m was public knowledge, FE colleges were reluctant to fund programs provided by the CEL partner organizations. Plus they felt they were being "fleeced" by higher education (HE), a sector much wealthier and better funded than FE.

Given all this, it was no surprise that achievements by April 2004 were dismal at best:

- 90 participants versus a goal of 500
- All of the first year £6.2m spent
- No assets owned by CEL
- Most of the income paid to partners for development work
- A management team created from senior staff of partners but not working collectively as a CEL team; the main motivation for staff lay in creating value for partners
- Major research program initiated and themes decided for the £3m investment over three years
- No additional income secured; 100 percent dependency on government funding
- Only five product lines in place

A New CEO: From Disarray to Repair and Trust

In April 2004 a new CEO, Lynne Sedgmore, took over the leadership role of CEL. Lynne had received the CBE award (within the Order of the British

Empire) in January 2004 for services to the Further Education sector, was a former FE principal (college president), and was well known and respected. She had entered the FE arena in 1980 and had strong and powerful networks. Lynne's previous experience as principal and chief executive of Guilford College, one of FE's leading colleges, had established her reputation as a leadership thinker and practitioner. She also had the trust of the FE colleges.

For Lynne, CEL was the culmination of a lifelong spiritual journey, her continual quest for spiritual wholeness, and a deep inquiry into how she could integrate her spirituality, leadership, educational profession, and organizational life. Her work in Further Education had been a true and well-loved professional vocation since 1982 and had been a place of spiritual integration and growth since 1989. Over the years she has come to the realization that "work is worship" and the place where she manifests her love of and service to others. As her career progressed, she became certain that there is an inner longing in every person's heart for meaning, purpose, and ultimately the transcendent, however buried or unconscious that may be for some. This knowing compelled her to want to make a difference in the way she led others. Like many of her colleagues, she spent a considerable amount of time in the workplace, and she felt that the workplace was for many their primary community outside the family.

Despite all the issues she inherited, Lynne viewed her new role as her "dream job," and she had a huge appetite and passion to make the long-awaited FE Leadership Centre a success. She also had a strong sense of an injustice being done to FE and her colleagues by the partners. Indeed, her love and passion for the possibility of the new Centre was the core driver for tackling all the difficult issues involved in this new role.

Before starting, Lynne performed a pre-appointment analysis and assessment by talking to staff and analyzing all available CEL information. During the period from January to April 2004 before she took on her CEO role, Lynne met with key players in the Centre to ascertain the situation. She observed the following: a poor relationship between the ministry-level civil servants and the CEL senior leadership team, spending of the total annual budget by partners and under-achievement of targets, significant tensions among partners, particularly on their pedagogies of management and leadership development, and insufficient development of new company structures, procedures, and processes to operate as an autonomous entity (for example, inability to offer her a CEL employment contract and pension scheme).

Although Lynne discovered an incredibly motivated, experienced, and committed board and senior management team, there was a lack of employee commitment to the new organization. The operating teams that were assigned to CEL still reported to their home organizations, so naturally their primary loyalties lay with them. She also became aware that CEL was legally a subsidiary of the Learning and Skills development Agency (LSDA) rather than an independent corporate entity. This had not been made clear to her during the interview and appointment process. Lynne had taken her new appointment with the understanding that she had been appointed CEO of a national autonomous independent agency. This revelation was a devastating blow. However, even after this revelation, she made it clear that she needed a full and free rein to undertake what needed to be done. She also found key allies in a few staff members who shared a similar vision and supported her in many ways from behind the scenes.

As a result of these observations she commissioned a formal audit of the organization and its first twelve months of operation and delivery before her arrival. This resulted in a "red alert" audit that disclosed major issues of:

- Financial compliance
- Lack of assets in CEL
- Low value for money
- Potential conflict of interest in governance structures
- No staff employed by CEL
- Contract overly favorable to partners
- Tensions and lack of trust in working relations

Upon taking the reins Lynne immediately began working on CEL's corporate vision and values. She also insisted on being the first employee directly employed by CEL even though her employment conditions were less favorable than being employed by one of the partners. This initial attempt to create a strong CEL corporate identity was thwarted because partner interests still dominated and resulted in too much game playing. After six months she decided to abandon an integrated approach in the interest of achieving performance goals and, for the time being, allowed each partner to focus on their areas of strength. As a result, CEL's vision, values, and aims were established with little worker consultation due to CEL's rigid silo structure, partner mentality, and the need to achieve performance goals in order not to be closed down the following year. Instead Lynne developed CEL's vision, values, and aims herself, with input from the chair, the senior team, and those few staff members who shared her vision for CEL. During this period, she consistently made it clear this was not her preferred leadership style but that the circumstances demanded it since, without adequate program delivery, CEL would not continue beyond March 2006. She asked for trust on the matter and promised to be held accountable in the next phase of CEL if her style did not change.

As a result of these consultations CEL adopted the following (Centre for Excellence in Leadership 2004):

CEL's Vision:

- World-class educational leadership for every learner.
- Outstanding leaders, providers, and partnerships.
- Inspired learning, learners, employers, and skills development.

CEL's Collective and Formally Agreed Values:

- *Learner focused.* We empower and enable everyone we work with to achieve their full leadership potential.
- *Professional.* We are passionate, energetic, and dedicated professionals who deliver high standards and performance.
- *Reflective.* We are reflective practitioners continually improving our professionalism and seeking feedback.

- *Collaborative.* We are a partnership organization and believe in sharing our learning and expertise.
- *Creative.* We think outside the box and constantly seek innovative ways of seeing the world. We strive constantly to learn and improve and create an open and supportive culture.
- *Diverse.* We celebrate and respect our differences alongside ensuring inclusivity and equality of opportunity.

CEL's Strategic Aims:

- To improve the overall standard of leadership in the FE sector.
- To improve leadership of provider performance for learner and employer success.
- To improve the diversity profile of sector leaders.
- To improve the supply of leaders to ease the succession crisis.
- To improve the quality and impact of research on leadership within the sector.

With the support, understanding, and participation of FE leaders and based on the CEL guiding publication *Leading the Way*, Lynne instigated an extensive client-services development program. During this period, she gave sixty-four presentations in nine months and formed formal partnerships with twenty-two FE organizations. In addition each founding partner was given clear business and performance goals.

Next she introduced processes to foster an internal CEL culture of commitment and service to FE customers so that staff could choose to belong to CEL or not. Out of this effort, a new CEL-focused organization began to emerge. CEL's emerging values and practices, and the realization that they could make a significant contribution to FE leaders and to CEL, caused many to abandon their comfortable contract status and choose to be employed directly by CEL—a brave and important move on their part.

During this period Lynne and her team were able to convince DFES to revise the whole funding base of CEL. The new commitment included a revised budget of £15m for 2005–2007 (rather than the £2m already committed for 2005–2006) and to extend the financial self-sufficiency goal out twelve months to March 2007. A major factor in this decision was the fact that CEL had far exceeded their participant goal of training 500 participants by nearly 2,000. There was also a significant increase in customer satisfaction and a commitment to provide service to 8,000 participants the following year for an investment of £7.5m, which signaled a big step in delivering significantly improved value for the money invested.

From the beginning it had always been made clear that CEL had to ultimately be financially self-sufficient. To accomplish this, CEL also committed to raising the level of additional funds from alternative sources, including the private sector. Another major challenge to achieving financial independence was the reluctance of FE organizations to pay market-rate fees for CEL's programs. For example, the aspiring principal's senior management program cost £6k. In other sectors and business schools, a comparative program cost between £12k and £24k.Even when this was pointed out, FE organizations refused to pay more. Indeed they continued to insist that £6k was exorbitant, despite many discussions with the Advisory Group and key stakeholders. Although this attitude was understandable, since the FE organizations in general were both underfunded and not accustomed to investing significant sums in the development of its senior managers, it still was a major roadblock to CEL's goal of self-sufficiency.

After receiving the approval for two years of additional funding, CEL reorganized into a charitable trust, reconstituted its board, and canceled the primary contract with the partners; in doing so it became an independent organization that could contract with any partner based on need. In addition, CEL would no longer be a formal subsidiary of LSDA. A new CEL board was formed comprised of highly respected and influential people from a range of sectors, including health, local authorities, FE, and the charity sector.

Based on the hard work by Lynne and her senior leadership team, CEL was able to move from the red alert audit status to a green status in a period of twelve months. CEL began to receive public support and endorsement from the new secretary of state for education, Alan Johnson. The new minister for higher and further education, Bill Rammell, was a frequent speaker at CEL events and encouraged the entrepreneurial activity of CEL. Prime Minister Tony Blair wrote a complimentary foreword for the CEL 2006–2007 annual review. All this meant that ministers and senior civil servants could now give unconcealed support to CEL without fear of embarrassment.

CEL began to offer high-profile conferences and events that were creative, imaginative, and well attended. These included unusual venues across the country, which differentiated CEL from other national organizations. Examples included the beautiful rooftop gardens in the Kensington neighborhood of London; the Globe Shakespeare Theatre; a famous oval cricket grounds; beautiful country manor houses; a haunted hotel; the Tower of London; and a Thames riverboat cruise, with the Tower of London Bridge opening especially for the guests.

Lynne also introduced staff strategic forums and annual staff retreats where difficult and unspoken issues could be raised to create open dialogue and a sense of community. External facilitators were brought in to enhance and support team processes. Employees were provided access to a coach or mentor with an annual staff budget of £3,500 per person, a much higher investment in their people than the national benchmark of £300 per person per year spent in universities. This reinforced CEL's strong value that a leadership development centre should invest in its own staff and model positive staff development, especially if, as in CEL's case, an adequate financial surplus was being generated and performance targets were being met or exceeded.

Lynne recognized that staff participation in developing creative ideas, innovation, and the overall strategic direction of CEL was critical if CEL was to achieve its goal of self-sufficiency. She knew that the key to CEL's success was the appointment of high-performing, highly dedicated staff members. It was widely acknowledged among FE organizations that poor staff performance was too frequently ignored. To counter this common occurrence, CEL created a bonus program to reward high performance that included rewards for modeling CEL's vision and cultural values. Anyone who did not "fit" the culture or who did not meet performance standards was first dealt with through peer pressure. If this failed, workers were counseled fairly and supportively through the formal HRM capability and disciplinary procedures. Although some staff left CEL feeling that the culture did not suit them or that they should have been treated differently, most related stories of how CEL had impacted positively on their lives and how the wide range of individuals in CEL had made a huge difference to them as professionals and as human beings.

The remaining employees were empowered to co-create changes to their jobs within their teams. Initiatives became bottom up, as well as top down. Lynne acquired a coach to assist her through the difficult period of reconfiguring CEL as part of her leadership-development process. This also signaled to staff the importance of using staff development resources for coaching if they so desired. Lynne chose a coach who could also respond to and support her spiritual and inner life while helping her integrate professional development and organizational needs. With her coach's help, Lynne introduced a series of strategy forums with the aim of democratizing strategy within CEL so that it involved all staff at every level and was no longer the sole domain of the top leaders and the board.

All of these initiatives worked to steadily improve CEL's performance and stakeholder effectiveness. The fractious relationship with government had been repaired, many partnerships were now in place, the demand for CEL's programs increased dramatically, and customer satisfaction was at an all-time high. This was reflected in CEL's April 2006 status report (Centre for Excellence in Leadership 2006):

- 12,000 participants versus the goal of 10,000.
- Customer satisfaction of 95 percent.
- 25 product lines and generated surplus of £1m.
- Additional income of £3m and reduced dependency on core grant to 70 percent.
- Overall budget of £11m.

- Staff expansion to 50 full-timers and 200 associates.
- Extensive impact surveys and reports on added value and impact of CEL's work across the sector.

CEL: MAXIMIZING THE TRIPLE BOTTOM LINE THROUGH SPIRITUAL LEADERSHIP

In April 2006, with the exception of the chair and one board member, a new CEL board and senior team were assembled and four new executive and six nonexecutive members were appointed. During the next two years, Lynne delivered on her promise to more fully engage staff. CEL employees were formally invited to help co-create the organization they wanted CEL to be. This process resulted in staff participating at every level with renewed responsibility, accountability, and trust. The strategic forums and staff retreats became more powerful, creative, and collective. Junior employees were encouraged to step up into leadership roles. The CEL Advisory Group, initially established at CEL's inception, became more proactive in providing the executive leadership team with helpful and supportive advice on the development of CEL's portfolio, as well as lobbying for more long-term financial support.

The Spirit at Work Award

In October 2007 CEL won the International Spirit at Work Award. CEL received the award for its programs on workplace spirituality, its commitment to spiritual leadership, and its focus on reflective practice, and for its work in creating a new paradigm for organizational performance —one that values the Triple Bottom Line through an emphasis on employee well-being and social justice, while maintaining superior financial performance.

CEL's commitment to workplace spirituality included the intellectual, physical, social, emotional, and spiritual dimensions. Spirituality was exercised in a very broad, pluralistic manner within CEL and incorporated both horizontal and vertical dimensions. The horizontal dimension of spirituality speaks to issues of how spirituality is addressed within the organization. Conversations among staff about soul needs, personal fulfillment, and spiritual aspirations were common. There was no desire by CEO Lynne Sedgmore or the senior team to control or monitor such exchanges. The intention and aspiration was that spirit would flow and manifest easily into the spaces arising to allow it in, and within those spaces, what will be, will be.

In addition, a structured discourse on the horizontal dimension was encouraged through a values clarification process. With the aid of an external facilitator, values were debated, articulated, and agreed upon using a range of staff focus groups, forums, questionnaires, away days, and formal meetings. This collective approach modeled CEL's core value of partnership and collaboration. The collective definition of spirituality in CEL through this discourse was best described as "connection with and experience of a higher power, others, and/or nature enabling inner peace, strength, harmony, love, meaning, wisdom, joy and right action." (Centre for Excellence in Leadership 2007; Centre for Excellence in Leadership, "Living Spirituality in the Workplace" 2008)

The range of spiritual approaches and practices favored and practiced by staff included agnosticism, atheism, what might be defined as "new age," green spirituality, and orthodox faith traditions. This diversity allowed for an open discourse of the vertical dimension. Inevitably, amid the cultural values debate, vertical dimension questions concerning spiritual and religious practices emerged. The vertical dimension was encouraged through individual coaching (all staff are entitled to a personal development coach). Lynne talked openly about the significance of the vertical dimension and the role of reflective practices in her life. She says she cannot remember a time when she was not asking spiritual/religious questions, nor could she imagine her life without such focus and exploration through an inner life practice based in prayer and meditation.

In her role as chief executive of CEL, Lynne Sedgmore became widely recognized for developing a model of organizational spirituality and practicing spiritual leadership. She gave national keynote speeches and facilitated workshops and "conversations" for Surrey University, the Ethelberg Centre, National Ecumenical Agency in Further Education (NEAFE), the

United Nations, and Findhorn. She chaired the UK Interfaith Seminary and published four articles sharing her experiences and views on workplace spirituality.

Measuring CEL's Organizational Spiritual Leadership
and the Learning and Growth Balanced Scorecard category

As part of its commitment to the Triple Bottom Line, CEL commissioned a longitudinal research project as a way to validate and confirm CEL's commitment to workplace spirituality and organizational spiritual leadership, and as evidence of the link between spirituality, well-being, and high performance. A key aspect of the study was the use of the organizational Spiritual Leadership Survey (covered in detail in the previous chapter). Results of the survey are summarized in Figure 8.6. Given in this figure are the averages for the two survey administrations (November 2006 and April 2008) for inner life, spiritual leadership (vision, hope/faith, and altruistic love), spiritual well-being (calling and membership), two learning and growth measures (life satisfaction and organizational commitment), and a measure of unit productivity. An asterisk denotes that there is a statistical significant difference between averages for the responses on that variable from 2006 to 2008.

The survey questionnaire utilized a 1 through 10 (from strongly disagree to strongly agree) response set. The bar graphs depict the dispersion of responses for these measures. Responses between 1.00 and 4.99 represent "disagree." "Neither" is the percentage of respondents with an average response value between 5.00 and 6.99. The "agree" percentage represents response values between 7.00 and 10.00. Based on previous experience and research, organizations would want all their employees to have high average response scores (above 7) and report moderately high (above 60 percent) percentage levels of "agree" for all nine variables of the Spiritual Leadership Model. These levels have been found to indicate high levels of spiritual leadership. Moderate or low levels (below 60 percent) on responses indicate areas for possible intervention for organizational development.

Results confirmed the spiritual leadership model and that CEL demonstrated high levels of organizational spiritual leadership. Averages for all

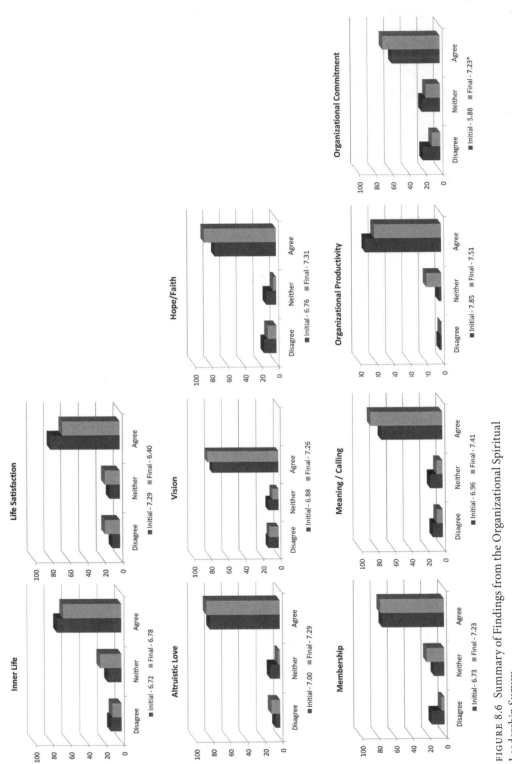

FIGURE 8.6 Summary of Findings from the Organizational Spiritual Leadership Survey

variables except inner life (6.88) were above 7.0 on the final survey administration. The percentage of "agree" responses, with the exception of organizational commitment, were above 60 percent for both surveys (the "agree" percentage for organizational commitment in 2006 was 58 percent). However, organizational commitment saw a significant increase in its average score, from 5.88 to 7.23 from 2006 to 2008. This significant increase is most likely due to the ongoing success of the CEL initiatives based in organizational spiritual leadership that were implemented during this period.

CEL's Commitment to Sustainability

As further evidence of its commitment to the Triple Bottom Line, both CEL and the FE sector had publically stated that they had an important role to play in embedding sustainable development in all CEL programs as an integral element of leadership development. In its strategy for sustainable development, "Leadership for Sustainability: Making Sustainable Development a Reality for Leaders," CEL defined sustainable development as "development which meets the needs of the present without compromising the ability of future generations to meet their own needs." In shaping its role and contribution to the sustainable development agenda, CEL identified a pressing need for FE leaders to be equipped with the knowledge, skills, and understanding to provide leadership for sustainable development. CEL defined such leadership as promoting and supporting sustainable development principles at all organizational levels (Centre for Excellence in Leadership, "Leadership for Sustainability" 2008).

To insure that sustainable development was imbedded in its programs, CEL initially met with leaders and other interested stakeholders in a number of forums to jointly explore the relationships between sustainable development and leadership. The result was two research projects, a sustainability conference, and a consultation seminar that provided the foundation for the development of CEL's sustainable development strategy, which was presented at the House of Lords on November 15, 2007. The strategy set out how CEL would support FE leaders in developing their capability to be "leaders for sustainability" by building (1) CEL's capacity for sustainability,

TABLE 8.1

CEL's Balanced Scorecard, Customer Perspective

Customer Perspective
By this we mean the perspectives of the institutions and individuals that we serve. To be successful, how should we appear to our customers and key stakeholders?

Goals	Measures	Indicators
Overall customer satisfaction is achieved	Goal 85% in line with DfES requirements	98% customer satisfaction achieved
Participants recognize CEL as delivering programs, services, and interventions that meet their specific needs	% of CEL participants describing their experience as good or very good.	98% customer satisfaction achieved
Customers consider CEL to be a value for money supplier	Average % of CEL customers describing the services received as good or very good value for money in relation to the services provided increasing year on year.	98% customer satisfaction achieved. Reduced contractor overheads achieved.
CEL is seen as actively supporting and promoting diversity	Numbers using CEL subsidy; strong diversity strategy; number of individuals from under-represented groups participating in CEL programs and services.	For the first quarter, 283 individual subsidies have been granted, a record high for a first quarter.

SOURCE: "Living Spirituality in the Workplace: The CEL Way," Centre for Excellence in Leadership, 2008. http://www.centreforexcellence.org.uk/usersdoc/livingspiritualityworkplace.pdf (accessed January 14, 2008).

(2) partnerships with key stakeholders that were committed to sustainability development, (3) leadership capability for developing sustainable organizations, and (4) sustainability practices.

CEL Moves Toward the Spiritual Leadership Balanced Scorecard Business Model

CEL began to develop a prototype of the Spiritual Leadership Balanced Scorecard Business Model that reflected its commitment to employee well-being, sustainability, and performance excellence. Performance measures were developed for all internal programs as well as for key external stakeholders. Due to space limitations, only the major critical results for the key focus areas of customers, people and internal business processes, continuous improvement, and financial performance for the first quarter (April 1 to June 30) of 2008 are reviewed. CEL had a green

TABLE 8.2

CEL's Balanced Scorecard, Internal Business Process Perspective

Internal Business Process Perspective
To be successful, which business processes should we be good at?

Goals	Measures	Indicators
Quality assurance	Year-on-year reduction on % of noncompliances in quality audits and % of customer complaints; year-on-year increase in compliments	0 formal complaints
Appoint, retain, and develop high-quality employees and associates	% of recruitment offers declined; annual employee/associate turnover rate; average number of training interventions per capita; internal promotions as % of all appointments; sickness rates	In this quarter, we have had 4 new starters and 5 leavers = turnover rate of 7.6% 6 new roles were offered, 2 of which were internal transfers and 0 were internal promotions.
Promote diversity at all levels and roles in the organization	Workforce monitoring in relation to national benchmarks of ethnicity, gender, age and disability	Internal monitoring reveals our workforce average for this quarter is: 73.5% female 88% full-time 69% white British /Irish /any other white background

SOURCE: "Living Spirituality in the Workplace: The CEL Way," Centre for Excellence in Leadership, 2008. http://www.centreforexcellence.org.uk/usersdoc/livingspiritualityworkplace.pdf (accessed January 14, 2008).

light status (target goals met or exceeded) for their customer, internal business process, continuous improvement, and financial balanced score-card performance categories during this period.

The Customer Perspective: CEL as a hybrid public/private sector organization exists to provide services that meet the policy imperatives of government and the needs of our stakeholders and customers. It is critical that CEL has clear strategies for meeting customer needs and, in turn, has performance measures that will help assess customer and stakeholder expectations, perceptions, and levels of satisfaction. Such measures will assist CEL in retaining a clear customer focus on such expectations by tracking performance in meeting them.

The People and Internal Business Process Perspective (Learning and Growth): The Results of the longitudinal spiritual leadership study confirmed that CEL demonstrated high levels of organizational spiritual leadership that led to high levels on the key learning and growth organi-

TABLE 8.3

CEL's Balanced Scorecard, Continuous Improvement Perspective

Continuous Improvement Perspective
To be successful how will we sustain our ability to learn and to improve?

Goals	Measures	Indicators
Sector ownership of CEL	Evidence gathered from stakeholders across the learning and skills sector via a wide and inclusive range of intelligence-gathering activities will enable CEL to be innovative and creative in the creation and development of programs and services for 2006–2008.	Quarterly meeting of CEL's advisory group and ongoing interactions with the sector inform development; repeat business levels increased.
Achievement of value for money is proactive and ongoing	Business planning and performance review is at the heart of the regular monitoring and evaluation of the objectives and activities contained in the 2006–2008 business plan to ensure that a process of continuous quality improvement is proactive and ongoing.	Open tender process initiated March 2007 to achieve improved quality and value for money.
CEL's contribution to the development of the FE system is effectively articulated in the improvement strategy coordinated by QIA.	Activities accurately presented in the improvement strategy; CEL's status as a key partner is clear.	CEL has contributed to the improvement strategy through their relationship with QIA and is working toward the new organization, LSIS.

SOURCE: "Living Spirituality in the Workplace: The CEL Way," Centre for Excellence in Leadership, 2008. http://www.centreforexcellence.org.uk/usersdoc/livingspiritualityworkplace.pdf (accessed January 14, 2008).

zational commitment and life satisfaction variables. In addition, to provide quality and cost-effective services and Value for Money, CEL must identify the key people and business processes it needs to be good at and then measure its performance in undertaking those processes. This perspective will encourage our directors and managers to identify performance of the key business processes; in the context of overall strategy, to assess current performance in undertaking those processes; and to establish goals for improving performance.

The Continuous Improvement Perspective: To achieve continuous improvement with a learning organization perspective in delivering quality, cost-effective services, CEL needs to ensure that it is able to learn and to improve from both an individual and organizational perspective to

TABLE 8.4

CEL's Balanced Scorecard, Financial Perspective

Financial Perspective
To be successful, how should we appear to those who provide our financial resources?

Goals	Measures	Indicators
Deliver to CEL's annual budget agreed by the board	Difference of income over expenditure; positive cash flow	Estimated full year is surplus of £118k against budget of £65k.
Diversify income streams	Maximize share of college market; increase market share of developing markets in ACL and WBL to achieve financial self-sufficiency incrementally year on year.	CEL has or is engaged with more than 300 of the 389 FE colleges, representing more than 75% of all FE colleges.
Work toward financial self-sufficiency	Return from sales meets a greater percentage of CEL's operational overhead costs	The year-to-date dependency on DfES Strategic Project grant was 49%, which is against the budgeted figure of 58%.
Ensure that all programs and services achieve contribution set out in annual business plan	Monthly review and quarterly reconciliation at business planning meetings.	The overall budgeted contribution goal of 34.2% at the end of Q3 was exceeded with an actual total contribution of 36.8%.

SOURCE: "Living Spirituality in the Workplace: The CEL Way," Centre for Excellence in Leadership, 2008. http://www.centreforexcellence.org.uk/usersdoc/livingspiritualityworkplace.pdf (accessed January 14, 2008).

demonstrate value for money. It is important to measure CEL's ability to learn, to cope with change, and to improve through its people, its systems, and its infrastructure.

The Financial Perspective: CEL continues to require key measures of its financial performance, but, again, this needs to be directly linked to the overall goals in order to help CEL from being solely financially driven mission driven.

Performance outcomes as of April 2008 included:

- 80 full-time staff members, 250 associates.
- Customer satisfaction of 97 percent.
- Nearly 40,000 participants through CEL in five years.
- Surplus of £1m in 2006–2007, surplus of £1.5m in 2007–2008, all reinvested in the further development of CEL's activities.
- 32 product offerings.

- Received International Spirit at Work Award.
- Organizational spiritual leadership and stakeholder perception surveys very positive.
- Overall budget at £16m annually in 2006–2007 and 2007–2008.
- Financial dependency at 50 percent.
- High staff morale, strong stakeholder engagement.
- Powerful impact studies on college performance and inspection results.
- High and positive media profile.

The Death of CEL: Bureaucracy Prevails

Even as CEL was rapidly moving toward its ultimate goal of financial self-sufficiency, a political storm was brewing. Another national FE organization that focused on quality improvement was perceived as failing. The politics dictated that a solution had to be found, and quickly, before this became a serious problem and embarrassment. The FE sector recently had a review in which a strong recommendation was made to simplify the national FE organizations. The need to reduce the number of national organizations—plus a genuine move across all public sectors to put leadership, quality, continuous improvement, and innovation together—made a strong political case that this would be a merger made in heaven. Thus, a merger of CEL and the quality improvement organization became a political inevitability. One of the reasons stated for the merger was that CEL had not achieved financial self-sufficiency, as was originally planned, despite the fact that it had already achieved 50 percent nondependency and was predicting financial self-sufficiency by 2011.

CEL was forced to enter into complex and difficult merger negotiations with an organization that had a much larger budget of £125m (CEL's was £16m per year) and a radically different culture and mind-set; it was highly bureaucratic, with formalized, sometimes rigid, procurement procedures that were slow to respond to innovative initiatives. CEL, on the other hand, was a learning organization that was swift, responsive, continually initiating and learning; it was customer focused, but with processes and formal procedures that were adequate to the task and no more. The CEL senior team introduced procedures only as were necessary to make the business effective. However, the more bureaucratic and powerful merging organization viewed CEL's procedures as inadequate, although all audit reports were good and performance metrics exceeded all expectations.

The merger deliberation took considerable time and was deeply painful since it turned out the two organizations' cultures were so different that they could not dialogue effectively. Even two sets of consultants were unable to resolve the fundamental cultural differences between the two organizations. The major argument put forward by the larger organization— that CEL failed to comply sufficiently with mandated detailed and bureaucratic procedures and processes—proved fatal for CEL as the merger progressed. While CEL's exceptional accomplishments and profitability were acknowledged by practitioners, consumers, key stakeholders, and the ministers, the civil servants inevitably began to view CEL negatively due to its perceived underdeveloped and inadequate bureaucratic processes. As a result CEL's chair, CEO (Lynne Sedgmore), the deputy CEO, and the finance director all decided, after much painful soul searching, not to go forward into the new organization. Lynne chose to stay with CEL until the merger came into effect and not to seek alternative employment. As a mark of respect, the minister of FE and civil servants offered her a two-day-a-week FE project working directly with the minister.

As the difficult merger progressed, CEL continued to exceed their profit and performance goals. On October 1, 2008, CEL and the quality agency merged to form a new sector-owned organization dedicated to supporting quality improvement and leadership development in the further education and skills sector. CEL is now part of the Learning and Skills Improvement Service (LSIS) with a new chair, board, and CEO. Five of the original CEL senior team members stayed on as members of the LSIS senior team.

A new chair of LSIS was appointed in January 2009. A CEO was recruited in February and appeared ready to take the job but, after an initial assessment of the role, decided not to take up the appointment. An interim

CEO was put in place for three months from March to June 2009. A third CEO was then appointed in June 2009 after a national search. He left in August 2010. A fourth CEO, who was then hired without a national search, retired in March 2011. The fifth LSIS CEO is now in place at the time of writing.

The Legacy of CEL

Once the merger was inevitable, the leadership team, staff, and board of CEL were very keen to articulate and leave a legacy in the merged organization to safeguard some of the best aspects of CEL culture, performance, and approaches. The legacy was focused through the written word, lived experience, and spirit of the people who had created and lived the reality and power of CEL. A document, "CEL as a High-Performing Organization" was published, and the CEL board also funded a range of academic articles and a book as part of the written legacy (Centre for Excellence in Leadership, "CEL as a High-Performing Organization" 2008). All staff received a silver star paperweight as a gift to mark the end of CEL with a note saying "Thanks for being a CEL star and best wishes for the future." CEL also bought a star in the sky and named it the "CEL star" with everyone having a certificate of exactly where this star is in the stellar constellation so they can link to CEL at any time by gazing at this star. (All of these activities were funded personally by Lynne and the deputy CEO, not CEL public funds.)

The living legacy of the CEO, deputy CEO, and key members of the executive leadership team and other staff continues in different ways. Many of those who left CEL are still heavily committed and passionate about CEL and the FE sector. Based on the book *The Starfish and the Spider* (Beckstrom and Brafman 2006) CEL's leadership team embraced the idea of the starfish. This is the notion that parts of a starfish may break off but the starfish will heal again, leaving the piece that has broken away but still a part of the original starfish. The leaders and staff who have stayed and moved into the merged organization continue to support and integrate the best of CEL and their own individual professional and contribution into the new organization. Some agreed that they would meet regularly with the remaining leaders in the merged organization. They also committed to taking the CEL energy, spirit, values, and expertise into their new jobs and to support each other as much as possible. A number of CEL staff members are currently in positions within other national FE agencies. Their passion for organizational spiritual leadership is enabling them to share their experience of a living CEL legacy.

Although most were sad that the merger happened, they felt CEL had changed their lives for the better. The key sentiment was that their experience and learning within CEL could never be taken away, whatever happened to them into the future. Many said that they had found a new way of being and a renewed sense of community in organizational life and that they could take the experience and spirit of CEL with them wherever they went into the future.

Perhaps CEL's greatest legacy lies in the more than 1,160 different organizations and nearly 40,000 individual participants who experienced CEL's unique culture and approach to leadership training. CEL became known as an organization that embraced workplace spirituality. CEL even advertised this as a core strength (Centre for Excellence in Leadership, "Living Spirituality in the Workplace" 2008). CEL also provides an excellent example of an organization that was beginning to implement the Spiritual Leadership Balanced Scorecard Business Model to maximize the Triple Bottom Line. The two surveys administered over a two-year period revealed high levels of spiritual leadership (hope/faith, vision, and altruistic love) and spiritual well-being (calling and membership), which then positively influenced CEL's key learning and growth, continuous improvement, customer, and financial performance balanced scorecard categories.

During CEL's five years of existence, Lynne Sedgmore guided CEL through its spiritual journey toward organizational spiritual leadership transformation. Lynne led CEL into the purgative way (see Chapter 3) to help its people appreciate the benefits of workplace spirituality. However, difficulties with CEL's initial partnering structure quickly brought CEL into the "first night of the dark soul." Lynne responded and carried CEL into the illuminative way by making short-term concessions to ensure the survival of CEL but making it clear that she would stay true to the vision and values she and her team articulated for CEL. Once survival seemed assured, Lynne and her team embarked on a vigorous course of action to move the entire organization into the illuminative way. This included an emphasis on the sustainability and strategic performance measurements of spiritual leadership and the balanced scorecard learning and growth, quality, customer satisfaction, and financial performance categories. CEL was fast becoming a sustainable organization that maximized the Triple Bottom Line.

It might seem that CEL did not weather its "second dark night of the soul." It appears that the politics of the situation that resulted in the merger of CEL with a much larger and traditionally bureaucratic organization led to its leaders giving up and to CEL's demise. And perhaps CEL was doomed from the beginning because the goal of self-sufficiency was impossible since its operation was so foreign to the highly bureaucratic civil service environment in the United Kingdom. Yes, one can argue that this experiment in implementing workplace spirituality through organizational spiritual leadership to maximize the Triple Bottom Line was a failure. However, one can also argue that the apparent demise of CEL and its key leadership team has only served to foster further growth in implementing workplace spirituality through spiritual leadership. A core group from CEL still serves in the new organization with the hope of furthering its transformation. And both those who stayed and those who left, including Lynne Sedgmore, have emerged out of this second dark night with a renewed sense of their vision and spiritual values, new energy, and a revitalized commitment to a higher good, a new way of being, a better way of behaving, and a new sense of community and energy as they take the experience and spirit of CEL with them wherever they go.

CONCLUSION

There is increasing public pressure from community and environmental stakeholders for boards of directors and CEOs to stop their obsessive emphasis on maximizing shareholder wealth. The search for this new ethos is evidenced by the growing public and business interest in building sustainable organizations. Leaders of sustainable organizations recognize that they operate in a global, interdependent world that includes powerful stakeholders that can threaten the organization's success, if not its very survival. This is a new breed of Conscious Capitalist that recognizes the power of purpose over profit and the need to serve stakeholders other than investors and management. Conscious Capitalists embody the idea that profit and financial success can coexist with an equal focus on employee well-being, social justice, and environmental stewardship—the Triple Bottom Line.

The Spiritual Leadership Balanced Scorecard Business Model emphasizes organizational spiritual leadership and stakeholder satisfaction as key to maximizing the Triple Bottom Line. Employee learning and growth is the central balanced scorecard performance category because it is a leading indicator that drives the other performance categories. Employees who have a sense of well-being and are committed, productive, and socially responsible will strive to continuously improve organizational processes and produce quality products and services that satisfy key customers and other stakeholders who, ultimately, drive financial performance. In turn, the learning and growth category is driven by the organizational spiritual leadership process.

Although short-lived, the Centre for Excellence in Leadership offers an example of an organization that made significant progress toward implementing the Spiritual Leadership Balanced Scorecard Business Model. Central to CEL's success was CEO Lynne Sedgmore, who has a strong commitment to implementing workplace spirituality through organizational spiritual leadership. Lynne and her leadership team worked hard to recruit and select staff members who were highly creative, articulate, and autonomous individuals who had a strong desire for continual learning, improvement, and self-reflective skills. Rather than attempting to define spirituality, CEL's approach was to encourage and allow everyone to explore and articulate their own way of being spiritual, not only in their work, but also in their whole lives. They believed strongly that it was important to respect the right of each individual to choose how and whether to engage in spiritual expression at work.

During this period, Lynne's situation was similar to what many leaders face in trying to create a sphere of influence for implementing organizational spiritual leadership when the leader and their core unit or group of followers are imbedded in a larger hostile organizational or external stakeholder environment. In these situations, it is important to act as the guiding leader and accept apparent organizational failure not as a fiasco and the end but, instead, as an evitable part of both the individual and organizational spiritual journey.

Practical Tools

For those interested in maximizing the Triple Bottom Line, the major tools introduced in this chapter include the following:

The **balanced scorecard categories** provide an overall framework or set of categories for establishing a performance measurement system to ensure that strategies are balanced and that financial results are driven by employee learning and growth, quality products and services, and customer and stakeholder satisfaction.

The **Spiritual Leadership Balanced Scorecard Business Model** utilizes organizational spiritual leadership as the driver of the balanced scorecard categories to maximize the Triple Bottom Line.

Chapter Nine

Co-Creating a Conscious, Sustainable World Through Spiritual Leadership

Albert Einstein's famous statement "Problems cannot be solved at the same level of awareness that created them" has never been truer (McGinnis n.d.). Geopolitically, we face seemingly endless and intractable conflicts rooted in religious and political interests that defy solution through the United Nations or any other multinational effort. In the national and international economic arena, real estate and stock market bubbles perpetrated by greedy individuals and organizations threaten a global great depression that is bankrupting entire nations.

What level of thinking and action will it take to make a change? Or is it not thinking at all, but a focus on being that is necessary? We find one possible solution in Eckhart Tolle's *A New Earth: Awakening to Your Life's Purpose*, which underlies much of what we've discussed in terms of personal spiritual leadership and maximizing the Triple Bottom Line through organizational spiritual leadership (Tolle 2005).

A New Heaven and a New Earth

In both personal and organizational spiritual leadership, a new earth begins with developing an inner life based on mindfulness. But is humanity ready for such a wide-scale transformation of consciousness? The possibility of such a transformation is the central message from all of the great wisdom teachers, such as Buddha, Jesus, and Mohammed. And yet human beings have not been ready to take up the call to mindfulness. If humanity is now ready as never before, is there enough of a critical mass to create the family, community, national, and global economic and political organizations necessary to reinforce what is, according to Tolle, our next evolution as a species? And what can *you* do to bring about and accelerate this shift? How can you use the models of spiritual leadership as a guide to facilitate and institutionalize a new emerging consciousness?

This book's main purpose is to act as a catalyst in providing new models, methods, and tools for engaging the world and contributing to a shift that has, hopefully, already begun in you. Not everyone is ready yet, but each person who awakens has the potential to lead others in this transformation.

Two Truths of the Human Condition

Insanity as the "Normal" State of Mind

There are two core insights or truths that most of humanity's ancient religions and spiritual traditions agree on. The first truth is the realization that the "normal" state of mind contains a strong element of dysfunction or even madness due to the essential nature of the human condition, which we explored in detail in Chapters 3 and 6. This dysfunction manifests as a form of collective mental illness that Hinduism calls Maya, the veil of delusion. In Buddhism, the mind in its normal state generates Dukkha, which is translated as suffering, dissatisfaction, or misery. The normal collective state of humanity in Christianity is one of "original sin." This collective manifestation of the insanity that lies at the heart of the human condition and the organizations created by it constitute the greater part of human history. The achievements of humanity in terms of the arts and sciences are impressive and undeniable. Recent advances in science and technology have enabled us to do and create things that would have been considered miraculous only two hundred years ago. Yet the very collective intelligence that underlies all this is tainted by madness, for it has also created great weapons and organizations to wage war. This very science and technology also underlies a different form of unprecedented violence that humans are inflicting on other life forms and the planet itself—witness the destruction of oxygen-producing forests and other plant and animal life as well as the poisoning of our planet's rivers, oceans, and air.

Adding to this madness is the emerging global obsession, driven by the Western capitalist paradigm, with consumerism and materialism. This overemphasis on material gain reflects an underlying assumption that we can consume and acquire our way into happiness and life satisfaction. Yet it is a fact of nature that material gain can only provide satisfactions limited to the level of our senses. If human beings were no different from animals this would be fine. However, it is obvious that our needs are more than sensual. No, an economic revolution is not enough. What is needed is a spiritual revolution.

Spiritual Revolution

A second truth arises out of all this bad news about the human condition: the good news of the possibility of a spiritual revolution leading to a radical transformation of human consciousness—the possibility of a new earth. In Hindu and Buddhist teachings, this transformation is called enlightenment and the end of suffering. In his teachings, Jesus terms this concept "salvation." Some traditions call it "liberation" or "awakening." This call for a spiritual revolution is, at its heart, a call for a radical transformation in our habitual preoccupation with self, grounded in our ego. It is a call to turn toward and embrace the wider community of beings with whom we are connected and to engage in conduct that recognizes others' interest alongside our own.

A recent ten-week event that featured Eckhart Tolle discussing *A New Earth* and answering questions from an Internet-based audience drew millions (Minzesheimer 2011). This provides evidence that a significant contingent is beginning to recognize that humanity is faced with a stark choice: evolve or die. As we evolve spiritually, we no longer derive our identity or a sense of who we are from an incessant stream of thinking. A sense of liberation emerges with the realization that we are not the "voice in our heads" but beings who can witness that. This is the awareness beyond thought that can be experienced in the simplest of breathing meditations, the space in which thoughts—or emotions or sense perception—happen. This awareness marks an important beginning. It is foretold in most religious and spiritual traditions. For example, the Bible speaks to the collapse of the existing world order and the arising of "a new heaven and a new earth" (Isaiah 65:17; Revelation 21:1). This "new heaven" is not a place; it refers to the realm of inner awareness—the emergence of a transformed state of human consciousness. The "new earth" is its reflection in the physical world. Both of these are first manifested at the individual level and ultimately at the organizational and societal levels as a critical mass of collective consciousness are achieved.

Aligning Your Inner and Outer Purpose Through Spiritual Leadership

Eckhart Tolle argues that you have two purposes—an inner purpose that is primary and concerns being, and an outer purpose that concerns doing. The two, however, are inseparable, like the head and tail of a coin. It is impossible to speak of one without referring to the other. Your inner purpose is to develop your inner life to become conscious and awaken through mindfulness. You also share that purpose with every other person on the planet because, given its current stage of evolution, this is the greater purpose of humanity. While your inner purpose is an essential part of the whole, your outer purpose can change over time and varies considerably from person to person. Finding and being in alignment with your inner purpose is the foundation for living and fulfilling your outer purpose and is essential for effective personal and organizational spiritual leadership. Without this alignment we are unlikely to realize joy, peace, and serenity in life independent of our circumstances, although we can still achieve and acquire much through effort, struggle, determination, cunning, or sheer hard work.

This is because outer purpose alone is always relative, unstable, and impermanent. As long as you are not present or are unaware of the power of living in the moment, you will seek meaning by doing, which can only be fulfilled in the future though goal attainment. For example, if caring for your children gives meaning to your life, what happens when they grow up? There is also a flip side to seeking fulfillment purely through goal attainment. If making it to the top of your field or profession gives meaning, then "making it" is only meaningful as long as there are many others who don't make it or must fail before your life can have meaning.

The bottom line is that you cannot become successful. You can only *be* successful. Success can never be more than a successful present moment in which doing becomes infused with the timeless quality of being. Therefore it is not your goals or actions that are paramount but the state of consciousness out of which they manifest. Once your inner life foundation is in place, your outer purpose becomes rooted in doing the "next right thing" moment to moment, charged with spiritual power and in alignment with a new earth.

Inner Life and Inner Purpose

What are some things you can do to nurture your inner life as well as work to provide an organizational context for fostering workers' inner life? Examples of people with strong inner-life practices featured in this book include Robert Ouimet of Cordon Bleu-Tomasso and Lynne Sedgmore of the Centre for Excellence in Leadership. For you, a start might be, as we discussed in Chapters 3 and 6, to seek the realization of the Level III Way of Knowing and Being by cultivating an inner life through a spiritual practice such as a simple breathing meditation or centering prayer. In doing so you will develop the capacity to be mindful and present from moment to moment and experience the awareness beyond thought, emotions, and physical sensations.

If you are already actively working to cultivate your inner life and mindfulness, you might commit to deepen your practice (for example, through spiritual retreats, finding a spiritual guide or sponsor, and/or becoming more active and committed to a spiritual or religious community) to more fully experience the Levels II and I of Knowing and Being and the Unitive Way on the Three-fold Path of Spiritual Transformation.

This is the point at which one's ego and life become dedicated to a higher good through hope/faith in a vision of love and service of others. In doing so you'll begin to experience union with your higher power, or the non-dual, in Level I and be more dedicated to a higher good and available to the needs of other people and your organization.

Inner life is also an important facet of workplace spirituality. It entails seeing the workplace as populated by people who have both a mind and a spirit and believing that the development of the spirit is as important as the development of the mind. Depending on your role and position in your organization, there are a number of management practices that you might implement that support employees' inner life. A number of these were discussed through the case studies we offered in earlier chapters. These include:

- A brief moment of silence before meetings
- A room for inner silence; spiritual support groups
- Corporate chaplains for confidential inner spiritual guidance and support
- Providing employees with coaching and mentoring opportunities from technical and leadership development to personal vision statements
- Supporting a context for conversations among workers about soul needs, personal fulfillment, and spiritual aspirations
- A library that loans employees spiritual and religious materials

There should be no effort to control or monitor these practices. While you might be a role model and be a leader in their implementation, workers should be free to choose whether or not to explore and nurture their inner life.

Spiritual Leadership and Outer Purpose

In committing to the spiritual journey, cultivating your inner life, and seeking to awaken through mindfulness, you fulfill your inner purpose. This provides the source for both personal and organizational spiritual leadership, which is the foundation for discovering, living, and fulfilling your outer purpose through hope/faith in a vision of service of others through altruistic love. Personal spiritual leadership satisfies your needs for spiritual well-being thorough calling and membership, which fuels higher levels of personal commitment and productivity, psychological well-being, and life satisfaction. Exercising organizational spiritual leadership satisfies both you and your followers' needs for spiritual well-being, which fosters higher levels of organizational commitment and productivity, employee well-being, corporate social responsibility/sustainability, and financial performance: the Triple Bottom Line.

One example of how to develop personal spiritual leadership is the Alcoholics Anonymous Twelve-Step program we outlined in Chapter 6. Most, if not all, of the world's spiritual and religious traditions emphasize a similar process or program for spiritual development. Regardless of which spiritual or religious practice or tradition you choose to follow, you are committing to developing personal spiritual leadership through a spiritual journey that requires the transformation from self-centered to other-centered in loving and serving others to experience the oneness of Being.

In Chapter 6 we also provided an example of how to develop your personal spiritual leadership through a personal mission statement. A personal mission statement serves as your personal constitution; it is the expression of your outer purpose. It becomes the standard by which you measure everything in life. It also provides an action plan for developing the qualities of spiritual leadership and spiritual well-being that we covered in detail in Chapters 4 and 5.

The process inherent in creating a personal mission statement is as important as the product. Writing or reviewing a personal mission statement forces you to think through your priorities deeply and carefully and to align your inner values, attitudes, and behavior with your outer purpose. As you begin to live your life according to your personal mission statement you have a sense of vision and purpose, and a mission of love and service of others grounded in altruistic values that provide intrinsic motivation and excitement for your life and what you are trying to do in fulfilling your outer purpose.

Organizational spiritual leadership is also an expression of your outer purpose. We covered how to implement organizational spiritual leadership in Chapter 7 and explained how organizational spiritual leadership is the driver of the Spiritual Leadership Balanced Scorecard Business Model, presented in Chapter 8. Organizational spiritual leadership requires you and your team to create vision and value congruence within and across organizational levels as well as to develop effective relationships between the organization and key stakeholders. To facilitate this congruence, we offered several ongoing practices in Chapter 7 that are crucial for the implementation of organizational spiritual leadership, including administering the organizational Spiritual Leadership Survey, carrying out a vision/stakeholder effectiveness analysis, conducting organizational development interventions and skills training, and aligning changes with key organization design variables.

Cordon Bleu-Tomasso, Interstate Batteries, Maxwell, Locke, and Ritter, and the Centre for Excellence in Leadership—the organizations we have worked with and featured in this book—provide specific practices for that work to reinforce one or more components of the organizational Spiritual Leadership Model. They include:

- Addressing workplace spirituality issues through a structured values clarification process using a range of staff focus groups, forums, questionnaires, away days and formal meetings.
- A competitive compensation and benefits package.
- Coupling profit sharing and open book management to facilitate transparency in the development of the annual operating plan and administration of a shared bonus.
- Staff participation in developing creative ideas, innovation, and the overall strategic direction of the organization.
- Different career tracks, including part-time, with varying levels of commitment, for workers who have heavier family obligations.
- Strategic forums and annual staff retreats with external facilitators to enhance and support team processes so that difficult and unspoken issues can be raised to create open dialogue and a sense of community.

- An egalitarian environment whereby leaders and workers roll up their sleeves, relinquish preferred parking spaces, move from window offices, and fly coach with their people.

- Empowering employees to co-create changes to their jobs within their teams so that the source of initiatives became bottom-up, as well as top-down.

- A dinner for four and pre-hiring Interviews that link the spouse or significant other and the family to the organization and the hiring process.

- Meetings between three employees and a high-ranking manager in which participants choose the subjects to discuss.

- An annual one-on-one personal conversation between one person having authority over the other to reflect together on the previous year and exchange thoughts about concrete events that have both negatively and positively marked their interpersonal relations.

- Taking great care to help the people asked to leave the organization by giving them access to their offices and the resources of the firm until they have found another job.

- Meetings between laid-off or dismissed employees with the manager who dismissed them at least twice in the first twelve months following their departure.

- A family-friendly workplace that supports flexible work schedules.

- Commitment to employee wellness and spiritual well-being by establishing a wellness team to ensure that all employees have the opportunity to take advantage of activities that promote healthy behaviors and positive attitudes.

- An Employers Support Parenting (ESP) brag bulletin board in a common area.

- Paid time off to attend school events as well as time to deal with issues surrounding aging parents, grandparents, and/or grandchildren.

- A program for employees to help one another through times of financial need, parenting, death, illness, and many other life challenges.

- An e-mail prayer chain.
- A "gesture" whereby some employees are called on to contribute and share with others by serving meals to street people, working in a prison or hospital, or collecting clothes, toys, or food to be distributed to those in need.
- A "Prize of the Heart" for a person who has over the years exhibited behavior that radiates joy for life, helping others, compassion, and human dignity.
- Bringing in inspirational and educational speakers.
- A monthly free pizza get-together that features spiritual speakers.
- Annual to bi-annual administration of the Spiritual Leadership Survey.

Taken together, these practices provide tools for helping you to further develop your personal and organizational spiritual leadership and as well as define, refine, and align your inner and outer purpose.

Co-Creating a Conscious, Sustainable World Through Spiritual Leadership

Mother Theresa once said that the poverty she saw in the West was much greater than poverty she dealt with in the slums of Calcutta because the West suffers from spiritual poverty. This is the great challenge, especially as the pace of life continues to accelerate and our world grows ever more connected, chaotic, and unpredictable. To add to this, more and more leaders are faced with questions for which their training has not prepared them:

- How can I plan when everything around me is changing constantly?
- How can I find and align my vision, purpose, and mission in life with my work?
- Where can I find meaning and calling in life and make a difference in the lives of others?
- What do I have to do as a leader to help establish as well as be a member of a work community in which I feel I belong and am loved, understood, and appreciated just as I am?

- How do I maintain my values and love and serve others and do my part to co-create a sustainable world when temptations to only serve my selfish needs abound?

Taken together, the spiritual leadership models, methods, tools, and practices can help address this challenge and provide answers to these seemingly intractable questions. They may also provide a way to bring into being a new heaven and a new earth that is conscious and where inner purpose is aligned with outer purpose. To do so, it is important to understand the importance of personal and organizational spiritual leadership in creating this alignment. Then we can use this knowledge to unleash the great potential of the human spirit that is universal and everywhere, no matter the culture, organization, group, or person.

Another major issue that needs to be addressed to meet this challenge and answer these questions is how to co-create a conscious, sustainable world that works for everyone. But what does sustainable mean within this context? Why is it important and, if it is, how can it be realized? The answer may lie in a focus on seven-generation sustainability.

Seven-generation sustainability urges the current generation of humans to live and work for the benefit of the seventh generation into the future. It originated with the Great Law of the Iroquois, which holds it appropriate to think seven generations ahead (a couple hundred years into the future) and decide whether the decisions people make today will benefit their children seven generations into the future. The original language is as follows:

> In all of your deliberations in the Confederate Council, in your efforts at law making, in all your official acts, self-interest shall be cast into oblivion. Cast not over your shoulder behind you the warnings of the nephews and nieces, should they chide you for any error or wrong you may do, but return to the way of the Great Law, which is just and right. Look and listen for the welfare of the whole people and have always in view not only the present but also the coming generations, even those whose faces are yet beneath the surface of the ground—the unborn of the future Nation. ("Seven-generation Sustainability" 2011)

From the perspective of seventh-generation sustainability individuals and organizations should look ahead and make every decision relate to the welfare and well-being of the seventh generation to come in asking "What about the seventh generation? Where are we taking them? What will they have?"

The Spiritual Leadership Balanced Scorecard Business model and the case example of the Center for Excellence in Leadership (CEL) in Chapter 8 can serve to illustrate the spirit of seventh-generation sustainability. It is reflected in the CEL's strategy for sustainable development and the definitions of sustainability and sustainable development in *Leadership for Sustainability: Making Sustainable Development a Reality for Leaders* (Centre for Excellence in Leadership 2008):

- Sustainability is a state of existence where social well-being and quality of life are maintained without degrading the ecological systems upon which life depends.

- Sustainable development meets the needs of the present without compromising the ability of future generations to meet their own needs. It is a process whereby one assesses the social, environmental, and economic aspects of any action or decision in order to achieve an outcome that is as close to sustainability as possible.

CEL believed that leadership support and development was essential for the implementation of sustainability and sustainable development. They asserted that there was a need for leaders at all levels to sponsor, drive, endorse, and support sustainability and sustainable development activity as part of demonstrating their commitment to the Triple Bottom Line. CEO Lynne Sedgmore and many staff members of CEL had a huge passion for this topic. Two staff members, in particular, were sustainability champions and provided a powerful example of employees taking the initiative, with full autonomy and backing from the senior managers, to ensure that CEL modeled and encouraged sustainability for all stakeholders, including the learners it trained as well as Further Education (FE) sector leaders.

CEL sought to engage and collaborate with their strategic partners in the development of a sustainability strategy. Lynne and her leadership team initially met with leaders and other interested stakeholders who supported sustainability. As one of the founder members of the Sustainability Integration Group (SIGnet), CEL benefited from the insights and experiences of a range of colleagues, many of whom were in the process of developing or were implementing sustainable development action plans. These stakeholders were among the first to hear and comment on CEL's earliest thinking on a sustainable development strategy. As work on the strategy progressed, valuable partnerships were established with other stakeholders committed to sustainability.

The model for sustainable development that emerged from these collaborations identified four distinct but inter-related objectives that provided the foundation for CEL's sustainable development activities.

- **Build CEL.** Develop CEL's own capacity and practice both to support other organizations and to become more sustainable itself.
- **Build leadership.** Support the development of leaders' and organizations' capacity and capability to be leaders for sustainability.
- **Build partnership.** Actively contribute to policy development and practice in sustainable development at the sector (industry) level.
- **Build practice.** Lead, support, and contribute to debate, discussion, and improvement in leadership for sustainability.

While leadership was a core theme of CEL's strategy for sustainable development, at its heart was the development of learners' knowledge, skills, and qualities to understand and demonstrate sustainable development as citizens; this is the development of what often is described as "sustainability literacy." Leaders at all levels played an instrumental role in making this happen. Building CEL was desirable in itself, but its main purpose for sustainable development was that it would make CEL better equipped to meet the other three objectives. By building practice, CEL would build leadership. Building partnerships would improve the quality and impact of everything that the leaders from CEL's programs do to achieve the other objectives. Leaders and partners could then work to implement sustainable development strategies that influence FE sector teaching and learning, learners, employers and their operations, and the communities they serve.

The logical next step for CEL was to move to a form of the Spiritual Leadership Balanced Scorecard Business Model to make sure it placed a balanced emphasis on sustainability as part of a Triple Bottom Line that also stressed employee well-being and performance excellence. In doing so CEL also recognized the importance of spiritual leadership as the ultimate driver of the Triple Bottom Line and the necessity of measuring it regularly as part of the learning and growth category.

A Call to Action

Throughout this book we've made the case that today's leaders are facing a spiritual threshold they must cross if they are to be successful in these turbulent times. This calls for a "new earth" based on models of personal spiritual leadership as well as business models driven by organizational spiritual leadership that facilitate the alignment of inner and outer purpose. These models are spiritual because they are based on principles that have been the focus of religious and spiritual inquiry and practice for thousands of years.

If you feel motivated to be a part of the new earth and want to be one the leaders working to co-create it, you may be asking, "I'm just one person. How do I help?" or "How can I get started?"

The answer is to first work on your personal spiritual leadership. This means committing to the spiritual journey and an inner-life practice to become more mindful, conscious, and aware moment to moment. It also means developing and living a personal mission statement as the foundation for hope/faith in your vision for loving and serving others to satisfy your needs for spiritual well-being through calling and membership and, as a result, experience higher levels of personal commitment and productivity, psychological well-being, and life satisfaction. It may also mean finding a coach, mentor, sponsor, or spiritual guide to aid and provide counsel as your journey unfolds.

You can also work to develop the qualities of organizational spiritual leadership. Doing so does not mean you have to be a CEO, member of the top leadership team, or in any management or leadership position. Everyone, including janitors and the lowest-paid clerical workers, has a sphere of influence and stakeholders they must satisfy. And no matter how toxic your organization or how far down in the catacombs you are buried in it, you can exercise organizational spiritual leadership if you have begun to work on your personal spiritual leadership. One does not have to be developed fully before the other, and they can both be practiced simultaneously. After all, every success and failure is part of the spiritual journey and an opportunity for spiritual growth.

One way to start would be to look for an issue that needs an idea champion. It can be anything from taking the initiative to organizing the firm's Christmas party to volunteering to serve on or lead a committee or initiating a recycling program for wastepaper and plastic. Anything that is an opportunity to love and serve others is a candidate. Articulate a vision for your project and then engage others to join and help further refine it. In doing so, do your best to show care and concern for all through altruistic love. If successful, this will fuel hope/faith in the vision and jumpstart the intrinsic motivation process inherent in spiritual leadership to satisfy your and your team members' needs for spiritual well-being through calling and membership that will fuel high levels of organizational commitment and productivity. Also conduct a vision/ stakeholder effectiveness analysis to reinforce the team's vision, purpose, mission, and cultural values. Then identify high-power and/or high-importance stakeholders whose expectations must be met if the project is to be successful. Develop goals and strategies to address any stakeholder issues related to unmet expectations. This does not have to be a formalized ritualistic process. Nor do you even have to tell your people the name of what you are doing. Just be the one who leads the process. The other members will find it logical and compelling once you outline the basic purpose of the exercise.

If you wish to exercise personal and organizational leadership to influence sustainability and sustainable development, you can draw on the CEL example discussed earlier. For instance, you could become a sustainability champion and work with others who share your passion to undertake an initiative to influence your organization to be a role model on some aspect of sustainability. Or if you are in a formal position of influence or can enlist the support of such a person, you could seek to sway your organization to implement a version of the CEL model for sustainable development in building organizational capacity for sustainability, leaders' capability to practice and support sustainability, partnerships for sustainability within an industry, and support and contribution to the dialogue for improvement in leadership for sustainability.

CONCLUSION

The leaders of the organizations that we studied in this book—Tomasso Corporation, Interstate Batteries, MLR, and CEL—are exemplars of both personal and organizational leadership and, to some extent, the Spiritual Leadership Balanced Scorecard Business Model. These leaders would all say that the most important change is personal. Little or nothing would have changed in their organizations if they had not changed. Each in their own way exemplifies the struggle to find and align their inner and outer purpose; to overcome their emotional programming and cultural conditioning; to embrace the spiritual journey and levels of knowing and being; and to connect to their higher power, or the nondual, through love and service of others. In managing difficult personal transitions, they also engaged in changing their organizations to enable the alignment of its inner and outer purpose. In doing so they created organizations that embraced change through empowered teams, fostered collaboration, and institutionalized participative processes and new ways of thinking.

These leaders and their organizations foretell of a new earth being built from the individual, team, and organizational levels up. In the past, families, communities, and even nations could exist more or less independently of one another. If they took into account the well-being of their neighbors, so much the better. Yet their survival was not dependent on this kind of perspective. Today's reality is much different. The modern world is such that the interests of our community or nation can no longer lie only within the confines of those boundaries. When we shift our basis of concern to others' well-being we can, and should, develop a sense of what the Dalai Lama calls "universal responsibility." Developing such a sense of responsibility helps us become sensitive to all others—not just those closest to us. We come to see the need to care for the countries and people who suffer most from disease and poverty. We recognize the need to help all others pursue happiness and avoid suffering. And we become aware of the fundamental oneness of the human family and the joy, peace, and serenity inherent in love and service of others.

Together, through development of our personal spiritual leadership, organizational spiritual leadership, and the use of the Spiritual Leadership Balanced Scorecard Business Model, we can take responsibility for co-creating spheres of influence and organizations committed to maximizing the Triple Bottom Line. Together we can foster oneness of the human family. Einstein's statement is true. This means that the seemingly intractable problems that are preventing global transformation and union, peace, and sustainability cannot be solved at the geopolitical and national levels. Perhaps though they can be solved through individuals, teams, and organizations committed to spiritual leadership that, collectively, could generate a critical mass for the chain reaction necessary to co-create a conscious, sustainable world that works for everyone.

Bibliography and Selected Readings by Chapter

CHAPTER 1

Aburdene, P. *Megatrends 2010*. Charlottesville, VA: Hampton Roads, 2005.

Baldrige National Quality Program. 2005. *Criteria for Performance Excellence.* Washington, DC: National Institute of Standards and Technology, Department of Commerce.

Benefiel, M. "The Second Half of the Journey: Spiritual Leadership for Organizational Transformation." *The Leadership Quarterly*, 16 (5) 2005: 723–747.

Collins, J. *Good to Great: Why Some Companies Make the Leap . . . and Others Don't*. New York: Harper Business, 2001.

Duschon, D., and D. Plowman. "Nurturing the Spirit at Work: Impact on Work Unit Performance." *The Leadership Quarterly*, 16 (5) 2005: 807–833.

Fry, L. "Toward a Theory of Spiritual Leadership." *The Leadership Quarterly*, 14 (3) 2003: 693–727.

———. "Introduction to the Special Issue: Toward a Paradigm of Spiritual Leadership." *The Leadership Quarterly*, 16 (5), 2005: 619–622.

———. "Toward a Theory of Ethical and Spiritual Well-Being and Corporate Social Responsibility Through Spiritual Leadership." In *Positive Psychology in Business Ethics and Corporate Responsibility*, ed. R. Giacalone, C. Jurkiewicz, and C. Dunn, 47–83. Greenwich, CT: Information Age Publishing, 2005.

———. "Spiritual Leadership: State-of-the-Art and Future Directions for Theory, Research, and Practice." In *Spirituality in Business: Theory, Practice, and Future Directions*, by J. Biberman and L. Tischler, 106–124. New York: Palgrave, 2008.

Fry, L., and M. Cohen. "Spiritual Leadership as a Paradigm for Organizational Transformation and Recovery from Extended Work Hours Cultures." *Journal of Business Ethics*, 84 (9) 2009: 265–278.

Fry, L., and J. Slocum. "Maximizing the Triple Bottom Line Through Spiritual Leadership." *Organizational Dynamics*, 37 (1) 2008: 86–96.

Fulmer, R. "The Challenge of Ethical Leadership." *Organizational Dynamics*, 33 (3), August 2004: 307–317.

Giacalone, R., and C. Jurkiewicz. "Toward a Science of Workplace Spirituality." In *Handbook of Workplace Spirituality and Organizational Performance*, by R. Giacalone and C. Jurkiewicz, 3–28. Armonk, NY: M. E. Sharpe, 2003.

Gladwin, Tom. n.d. http://www.sustainability.com/council/tom-gladwin. (Accessed June 5, 2012).

Kaplan, R., and D. Norton. *The Balanced Scorecard: Translating Strategy into Action*. Boston: Harvard Business School Press, 1996.

Mackey, J. "Conscious Capitalism: Creating a New Paradigm for Business." *Whole Planet Foundation*. 2007. http://www.wholeplanetfoundation.org/files/uploaded/John_Mackey-Conscious_Capitalism.pdf (accessed January 28, 2010).

Mason, R. "Spirituality and Information." In *Handbook of Workplace Spirituality and Organizational Performance*, by R. Giacalone and C. Jurkiewicz. Armonk, NY: M. E. Sharpe, 2003.

Matherly, L., L. Fry, and R. Ouimet. "A Strategic Scorecard Model of Performance Excellence Through Spiritual Leadership." Honolulu, HA: Academy of Management Conference, 2005.

Mele, D., and A. Corrales. *Tomasso Corporation: Including Spirituality in the Organizational Culture*. Barcelona, Spain: IESE Publishing, 2005.

Mitroff, I., and E. Denton. *A Spiritual Audit of Corporate America: A Hard Look at Spirituality, Religion, and Values in the Workplace*. San Francisco: Jossey-Bass, 1999.

Neal, J. "Leadership and Spirituality in the Workplace." In *Leadership Theory, Application, Skill Development*, by R. Lussier and C. Achua, 464–473. Boston: South-Western College Publishing, 2001.

Ouimet, J.-R. *Spirituality in Management Reconciles Human Well-Being–Productivity–Profits*. Montreal: Ouimet-Cordon Bleu, 2005.

———. *Everything Has Been Loaned to You*. Montreal, Canada: To God Go Foundation, 2009.

"Our Project: In Management, How to Reconcile Spirituality, Human Well-Being with Productivity and Profit." *Notre Project*. n.d. http://www.notreprojet.org/index.php?id=174. (accessed November 19, 2008).

Savitz, A. *The Harry Walker Agency*. n.d. http://www.harrywalker.com/speaker/Andrew-Savitz.cfm?Spea_ID=1095 (accessed November 17, 2009).

Savitz, A., and K. Weber. *The Triple Bottom Line: Why Sustainability Is Transforming the Best-Run Companies and How It Can Work for You*. New York: Wiley, 2006.

Schein, E. *Organizational Culture and Leadership*. San Francisco: Jossey-Bass, 2004.

"Shared Belief in the Golden Rule." *Religious Tolerance Organization*. n.d. http://www.religioustolerance.org/reciproc.htm (accessed November 11, 2009).

Snyder, C., and S. Lopez. *Handbook of Positive Psychology*. Oxford and New York: Oxford University Press, 2001.

Tenzin Gyatso, the 14th Dalai Lama. *Ethics for the New Millennium*. New York: Putnam, 1999.

CHAPTER 2

Ancona, G., T. Kochan, M. Scully, J. Van Maanen, and D. Westney. *Managing for the Future: Organizational Behavior and Processes*. Boston: South-Western College Publishing, 2004.

Bass, B. *Bass and Stogdill's Handbook of Leadership: Theory, Research, and Managerial Applications*, 3rd ed. New York: Free Press, 1990.

Bass, B., and P. Steidlmeier. "Ethics, Character, and Authentic Transformational Leadership." *The Leadership Quarterly*, 10 (2) 1999: 181–217.

Conger, J., and R. Kanungo. "The Empowerment Process: Integrating Theory and Practice." *Academy of Management Review*, 13 (3) 1988: 471–482.

Daft, R. *The Leadership Experience*, 4th ed. Mason, OH: Thompson South-Western, 2008.

Daft, R., and R. Lengel. *Fusion Leadership: Unlocking the Subtle Forces That Change People and Organizations*. San Francisco: Berrett-Koehler, 1998.

Deci, E., and R. Ryan. "The "What" and "Why" of Goal Pursuits: Human Needs and Self-determination of Behavior." *Psychological Inquiry*, 11 (4), 2000: 227–268.

Duschon, D., and D. Plowman. "Nurturing the Spirit at Work: Impact on Work Unit Performance." *The Leadership Quarterly*, 16 (5) 2005: 807–833.

Fleischman, P. *The Healing Spirit: Exploration in Religion and Psychotherapy*. Cleveland: Bonne Chance, 1994.

Freeman, R. *Strategic Management: A Stakeholder Approach*. Boston: Pitman, 1984.

Fry, L. "Toward a Theory of Spiritual Leadership." *The Leadership Quarterly*, 14 (3) 2003: 693–727.

———. "Introduction to the Special Issue: Toward a Paradigm of Spiritual Leadership." *The Leadership Quarterly*, 16 (5), 2005: 619–622.

———. "Toward a Theory of Ethical and Spiritual Well-Being and Corporate Social Responsibility Through Spiritual Leadership." In *Positive Psychology in Business Ethics and Corporate Responsibility*, ed. R. Giacalone, C. Jurkiewicz, and C. Dunn, 47–83. Greenwich, CT: Information Age Publishing, 2005.

———. "Spiritual Leadership: State-of-the-Art and Future Directions for Theory, Research, and Practice." In *Spirituality in Business: Theory, Practice, and Future Directions*, by J. Biberman and L. Tischler, 106–124. New York: Palgrave, 2008.

Fry, L., S. Hanna, M. Noel, and F. Walumba. "Impact of Spiritual Leadership on Unit Performance." *The Leadership Quarterly*, 22 (2) 2011: 259–270.

Fry, L., and L. Matherly. "Spiritual Leadership and Organizational Performance." Atlanta, GA: Academy of Management Conference, 2006.

Fry, L., and J. Slocum. "Maximizing the Triple Bottom Line Through Spiritual Leadership." *Organizational Dynamics*, 37 (1), 2008: 86–96.

Galbraith, J. *Organization Design*. Reading, MA: Addison-Wesley, 1977.

Kouzes, J., and B. Pozner. *The Leadership Challenge*, 2nd ed. San Francisco: Jossey-Bass, 2003.

Levy, R. "My Experience as Participant in the Course on Spirituality for Executive Leadership." *Journal of Management Inquiry*, 9 (2), 2000: 129–131.

McGill, M., and J. Slocum. "Management Practices in Learning Organizations." *Organizational Dynamics*, 21 (1)1992: 5–18.

Miller, K., and N. Miller. *In Search of an Abundant Life: Secrets of Success*. n.d. http://powertochange.com/discover/faith/miller/ (accessed April 24, 2010).

Miller, N. *Beyond the Norm*. Nashville: Thomas Nelson, 1996.

Miller, N. *Personal Testimony*. n.d. http://corporate.interstatebatteries.com/norm_miller/testimony/ (accessed April 26, 2010).

Moxley, R. *Leadership and Spirit*. San Francisco: Jossey-Bass, 2000.

Nyhan, R. "Changing the Paradigm: Trust and Its Role in Public Sector Organizations." *American Public Review of Administration*, 30 (1) 2000: 87–109.

Paloutzian, R., R. Emmons, and S. Keortge. "Spiritual Well-being, Spiritual Intelligence, and Healthy Workplace Policy." In *Handbook of Workplace Spirituality and Organizational Performance*, by C. Jurkiewicz and R. Giacalone, 123–136. Armonk, NY: M. E. Sharpe.

Pfeffer, J. "The Whole Truth and Nothing But: The Value of Honesty in Organizations." In *What Were They Thinking? Unconventional Wisdom About Management*, by J. Pfeffer, 122–127. Boston: Harvard Business School, 2007.

Ryff, C., and B. Singer. "From Social Structure to Biology: Integrative Science in Pursuit of Human Health and Well-being." In *Handbook of Positive Psychology*, by C. Synder and S. Lopez, 541–555. Oxford and New York: Oxford University Press, 2001.

Senge, P. *The Fifth Discipline: The Art and Practice of the Learning Organization*. New York: Doubleday, 1990.

Spreitzer, G. "Social Structural Characteristics of Psychological Empowerment." *Academy of Management Journal*, 39 (2), 1996: 483–504.

Thomas, G. "Just What Is Personal Leadership?" *Leading Today*. Feburary 2002. http://www.leadingtoday.org/Onmag/feb02/gt-feb02.html (accessed July 02, 2009).

CHAPTER 3

Almaas, A. *The Inner Journey Home: Soul's Realization of the Unity of Reality.* Boston: Shambala, 2004.

Bass, B., and P. Steidlmeier. "Ethics, Character, and Authentic Transformational Leadership." *The Leadership Quarterly,* 10 (2) 1999: 181–217.

Benefiel, M. "The Second Half of the Journey: Spiritual Leadership for Organizational Transformation." *The Leadership Quarterly,* 16 (5) 2005: 723–747.

———. *Soul at Work: Spiritual Leadership in Organizations.* Nashville: Seabury, 2005.

———. *The Soul of a Leader: Finding Your Path to Success and Fulfillment.* New York: Crossroads, 2008.

"Bernard Madoff." *Wikipedia.* n.d. http://en.wikipedia.org/wiki/Bernard _Madoff (accessed July 4, 2009).

Burrell, G., and G. Morgan. *Sociological Paradigms and Organizational Analysis.* Ashgate Publishing, 2007.

Collins, J. *Good to Great: Why Some Companies Make the Leap . . . and Others Don't.* New York: Harper Business, 2001.

Conger, J., and R. Kanungo. "The Empowerment Process: Integrating Theory and Practice." *Academy of Management Review,* 13 (3) 1988: 471–482.

Conn, W. *Christian Conversion: A Development Interpretation of Autonomy and Surrender.* Mahwah, NJ: Paulist Press, 1986.

Duschon, D., and D. Plowman. "Nurturing the Spirit at Work: Impact on Work Unit Performance." *The Leadership Quarterly,* 16 (5) 2005: 807–833.

Elgin, B. "Who Says CEOs Can't Find Inner Peace?" *Business Week,* September 1, 2003: 77–80.

Fry, L. "Toward a Theory of Spiritual Leadership." *The Leadership Quarterly,* 14 (3) 2003: 693–727.

———. "Toward a Theory of Ethical and Spiritual Well-Being and Corporate Social Responsibility Through Spiritual Leadership." In *Positive Psychology in Business Ethics and Corporate Responsibility,* ed. R. Giacalone, C. Jurkiewicz, and C. Dunn, 47–83. Greenwich, CT: Information Age Publishing, 2005.

———. "Spiritual Leadership: State-of-the-Art and Future Directions for Theory, Research, and Practice." In *Spirituality in Business: Theory, Practice, and Future Directions,* by J. Biberman and L. Tischler, 106–124. New York: Palgrave, 2008.

Fry, L., and M. Kriger. "Towards a Theory of Being-Centered Leadership: Multiple Levels of Being as Context for Effective Leadership." *Human Relations,* 62 (11), 2009: 1667–1734.

Fry, L., and L. Matherly. "Workplace Spirituality, Spiritual Leadership and Performance Excellence." In *Encyclopedia of Industrial Organizational Psychology*, by S. Rogelberg, 751–754. San Francisco: Sage, 2007.

Fry, L., and J. Slocum. "Maximizing the Triple Bottom Line Through Spiritual Leadership." *Organizational Dynamics*, 37 (1) 2008: 86–96.

Hatang, S., and S. Venter. "Memory: Using Memory to Create Social Justice." March 2011. http://www.nelsonmandela.org/index.php/memory/authorised_quotations_book/introduction/ (accessed 10 18, 2011).

Horton, W. *God*, 9th ed. New York: Association Press, 1950.

Keating, T. *The Human Condition: Contemplation and Transformation*. New York: Paulist Press, 1999.

Kriger, M., and B. Hanson. "A Value-Based Paradigm for Creating Truly Healthy Organizations." *Journal of Organizational Change Management* , 12 (4) 1999: 302–318.

Kriger, M., and Y. Seng. "Leadership with Inner Meaning: A Contingency Theory of Leadership Based on Worldviews of Five Religions." *The Leadership Quarterly*, 16 (5) 2005: 771–806.

Kurtz, E., and K. Ketcham. *The Spirituality of Imperfection: Storytelling and the Search for Meaning*. New York: Bantam, 1992.

Matherly, L., L. Fry, and R. Ouimet. "A Strategic Scorecard Model of Performance Excellence Through Spiritual Leadership." Honolulu, HI: Academy of Management Conference, 2005.

O'Neill, R. "Fool's Journey." n.d. http://www.tarot.com/about-tarot/library/boneill/fool-journey?code=aeclectic&feature=boneill-fool-journey& (accessed June 25, 2009).

Osborne, A. *Ramana, Maharshi, and the Path to Self-Knowledge*. Boston: Weiser Books, 1970.

Paul, L. "The Spiritual Journey of the Fool." n.d. http://www.bellaonline.com/articles/art29899.asp (accessed June 23, 2009).

Rohr, R. *Everything Belongs: The Gift of Contemplative Prayer*. New York: Crossroads, 2003.

Ryff, C., and B. Singer. "From Social Structure to Biology: Integrative Science in Pursuit of Human Health and Well-being." In *Handbook of Positive Psychology*, by C. Synder and S. Lopez, 541–555. New York: Oxford University Press, 2001.

Savitz, A. *The Harry Walker Agency*. n.d. http://www.harrywalker.com/speaker/Andrew-Savitz.cfm?Spea_ID=1095 (accessed November 17, 2009).

Shapiro, S., and L. Carlson. *The Art and Science of Mindfulness: Integrating Mindfulness into Psychology and the Helping Professions*. Washington, DC: American Psychological Association, 2009.

Smith, H. *The World's Religions: Our Great Wisdom Traditions.* San Francisco: Harper, 1991.

Tolle, E. *A New Earth: Awakening to Your Life's Purpose.* New York: Plume, 2005.

———. *The Power of Now: A Guide to Spiritual Enlightenment.* Novato, CA: Namaste Publishing, 1999.

Vaill, P. *Spirited Leading and Learning.* San Francisco: Jossey-Bass, 1998.

Walsh, J. *The Cloud of Unknowning.* Mahwah, NJ: Paulist Press, 1981.

"What is the Success Rate of Recovery in AA?" June 28, 2008. http://www.spiritualriver.com/what-is-the-success-rate-of-recovery-in-aa/ (accessed October 16, 2011).

Wilber, K. *A Theory of Everything: An Integral Vision of Business, Politics, Science, and Spirituality.* Boston: Shambhala, 2000.

———. *Integral Psychology: Consciousness, Spirit, Psychology, Therapy.* Boston: Shambhala, 2000.

Yukl, G. *Leadership in Organizations,* 6th ed. Englewood Cliffs, NJ: Prentice Hall, 2006.

CHAPTER 4

Allen, C. *The Miracle of Love.* Old Tappan, NJ: Revell, 1972.

"Amish School Shooting." *Wikipedia.* n.d. http://en.wikipedia.org/wiki/amish_school_shooting (accessed November 06, 2008).

BBPnews.com. "A Fun Workplace Can Be a Productive Workplace." *Bureau of Business Practice Newsletter,* 2001: 1–2.

Cameron, K. "Leadership Through Organizational Forgiveness." *University of Michigan.* n.d. http://www.bus.umich.edu/facultyresearch/research/tryingtimes/forgiveness.htm (accessed October 22, 2008).

Cassell, E. "Compassion." In *Handbook of Positive Psychology,* by C. Snyder and S. Lopez, 434–445. Oxford and New York: Oxford University Press, 2001.

Cochlan, G. "Love Leadership." *Personal Excellence,* 12 (11) , 2007: 3.

Collins, J. *Good to Great: Why Some Companies Make the Leap . . . and Others Don't.* New York: Harper Business, 2001.

Covey, S. *The Seven Habits of Highly Effective People: Powerful Lessons in Personal Change.* New York: Free Press, 1989.

Daft, R. *The Leadership Experience,* 4th ed. Mason, OH: Thompson South-Western, 2008.

Dourado, P. "Love and Leadership." *Changing Minds.* n.d. http://changingminds.org/articles/articles/love_and_leadership.htm (accessed November 06, 2008).

Driscoll, C., and M. McKee. "Restorying a Culture of Ethical and Spiritual Values: A Role for Leader Storytelling." *Journal of Business Ethics,* 73 (2) 2007: 205–217.

Duffner, P. "The Virtue of Patience." *The Rosary of Light and Life.* March 1994. http://www.pacifier.com/rosary-center.org/1147n2.htm (accessed October 2008).

Emmons, R. "Acts of Gratitude in Organizations." In *Positive Organizational Scholarship: Foundations of a New Discipline,* by K. Cameron, J. Dutton, and R. Quinn, 81–93. San Francisco: C. S. Berritt-Koehler, 2003.

———. "The Psychology of Gratitude: An Introduction." In *The Psychology of Gratitude,* by R. Emmons and M. McCullough, 3–16. New York: Oxford University Press, 2004.

Emmons, R., and C. Shelton. "Gratitude and the Science of Positive Psychology." In *Handbook of Positive Psychology,* by C. Snyder and S. Lopez, 459–471. Oxford and New York: Oxford University Press, 2001.

Ferris, R. "How Organizational Love Can Improve Leadership." *Organizational Dynamics,* 16 (4), 1988: 41–51.

Ford, R., F. McLaughlin, and J. Newstrom. "Questions and Answers About Fun at Work." *Human Resource Planning,* 26 (4) 2003: 18–33.

Fros, P. "Why Compassion Counts." *Journal of Management Inquiry,* 8 (2) 1999: 127–133.

Fry, L. "Toward a Theory of Spiritual Leadership." *The Leadership Quarterly,* 14 (3) 2003: 693–727.

———. "Spiritual Leadership: State-of-the-Art and Future Directions for Theory, Research, and Practice." In *Spirituality in Business: Theory, Practice, and Future Directions,* by J. Biberman and L. Tischler, 106–124. New York: Palgrave, 2008.

Fry, L., and M. Cohen. "Spiritual Leadership as a Paradigm for Organizational Transformation and Recovery from Extended Work Hours Cultures." *Journal of Business Ethics,* 84 (9) 2009: 265–278.

Fry, L., L. Matherly, and S. Vitucci. "Spiritual Leadership Theory as a Source for Future Theory, Research, and Recovery for Workaholism." In *Research Companion to Workaholism in Organizations,* by R. Burke, 330–352. New Horizons in Management Series: Northampton, MA, 2006.

Fry, L., and J. Slocum. "Maximizing the Triple Bottom Line Through Spiritual Leadership." *Organizational Dynamics,* 37 (1) 2008: 86–96.

Giacalone, R., and C. Jurkiewicz. *Handbook of Workplace Spirituality and Organizational Performance.* Armonk, NY: M. E. Sharpe, 2003.

Goleman, D. "What Makes a Leader?" *Harvard Business Review,* (January) 1998: 93–99.

Gunn, B. "Level 5 Leaders." *Strategic Finance,* 83 (8), 2002: 14–16.

Hazelden Foundation. *Humility.* Center City, MN: Hazelden Foundation Press, 1985.

How to Be Patient. n.d. http://wiki.com/be-patient (accessed October 16, 2008).

Hutchinson, S., A. LeBlanc, and R. Booth. "More Than 'Just Having Fun': Reconsidering the Role of Enjoyment in Therapeutic Recreation Practice." *Therapeutic Recreation Journal,* 40 (4) 2006: 220–240.

Joiner, J. "Humility: The Core of Servant Leadership." *Marketing Profs Daily Fix.* January 2007. http://www.mpdailyfix.com/2007/01/humility_the_core_of _servant_1.htm (accessed October 2008, 2008).

Kanov, S., S. Maitlis, M. Worline, J. Dutton, P. Frost, and J. Lilius. "Compassion in Organizational Life." *American Behavioral Scientist,* 47 (6) 2008: 808–827.

Karl-Marshall, K., L. Hall, and L. Harland. "Attitudes Toward Worplace Fun: A Three-Sector Comparison." *Journal of Leadership and Organizational Studies,* 12 (2) 2005: 1–17.

Kellet, J., R. Humphrey, and R. Sleeth. "Emphathy and Complex Task Performance: Two Routes to Leadership." *The Leadership Quarterly,* 13 (2) 2002: 523–544.

Kouzes, J., and B. Posner. *Encouraging the Heart.* San Francisco: Josey-Bass, 1999.

———. *The Leadership Challenge,* 2nd ed. San Francisco: Jossey-Bass, 2003.

Lewis, C. *The Four Loves.* New York: Harcourt, 1960.

Liliius, J., M. Worline, S. Maitlis, J. Kanov, J. Dutton, and P. Frost. "The Countours and Consequences of Compassion at Work." *Journal of Organizational Behavior,* 29 (8) 2008: 193–218.

Lundin, S., H. Paul, and J. Christensen. *Fish!* New York: Hyperion, 2000.

Maghroori, R., and E. Rolland. "Strategic Leadership: The Art of Balancing Organizational Mission with Policy, Procedures, and External Environment." *The Journal of Leadership Studies,* 4 (2) 1997: 62–81.

Maxwell, E. *Service, Prosperity, and Sanity: Positioning the Professional Service Firm for the Future.* Austin, TX: Maxwell, Locke, and Ritter, 1998.

McCain, J. "In Search of Courage." *Fast Company,* September 2004: 52–56.

McCullough, M., L. Root, B. Tabak, and C. Van Oyen Witvliet. "Forgiveness." In *Handbook of Positive Psychology,* ed. C. Snyder and S. Lopez, 427–436. Oxford and New York: Oxford University Press, 2001.

Molyneaux, D. "Blessed are the meek, for they shall inherit the earth—An Aspiration Applicable to Business?" *Journal of Business Ethics,* 48 (4) 2003: 347–363.

Morris, J., C. Bortheridge, and J. Urbanski. "Bringing Humility to Leadership: Antecedents and Consequences of Leader Humility." *Human Relations,* 58 (10) 2005: 1323–1350.

Niebuhr, Reinhold. *The Voice of Love.* n.d. http://www.thevoiceforlove.com/
serenity-prayer.html (accessed October 22, 2008).

Nyhan, R. "Changing the Paradigm: Trust and Its Role in Public Sector
Organizations." *American Public Review of Administration,* 30 (1) 2000:
87–109.

Openshaw, J. "A Little Love Goes a Long Way: A New Perspective on Leadership
Styles." *Market Watch.* 2007. http://www.marketwatch.com/news/story/story
.aspx?guid=%7B502dbe1c-a4fc-4230-a2dc-063a923bfa76%7D (accessed
November 06, 2008).

Pananski, M., and F. Yammarina. "Integrity and Leadership: Clearing the
Conceptual Confusion." *European Management Journal,* 25 (3) 2007:
171–184.

Peck, M. *The Road Less Traveled: A New Psychology of Love, Traditional Values,
and Spiritual Growth.* New York: Simon & Schuster, 1978.

Pfeffer, J. "The Whole Truth and Nothing But: The Value of Honesty in
Organizations." In *What Were They Thinking? Unconventional Wisdom
About Management,* by J. Pfeffer, 122–127. Boston: Harvard Business School,
2007.

Reave, L. "Spiritual Values and Practices Related to Leadership Effectiveness."
Leadership Quarterly, 16 (5) 2005: 655–687.

Robertson, K. *A Forgiveness Journal: Letting Go of the Past.* Colleyville, TX: Brie
Leadership Press, 2009.

Rutland, M. "Take the WEAK Out of Meek." *Ministry Today.* January/February
2004. http://cpanel.strang.com/~ministry/display.php?id=8446 (accessed
October 17, 2008).

Schein, E. "Organizational Culture." *American Psychologist,* 45 (2), 1990: 109–119.

———. *Organizational Culture and Leadership.* San Francisco: Jossey-Bass, 2004.

Smith, H. *The World's Religions: Our Great Wisdom Traditions.* San Francisco:
Harper, 1991.

Tangney, J. "Humililty." In *Handbook of Positive Psychology,* ed. C. Snyder and S.
Lopez, 411–419. Oxford and New York: Oxford University Press, 2001.

Tenzin Gyatso, the 14th Dalai Lama. *Ethics for the New Millennium.* New York:
Putnam, 1999.

Thompson, L., and P. Shanen. "Forgiveness in the Workplace." In *Handbook of
Workplace Spirituality and Organizational Performance,* by R. Giacalone and
C. Jurkiewicz, Armonk, 3–28. NY: M. E. Sharpe, 2003.

Tutu, D. *No Future Without Forgiveness.* New York: Doubleday, 1999.

Vincent, R. "The Virtue of Acceptance." *The Centric.* n.d. http//www.theocentric
.com/spirituality/Christian_living/the_virtue_of_acceptance.html (accessed
October 21, 2008).

Walson, S. F. "Courage Leadership: How to Claim Your Courage and Help Others Do the Same." *T&D*, 53 (8) 2003, August: 58–61.

Wein, S. "Is Courage the Counterpoint of Demoralization?" *Journal of Pallitive Care*, 23 (1) 2007: 40–43.

Whipple, R. "Leaders Can Create or Destroy Trust." *T&D*, 61 (4) 2007: 88–89.

CHAPTER 5

Alcoholics Anonymous. *Alcoholics Anonymous*. New York: Alcoholics Anonymous World Services, 2003.

Beagrie, S. "How to . . . Create Meaning at Work." *Personnel Today*, November 22, 2005: 31.

Bell, E. "Well-being and Work: Contribution or Contradiction." *Spirit in Work*, 2 2004: 3–5.

Biberman, J. "Life and Work as a Calling." *Interbeing*, 1 (1) 2007: 21–24.

"Carl Jung." *Wikipedia*. n.d. http://en.wikipedia.org/wiki/Carl_jung (accessed December 23, 2008).

Chalofsky, N. "Meaningful Work." *T+D*, 57 (2) 2003: 52–57.

Dalton, J. "Career and Calling: Finding a Place for the Spirit in Work and Community." *New Directions for Student Services* 93 (Fall) 2001: 17–25.

DeKlerk, J. "Spirituality, Meaning in Life, and Work Wellness: A Research Agenda." *International Journal of Organizational Analysis*, 13 (1) 2005: 64–89.

Diener, E., R. Lucus, and S. Oishi. "Subjective Well-being: The Science of Happiness and Life Satisfaction." In *Handbook of Positive Psychology*, by C. Snyder and S. Lopez, 63–73. Oxford and New York: Oxford University Press, 2001.

Fleischman, P. *The Healing Spirit: Exploration in Religion and Psychotherapy*. Cleveland: Bonne Chance Press, 1994.

Frankl, V. *The Doctor and the Soul*. New York: Vintage Books, 1986.

———. *Man's Search for Meaning*. New York: Pocket Books, 1985.

Fry, L. "Toward a Theory of Spiritual Leadership." *The Leadership Quarterly*, 14 (3) 2003: 693–727.

———. "Spiritual Leadership: State-of-the-Art and Future Directions for Theory, Research, and Practice." In *Spirituality in Business: Theory, Practice, and Future Directions*, by J. Biberman and L. Tischler, 106–124. New York: Palgrave, 2008.

Fry, L., and J. Slocum. "Maximizing the Triple Bottom Line Through Spiritual Leadership." *Organizational Dynamics*, 37 (1) 2008: 86–96.

Giacalone, R., and C. Jurkiewicz. *Handbook of Workplace Spirituality and Organizational Performance*. Armonk, NY: M. E. Sharpe, 2003.

Gorman, S. "Breaking the Mold: Accounting Firm Creates Program to Promote Employee Wellness." *Austin Business Journal*, August 2007: 17–23.

Kriger, M., and B. Hanson. "A Value-based Paradigm for Creating Truly Healthy Organizations." *Journal of Organizational Change Management*, 12 (4), 1999: 302–318.

Lickona, T. *Educating for Character.* New York: Bantam, 1991.

Maxwell, E. *Service, Prosperity, and Sanity: Positioning the Professional Service Firm for the Future.* Austin, TX: Maxwell, Locke, and Ritter LLP, 1998.

———. "Trust Should Be Paramount Among Professionals." *Austin Business Journal,* October 2008: 3–9.

McClurea, J., and J. Brown. "Belonging at Work." *Human Resource Development International,* 11 (1) 2008: 3–17.

Morrison, E., G. Burke III, and L. Greene. "Meaning in Motivation: Does Your Organization Need an Inner Life?" *Journal of Health and Human Services Administration,* 30 (1) 2007: 98–115.

Ohmann, O. "Skyhooks: With Special Implications for Monday through Friday." *Harvard Business Review,* 33 (3) 1955: 33–41.

Paloutzian, R., R. Emmons, and S. Keortge. "Spiritual Well-being, Spiritual Intelligence, and Healthy Workplace Policy." In *Handbook of Workplace Spirituality and Organizational Performance,* by C. Jurkiewicz and R. Giacalone, 123–136. Armonk, NY: M. E. Sharpe, 2003.

"The Power of Purpose Awards." *Templeton.* n.d. http://www.selfknowledge.org/whoweare/templeton_augie.htm (accessed December 25, 2008).

Ryff, C., and B. Singer. "From Social Structure to Biology: Integrative Science in Pursuit of Human Health and Well-being." In *Handbook of Positive Psychology,* by C. Synder and S. Lopez, 541–555. Oxford and New York: Oxford University Press, 2001.

Smith, H. *The World's Religions: Our Great Wisdom Traditions.* San Francisco: Harper, 1991.

Snyder, C., and S. Lopez. *Handbook of Positive Psychology.* Oxford and New York: Oxford University Press, 2001.

"Welcome to Heartland." n.d. http://heartlandcircle.com/HC-history.htm (accessed December 28, 2008).

"Wilfred Grenfell Quotes." n.d. http://thinkexist.com/quotation/real-joy-comes -not-from-ease-or-riches-or-from/410837.html (accessed November 2, 2008).

CHAPTER 6

Alcoholics Anonymous. *Alcoholics Anonymous.* New York: Alcoholics Anonymous World Services, 2003.

"Characteristics of Adult Children of Alcoholics." *U.S. Department of Human and Health Services Administration Center for Substance Abuse Prevention.* n.d. http://www.captus.samhsa.gov/central/documents/4AdultCh (accessed September 11, 2009).

"Contemplative Outreach." *Contemplative Outreach.* n.d. http://www .contemplativeoutreach.org (accessed September 30, 2009).

Covey, S. *Seven Habits of Highly Effective People: Powerful Lessons in Personal Change.* New York: Free Press, 1989.

"Fourth Step Inventory." n.d. http://www.royy.com/step4.pdf (accessed August 30, 2009).

Fry, L. "Toward a Theory of Spiritual Leadership." *The Leadership Quarterly,* 14 (3) 2003: 693–727.

——. "Spiritual Leadership: State-of-the-Art and Future Directions for Theory, Research, and Practice." In *Spirituality in Business: Theory, Practice, and Future Directions,* by J. Biberman and L. Tischler, 106–124. New York: Palgrave, 2008.

Fry, L., and J. Slocum. "Maximizing the Triple Bottom Line through Spiritual Leadership." *Organizational Dynamics,* 37 (1) 2008: 86–96.

Keating, T. *The Human Condition: Contemplation and Transformation.* New York: Paulist Press, 1999.

——. *Fruits and Gifts of the Spirit.* New York: Lantern Books, 2007.

——. *Divine Therapy and Addiction: Centering Prayer and the Twelve Steps.* New York: Lantern Books, 2009.

Kornfield, J. *Meditation for Beginners: Six Guided Meditations for Insight, Inner Clarity, and Cultivating a Compassionate Heart.* Boulder, CO: Sounds True, 2004.

Kurth, K. "Spiritually Renewing Ourselves at Work." In *Handbook of Workplace Spirituality and Organizational Performance,* by R. Giacalone and C. Jurkiewicz, 447–460. Armonk, NY: M. E. Sharpe, 2003.

Kurtz, E., and K. Ketcham. *The Spirituality of Imperfection: Storytelling and the Search for Meaning.* New York: Bantam, 1992.

Larsen, E. *Stage II Recovery: Life Beyond Addiction.* New York: HarperCollins, 1985.

Lovell, E. *Wisdom of the Tarot.* Van Nuys, CA: Astro-Analytics Publications, 1978.

Meyer, P. *Effective Personal Productivity.* Waco, TX: Leadership Management, 1994.

Paths to Recovery: Al-Anon's Steps, Traditions, and Concepts. Virginia Beach, VA: Al-Anon Family Groups, 1997.

Pennington, M., T. Keating, and T. Clarke. *Finding Grace at the Center: The Beginning of Centering Prayer.* Woodstock, VT: Skylight Paths, 2002.

Ronel, N. "From Self-help to Professional Care: An Enhanced Application of the 12-Step Program." *Journal of Applied Behavioral science,* 36 (1) 2000: 108–122.

Ryff, C., and B. Singer. "From Social Structure to Biology: Integrative Science in Pursuit of Human Health and Well-being." In *Handbook of Positive Psychology*, by C. Synder and S. Lopez, 541–555. Oxford and New York: Oxford University Press, 2001.

Salzberg, S. *Loving-kindness: The Revolutionary Art of Happiness*. Boston: Shambhala, 1997.

Senge, P., C. Scharmer, J. Jaworski, and B. Flowers. *Presence: Human Purpose and the Field of the Future*. New York: Currency Books, 2004.

St. Romain, P. *Reflections on the Serenity Prayer*. Liguori, MO: Liguori Press, 1997.

Thomas, G. "Just What Is Personal Leadership?" *Leading Today*. February 2002. http://www.leadingtoday.org/Onmag/feb02/gt-feb02.html (accessed July 02, 2009).

Tolle, E. *The Power of Now: A Guide to Spiritual Enlightenment*. Novato, CA: Namaste Publishing, 1999.

Warner, C. *Bonds That Make Us Free*. Ann Arbor, MI: Shadow Mountain, 2001.

CHAPTER 7

Ancona, G., T. Kochan, M. Scully, J. VanMaanen, and D. Westney. *Organizational Behavior and Orocesses*. Boston: South-Western College Publishing, 2004.

Berner, R. "P&G: New and Improved." July 07, 2003. http://www.businessweek.com/magazine/content/03_27/b3840001_mz001.htm (accessed May 17, 2009).

Brown, D., and D. Harvey. *An Experiential Approach to Organization Development*, 7th ed. Englewood Cliffs, NJ: Prentice Hall, 2005.

Bushe, G. "Advances in Appreciative Inquiry as an Organization Development Intervention." *Organization Development Journal*, 17 (2) 1999: 61–68.

Carmeli, A., and J. Schaubroeck. "Top Management Teams: Behavioral Integration, Decision Quality, and Organizational Decline." *The Leadership Quarterly*, 17 (6) 2006: 441–453.

Collins, J. *Good to Great: Why Some Companies Make the Leap . . . and Others Don't*. New York: Harper Business, 2001.

Collins, V. *The Key to Serenity and Peace of Mind*. St. Meinra, IN: Abbey Press, 1960.

Conger, J., and R. Kanungo. "The Empowerment Process: Integrating Theory and Practice." *Academy of Management Review*, 13 (3) 1988: 471–482.

Cummings, T., and C. Worley. *Organization Development and Change*, 9th ed. Boston: South-Western College Publishing, 2009.

Daft, R. *Organization Theory and Design*, 9th ed. Mason, OH: Thompson South-Western, 2007.

———. *The Leadership Experience*, 4th ed. Mason, OH: Thompson South-Western, 2008.

Daft, R., and R. Lengel. *Fusion Leadership: Unlocking the Subtle Forces That Change People and Organizations*. San Francisco: Berrett-Koehler, 1998.

Dhammananda, K. "Why Fear and Worry." *SG Box*. n.d. http://sgbox.com/sgboxinsight1.html (accessed May 17, 2009).

Filley, A. *Interpersonal Conflict Resolution*. Dallas: Scott, Foresman, 1975.

Filley, A., R. House, and S. Kerr. *Managerial Processes and Organizational Behavior*. Glenview, IL: Scott, Foresman, 1976.

Ford, R., and M. Fottle. "Empowerment: A Matter of Degree." *Academy of Management Executive*, 9 (3) 1995: 21–31.

Freeman, R. *Strategic Management: A Stakeholder Approach*. Boston: Pitman, 1984.

French, W., C. Bell, and R. Zawacki. *Organization Development and Transformation: Managing Effective Change*, 6th ed. Burr Ridge, IL: Irwin-McGraw-Hill, 2004.

Friedman, T. *The World Is Flat: A Brief History of the Twenty-first Century*. New York: Farrar, Strauss and Giroux, 2005.

Fry, L. "Toward a Theory of Siritual Leadership." *The Leadership Quarterly*, 14 (13) 2003: 693–727.

———. "Spiritual Leadership: State-of-the-art and Future Directions for Theory, Research, and Practice." In *Spirituality in Business: Theory, Practice, and Future Directions*, by J. Biberman and L. Tischler, 106–124. New York: Palgrave, 2008.

Fry, L., and M. Cohen. "Spiritual Leadership as a Paradigm for Organizational Transformation and Recovery from Extended Work Hours Cultures." *Journal of Business Ethics*, 84, (9) 2009: 265–278.

Fry, L., and L. Matherly. "Spiritual Leadership and Organizational Performance: An Exploratory Study." Atlanta, GA: Academy of Management Conference, 2006.

Fry, L., L. Matherly, and S. Vitucci. "Spiritual Leadership Theory as a Source for Future Theory, Research, and Recovery for Workaholism." In *Research Companion to Workaholism in Organizations*, by R. Burke, 751–754. Northampton, MA: New Horizons in Management Series, 2006.

Fry, L., M. Nisiewicz, S. Vitucci, and M. Cedilo. "Transforming City Government Through Spiritual Leadership: Measurement and Establishing a Baseline." Philadelphia: Academy of Management Conference, 2007.

———. "Transforming Police Organizations Through Spritual Leadership: Measurement and Establishing a Baseline." Philadelphia: Academy of Management Conference, 2007.

Fry, L., and J. Slocum. "Maximizing the Triple Bottom Line Through Spiritual Leadership." *Organizational Dynamics,* 37 (1) 2008: 86–96.

Fry, L., and J. Whittington. "Spiritual Leadership as a Paradigm for Organizational Transformation and Development." Honolulu: Academy of Management Conference, 2005.

Fry, L., S. Vitucci, and M. Cedilo. "Transforming the Army through Spiritual Leadership." *The Leadership Quarterly,* 16 (5) 2005: 835–862.

Galbraith, J. *Organization Design.* Reading, MA: Addison-Wesley, 1977.

Galbraith, J. *Organization Development.* San Fancisco: Jossey-Bass, 2006.

Giacalone, R., and C. Jurkiewicz. *Handbook of Workplace Spirituality and Organizational Performance.* Armonk, NY: M. E. Sharpe, 2003.

Gibson, D., and S. Barsade. "The Experience of Anger at Work: Lessons from the Chronically Angry." Chicago, IL: Academy of Management Conference, 1999.

Hazelden Foundation. *Humility.* Center City, MN: Hazelden Foundation Press, 1985.

Holder, P. "Fear . . . Your Worst Enemy." *Wingchun Center.* n.d. http://www .wingchuncenter/articles/art01.htm (accessed May 19, 2009).

Hoyle, J., and R. Slater. "Love, Happiness, and America's Schools: The Role of Educational Leadership in the 21st Century." *Phi Delta Kappa,* 82 (10) 2001: 790–794.

"Introduction to Consensus Decision-Making," n.d. http://theanarchistlibrary .org//HTML/Anonymous__Introduction_to_Consensus_Descision-Making .html (accessed November 15, 2008).

Joch, A. "Defuse Workplace Anger." *IT World.* 2001. http://www.itworld/ itwo305joch (accessed May 17, 2009).

Johnson, G., and W. Leavitt. "Building on Success: Transforming Organizations Through an Appreciative Inquiry." *Public Personnel Management,* 30 (1) Spring 2001: 129.

Jones, T., W. Felps, and G. Bigley. "Ethical Theory and Stakeholder-related Decisions: The Role of Stakeholder Culture." *Academy of Management Review,* 32 (1), 2007: 137–155.

Kilmann, T., and G. Killmann. *Introduction to Conflict and Teams: Enhancing Team Performance Using the TKI.* Mountain View, CA: CPP, Inc., 2004.

Kimes, M. "P&G's Leadership Machine." *Fortune,* April 13, 2009: 22.

Kotter, J. *Leading Change.* Boston: Harvard Business School Press, 1996.

Kriger, M., and B. Hanson. "A Value-based Paradigm for Creating Truly Healthy Organizations." *Journal of Organizational Change Management,* 12 (4) 1999: 302–318.

Labovitz, G. "Managing Conflict." *Business Horizons,* 23 (3) June 1980: 30–37.

Larson, E., and C. Hegarty. *From Anger to Forgiveness.* New York: Ballantine, 1992.

Lawler, E. "From the Ground Up: Six Principles for Building the New Logic Corporation." *Leadership Quarterly,* 16 (5) 2000: 655–688.

Levy, R. "My Experience as Participant in the Course on Spirituality for Executive Leadership." *Journal of Management Inquiry,* 9 (2) 2000: 129–131.

Lord, J. "Appreciative Inquiry and the Quest." *Philanthropic Quest International.* 2005. http://www.appreciative-inquiry.org/index.htm (accessed June 11, 2009).

Luthans, F., and B. Avolio. "Authentic Leadership Development." In *Postive Organizational Scholarship: Foundations of a New Discipline,* by K. Cameron, J. Dutton, and R. Quinn,. San Francisco: Berrett-Koehler, 2003.

Maghroori, R., and E. Rolland. "Strategic Leadership: The Art of Balancing Organizational Mission with Policy, Procedures, and External Environment." *The Journal of Leadership Studies,* 4 (2) 1997: 62–81.

Malone, P., and L. Fry. "Transforming Schools Through Spiritual Leadership: A Field Experiment." In *Ethics: The Heart of Leadership,* by J. Ciulla, 63–86. Westport, CN: Praeger, 2003.

McGill, M., and J. Slocum. "Management Practices in Learning Organizations." *Organizational Dynamics,* 21 (1) 1992: 5–18.

McManus, K. "Are You Afraid?" *Great Systems.* n.d. http://www.greatsystems. com/afraid.html (accessed May 17, 2009).

Messina, J. "Handling Resentment." *Live Strong.* n.d. http://www.livestrong.com /article/14691-handling-resentment (accessed May 17, 2009).

Morris, P. "Managing Workplace Anger." *Business Shrink.* n.d. http://www .businessshrink.biz/files/article3.htm (accessed May 17, 2009).

Mowday, R., L. Porter, and R. Steers. *Employee-Organization Linkages.* New York: Academic Press, 1982.

Moxley, R. *Leadership and Spirit.* San Francisco: Jossey-Bass, 2000.

Murphy, J. " Forgiveness and Resentment." *Midwest Studies in Philosophy,* 7 (1), 2008: 503–516.

Noel, M. "United States Military Academy Spiritual Leadership: Impact on Unit Performance." Term Paper. West Point: USMA, 2007.

Nyhan, R. "Changing the Paradigm: Trust and Its Role in Public Sector Organizations." *American Public Review of Administration,* 30 (1) 2000: 87–109.

Ouchi, W., R. Riordan, L. Lingle, and L. Porter. "Making Public School Work: Management Reform as the Key." *Academy of Management Journal,* 48 (6) 2005: 929–940.

"Our Project: Reconciliation of Human Well-being with Productivity and Profits." *Notre Project.* n.d. http://www.notreproject.org/homepage-our -project.html (accessed November 19, 2008).

P&G. "Sustainability . . . Improving Lives Now and for Generations to Come." *P&G.* n.d. http://www.pg.com/company/our_commitment/sustainability. html (accessed June 09, 2009).

Pfeffer, J. *The Human Equation: Building Profits by Putting People First.* Boston: Harvard Business School Press, 1998.

———. "Business and the Spirit: Management Practices That Sustain Values." In *Handbook of Workplace Spirituality and Organizational Performance,* by R. Giacalone and C. Jurkiewicz, 29–45. Armonk, NY: M. E. Sharpe, 2003.

"Procter & Gamble (P&G) Dividend Stock Analysis." *Dividend Growth Investor.* January 23, 2009. http://www.dividengrowthinvestor.com/2009/01/procter -gamble-pg-dividend-stock.html (accessed June 08, 2009).

"Quest." *Appreciative Inquiry.* 2004. http://www.appreciative-inquiry.org (accessed May 06, 2007).

Reingold, J. "The $79 Billion Handoff." *Fortune,* December 07, 2009: 81–86.

Schein, E. "Organizational Culture." *American Psychologist,* 45 (2) 1990: 109–119.

———. *Organizational Culture and Leadership.* San Francisco: Jossey-Bass, 2004.

Sellers, P. "Teaching an Old Dog New Tricks." *Fortune.* May 31, 2004. http:// money.cnn.com/magazines/fortune/fortune_archive/2004/05/31/370714/ index.htm (accessed June 08, 2009).

Senge, P. *The Fifth Discipline: The Art and Practice of the Learning Organization.* New York: Doubleday, 1990.

Sharkrani, S. "Teacher Turnover." *Michigan State University College of Education Report.* 2008. http://ww.epc.msu.edu/publications/report/teacher_turnover .pdf (accessed May 27, 2009).

Spreitzer, G. "Social Structural Characteristics of Psychological Empowerment." *Academy of Management Journal,* 39 (2), 1996: 483–504.

Thomas, K. "Conflict and Conflict Management." In *The Handbook of Industrial and Organizational Psychology,* by M. Dunnette. Chicago: Rand McNally, 1976.

Warren, L. "Worrying, worrying, worrying." *Plim Report.* 1998. http://www.plim .org.worry.html (accessed May 19, 2009).

Wasserman, T. "Seizing the Moment of Truth." *Brandweek,* October 10, 2005: 8–13.

Weitzel, W., and E. Jonsson. "Decline in Organizations: A Literature Integration and Extension." *Administrative Science Quarterly,* 34 (1) 1989: 91–109.

Whetten, D. "Organizational Decline: A Neglected Topic in Organizational Science." *Academy of Management,* 5 (4) 1980: 577–588.

Whetten, D., and K. Cameron. *Developing Management Skills,* 4th ed. Reading, MA: Addison-Wesley, 1998.

Whitney, D., and Trosten-Bloom. *The Power of Appreciative Inquiry.* San Francisco: Barrett-Koehler, 2003.

CHAPTER 8

Aldridge, J. "McJobs That All the Family Can Share." *Daily Telegraph*, Kent, UK, January, 26 2006: 1.

"Baldrige National Quality Program." *Criteria for Performance Excellence.* Washington, DC: National Institute of Standards and Technology, Department of Commerce, 1992–2005.

Bass, B., and P. Steidlmeier. "Ethics, Character, and Authentic Transformational Leadership." *The Leadership Quarterly,* 10 (2) 1999: 181–217.

Berner, R. *P&G: New and Improved.* July 07, 2003. http://www.businessweek. com/magazine/content/03_27/b3840001_mz001.htm (accessed May 17, 2009).

Beckstrom, R., and Brafman, O. "The Starfish and the Spider: The Unstoppable Power of Leaderless Organizations." Portfolio Hardcover, 2006.

Buchholz, R., and S. Rosenthal. "Spirituality, Consumption, and Business: A Pragmatic Perspective." In *Handbook of Workplace Spirituality and Organizational Performance*, by R. Giacalone and C. Jurkiewicz. Armonk, NY: M. E. Sharpe, 2003.

Cavanaugh, G. "Spirituality for Managers: Context and Critique." *Journal of Organizational Change Management,* 12 (3) 1999: 186–199.

Centre for Excellence in Leadership. "Leading the Way." Centre for Excellence in Leadership. 2004.

———. "Annual Review 2005–2006." Centre for Excellence in Leadership. 2006

———. "Ordinary Heros Extraordinary Company: Application for the Spirit at Work Award". Centre for Excellence in Leadership. 2007.

———. "Living Spirituality in the Workplace: The CEL Way." Centre for Excellence in Leadership. 2008.

———. "Leadership for Sustainability: Making Sustainable Development a Reality for Leaders," Centre for Excellence in Leadership. 2008.

———. "CEL as a High-Performing Organization." Centre for Excellence in Leadership. 2008.

Ciulla, J. " Leadership and the Problem of Bogus Empowerment." In *Ethics: The Heart of Leadership*, by J. Ciulla, 63–86. Westport, CN: Praeger, 1998.

"Conceptualizing Conscious Capitalism." *Bently University Web.* n.d. http:// www.bentley.edu/conscious-capitalism/index.cfm (accessed April 05, 2010).

Conger, J., and R. Kanungo. "The Empowerment Process: Integrating Theory and Practice." *Academy of Management Review,* 13 (3) 1988: 471–482.

"Conscious Business." *Wikipedia.* n.d. http://en.wikipedia.org/wiki/conscious_ business (accessed April 06, 2010).

"Conscious Capitalism." *C3: Catalyzing Conscious Capitalism.* n.d. http:// consciouscapitalism.com (accessed April 05, 2010).

Daniels, C. "Women v. Wal-Mart." *Fortune,* July 21, 2003: 79–82.

Deci, E., and R. Ryan. "The "What" and "Why" of Goal Pursuits: Human Needs and Self-determination of Behavior." *Psychological Inquiry*, 11 (4), 2000: 227–268.

Fayol, H. *General and Industrial Management*. New York: IEEE Press, 1984.

Ford, R., and M. Fottle. "Empowerment: A Matter of Degree." *Academy of Management Executive*, 9 (3) 1995: 21–31.

Freeman, R. *Strategic Management: A Stakeholder Approach*. Boston: Pitman, 1984.

Fry, L. "Toward a Theory of Spiritual Leadership." *The Leadership Quarterly*, 14 (3) 2003: 693–727.

———. "Toward a Theory of Ethical and Spiritual Well-Being and Corporate Social Responsibility Through Spiritual Leadership." In *Positive Psychology in Business Ethics and Corporate Responsibility*, ed. R. Giacalone, C. Jurkiewicz, and C. Dunn, 47–83. Greenwich, CT: Information Age Publishing, 2005.

———. "Spiritual Leadership: State-of-the-art and Future Directions for Theory, Research, and Practice." In *Spirituality in Business: Theory, Practice, and Future Directions*, by J. Biberman and L. Tischler, 106–124. New York: Palgrave, 2008.

Fry, L. , and L. Matherly. "Spiritual Leadership and Organizational Performance: An Exploratory Study." Atlanta, GA: Academy of Management Conference, 2006.

Fry, L., M. Nisiewicz, S. Vitucci, and M. Cedilo. "Transforming City Government Through Spiritual Leadership: Measurement and Establishing a Baseline." Philadelphia: Academy of Management Conference, 2007.

———. "Transforming Police Organizations Through Sprtual Leadership: Measurement and Establishing a Baseline." Philadelphia: Academy of Management Conference, 2007.

Fry, L., L. Sedgmore, and Y. Altman. "Maximizing the Triple Bottom Line and Spiritual Leadership: The CEL Story." Chicago: Academy of Management Conference, 2009.

Fry, L., and J. Slocum. "Maximizing the Triple Bottom Line Through Spiritual Leadership." *Organizational Dynamics*, 37(1) 2008: 86–96.

Fry, L., S. Vitucci, and M. Cedilo. "Transforming the Army Through Spiritual Leadership." *The Leadership Quarterly*, 16 (5) 2005: 835–862.

Fuchsberg, G. "Managing: Baldrige Awards Give More Weight to Results." *Wall Street Journal*, February 24, 1992: B1.

Garten, J. "A New Year: A New Agenda." *The Economist*, January 04, 2003: 44–56.

Gentry, C. "Off the Clock." *Chain Store Age* , February 2003: 33–36.

Giacalone, R., and C. Jurkiewicz. *Handbook of Workplace Spirituality and Organizational Performance*. Armonk, NY: M. E. Sharpe, 2003.

Giacalone, R., C. Jurkiewicz, and L. Fry. "From Advocacy to Science: The Next Steps in Workplace Spirituality Research." In *Handbook of the Psychology of Religion and Spirituality*, by R. Paloutzian and C. Park, 515–528. Newbury Park, CA: Sage, 2005.

Heinze, D., S. Sibary, and A. Sikula. "Relations Among Corporate Social Responsibility, Financial Soundness, and Investment Value in 22 Manufacturing Industry Groups." *Ethics and Behavior*, 9 (4) 2000: 331–347.

Hollander, E., and L. Offerman. "Power and Leadership in Organizations." *American Psychology*, 45 (2) 1990: 179–189.

Holt, S. "Wal-Mart workers' Suit Wins Class Action Status." *Seattle Times*, October 9, 2004: E1, E4.

"HR Challenges . . . I'm Loving It." *Personnel Today*, September 06, 2005: 11.

Kaplan, R., and D. Norton. "The Balanced Scorecard: Measures That Drive Performance." *Harvard Business Review*, 70 (1) 1992: 71–79.

———. *The Balanced Scorecard: Translating Strategy into Action*. Boston: Harvard Business School Press, 1996.

———. "Using the Balanced Scorecard as a Strategic Management System." *Harvard Business Review*, 74 (1) 1996: 75–76.

———. *Strategy Maps: Converting Intangible Assets into Tangible Outcomes*. Boston: Harvard Business School Press, 2004.

———. "Transforming the Balanced Scorecard from Performance Measurement to Strategic Management." *Accounting Horizons*, 15 (2) 2006: 87–104.

Kofman, F. *Conscious Business*. Louisville, KY: Sounds True, 2006.

Mackey, J. "Conscious Capitalism: Creating a New Paradigm for Business." *Whole Planet Foundation*. 2007. http://www.wholeplanetfoundation.org/files/uploaded/John_Mackey-Conscious_Capitalism.pdf (accessed January 28, 2010).

Mahoney, F., and C. Thor. *The TQM Trilogy: Using ISO 9000, the Deming Price, and the Baldrige Award to Establish a System for Total Management*. New York: AMACOM, 1994.

Malone, P., and L. Fry. "Transforming Schools Through Spiritual Leadership: A Field Experiment." In *Ethics: The Heart of Leadership*, by J. Ciulla, 63–86. Westport, CN: Praeger, 2003.

Mason, R. "Spirituality and Information." In *Handbook of Workplace Spirituality and Organizational Performance*, by R. Giacalone and C. Jurkiewicz, Armonk, NY: M. E. Sharpe, 2003.

"McDonalds's Ads Tout McJobs." *The Wall Street Journal* , September 22, 2005.

"McDonald's Targeted in Obesity Lawsuit." *BBC News World Edition*. November 22, 2002. http://news.bbc.co.uk/hi/americas/2502431.stm (accessed April 09, 2009).

"McDonald's to Fund Obesity Research." *Fast Food News.* September 14, 2006. http://www.foodfacts.info/blog/2006/09/mcdonalds-to-fund-obesity -research.html (accessed April 08, 2009).

McWilliams, A., and D. Seigel. "Corporate Social Responsiblity." *Academy of Management Review,* 26 (1) 2001: 117–127.

Mobely, L. "Personal Values and Corporate Ethics." In *Men in Decision Making: Social Ethics and the Policy of Society,* by A. Klose and R. Weiler, Freiburg: Herder, 1971: 1887–1199.

Nadesan, M. "The Discourse of Corporate Spiritualism and Evangelical Capitalism." *Management Communication Quarterly,* 13 (1) 1999: 3–42.

Nash, L. *Believers in Business.* Nashville, TN: Nelson, 1994.

Noe, E. "Did Childhood Obesity Worries Kill Disney-McDonald's Pact?" *ABC News.* May 08, 2006. http://abcnews.go.com/business/story?id=193751& page=1 (accessed April 08, 2009).

Ostas, D. "Deconstructing Corporate Social Responsiblity: Insights from Legal and Economic Theory." *American Business Law Journal,* 38 (2) 2001: 261–299.

Savitz, A., and K. Weber. *The Triple Bottom Line: Why Sustainability Is Transforming the Best-run Companies and How It Can Work for You.* New York: Wiley, 2006.

Sedgmore, L. "Christian Leadership as Ministry Within the Workplace." *Faith Business Ministry,* 4 (4) Winter 2000/2001: 29–33.

Spreitzer, G. "Social Structural Characteristics of Psychological Empowerment." *Academy of Management Journal,* 39 (2) 1996: 483–504.

Stacks, D. "The Miracle Worker." *Fast Company.* December 01, 2009. http://www .fastcompany.com/magazine/141/the-miracle-worker.html (accessed April 05, 2010).

Trevino, L., and K. Nelson. *Managing Business Ethics.* Hoboken, NJ: Wiley, 2004.

Weber, M. *The Protestant Ethic and the Spirit of Capitalism.* New York: Scribner's, 1958.

Western, S., and L. Sedgmore. "A Privileged Converstaion." *Journal of Management Spirituality and Religion,* 5 (3) 2008: 321–346.

"Whole Food's Market Values." *Whole Foods Market.* n.d. http://www. wholefoodsmarket.com/values/corevalues.php#supporting (accessed April 07, 2010).

Chapter 9

Centre for Excellence in Leadership. "Leadership for Sustainability: Making Sustainable Development a Reality for Leaders," Centre for Excellence in Leadership. 2008.

Fry, L. "Toward a Theory of Spiritual leadership." *The Leadership Quarterly*, 14 (3) 2003: 693–727.

———. "Toward a Paradigm of Spiritual Leadership." *The Leadership Quarterly*, 5 (16) 2005: 256.

———. "Toward a Theory of Ethical and Spiritual Well-Being and Corporate Social Responsibility Through Spiritual Leadership." In *Positive Psychology in Business Ethics and Corporate Responsibility*, ed. R. Giacalone, C. Jurkiewicz, and C. Dunn, 47–83. Greenwich, CT: Information Age Publishing, 2005.

———. "Spiritual Leadership: State-of-the-art and Future Directions for Theory, Research, and Practice." In *Spirituality in Business: Theory, Practice, and Future Directions*, by J. Biberman and L. Tischler, 106–124. New York: Palgrave, 2008.

Fry, L., and M. Kriger. "Towards a Theory of Being-centered Leadership: Multiple Levels of Being as Context for Effective Leadership." *Human Relations*, 62 (11) 2009: 1667–1734.

Fry, L., and J. Slocum. "Maximizing the Triple Bottom Line Through Spiritual Leadership." *Organizational Dynamics*, 37(1) 2008: 86–96.

McGinnis, B. "Einstein Believed in God, the Creator, the First Cause of Everything That Exists." *Patriot*. n.d. http://patriot.net/~bmcgin/peral -einsteinbelievedingod.html (accessed February 07, 2010).

Miklasz, B. "Drew Brees: Renaissance man." *St. Louis Post-Dispatch*. February 02, 2010. http://www.stltoday.com/stltoday/sports/columnists.nsf/ berniemiklasz/story/12CF8E6D7A270E9A862576BE00107C91 ?OpenDocument (accessed February 10, 2010).

Minzeshcimer, B. "Oprah Brings Tolle to the Classroom." November 21, 2011. http://www.usatoday.com/life/people/2008-03-02-oprah-tolle_N.htm (accessed November 11, 2011).

"Seven-generation Sustainability." September 13, 2011. http://en.wikipedia.org/ wiki/Seven_generation_sustainability (accessed November 18, 2011).

Tolle, E. *A New Earth: Awakening to Your Life's Purpose*. New York: Plume, 2005.

"Towards Leadership for Sustainability: The CEL Development Strategy." 2007. http://www.google.com/url?sa=t&rct=j&q=&esrc=s&source=web&cd=1& ved=0CCEQFjAA&url=http%3A%2F%2Fwww.eauc.org.uk%2Fsorted%2Ffiles %2Fleadershipforsustainability_1.pdf&ei=b2HKTuvQBeHosQK_yoxN& usg=AFQjCNHH_uXcZx1CCc83Mgx8foi52Wvfxw (accessed November 21, 2011).

Wheatley, M. *Finding Our Way: Leadership for Uncertain Times*. San Francisco: Barrett-Koehler, 2007.

Index